THE REAL PINK PANTHER

To my father, who raised me on The Goons and Peter Sellers.
Sorry, this book came too late.

'The Pink Panther series feels like one huge twelve-hour movie that took twenty years to shoot.'

Burt Kwouk

'Peter Sellers was a mercurial clown who could get you laughing one minute and cut your heart out with a bloody axe the next.'

Blake Edwards

THE REAL PINK PANTHER

Stories Behind the Classic Films

Robert Sellers

WHITE OWL
AN IMPRINT OF PEN & SWORD BOOKS LTD
YORKSHIRE – PHILADELPHIA

First published in Great Britain in 2025 by
PEN AND SWORD WHITE OWL
An imprint of
Pen & Sword Books Ltd
Yorkshire – Philadelphia

ISBN 978 1 03610 936 3

A CIP catalogue record for this book is available from the British Library.

Typeset in Times New Roman 11/14 by
SJmagic DESIGN SERVICES, India.
Printed and bound in the UK by CPI Group (UK) Ltd, Croydon, CR0 4YY.

The Publisher's authorised representative in the EU for product safety is
Authorised Rep Compliance Ltd., Ground Floor, 71 Lower Baggot Street,
Dublin D02 P593, Ireland.
www.arccompliance.com

For a complete list of Pen & Sword titles please contact

PEN & SWORD BOOKS LIMITED
George House, Units 12 & 13, Beevor Street, Off Pontefract Road,
Barnsley, South Yorkshire, S71 1HN, England
E-mail: enquiries@pen-and-sword.co.uk
Website: www.pen-and-sword.co.uk

or

PEN AND SWORD BOOKS
1950 Lawrence Rd, Havertown, PA 19083, USA
E-mail: uspen-and-sword@casematepublishers.com
Website: www.penandswordbooks.com

MIX
Paper | Supporting responsible forestry
FSC® C013604

CONTENTS

ACKNOWLEDGEMENTS

The author wishes to express his sincere thanks to the following people, all of whom gave their time and assistance with great generosity of spirit.

John Allenby, Vic Armstrong, Leslie Ash, Jeffrey Auerbach, Christophe Beck, Michael Birkett (2015 interview) Dyan Cannon, Gregg Champion, Cyd Child, Carol Cleveland, Brian W. Cook, Chris Coppel, Denise Crosby, John Dellaverson, Lesley-Anne Down, Joe Dunne, Mathew Dunne, Don E. FauntLeRoy, Adam Fields, Clive Francis, Mike Grady, Burt Kwouk (2003 interview), Valerie Leon, Shawn Levy, Monica Mancini, Peter Mullins, Daniel Peacock, Eric Pleskow, Michael Saltzman, Peter Samuelson, Catherine Schell, Terry Ackland-Snow, Elke Sommer, Graham Stark (2003 interview), Robert Wagner, Ted Wass, Tony White, Susan Wood, Harald Zwart.

Special thanks to Lance Richlin, son of Maurice Richlin, for allowing me access to his father's unpublished memoirs.

Chapter 1

THE PINK PANTHER

Around about March of 1962 screenwriter Maurice Richlin got a call from Blake Edwards asking if he could drop by and see him. Maurice agreed, keen to tell his friend about a new idea he had for a comedy movie. Blake had a few quick errands to run so he took Maurice for a spin through the Hollywood Hills in his brand-new Jaguar sports car as they talked. Blake told Maurice of a recent decision he had made to sign a four-picture deal with the Mirisch Company, a production outfit owned and run by three brothers: Walter, Marvin and Harold. The Mirisch brothers were on something of a hot streak with hits *Some Like It Hot* (1959), *The Apartment* (1960), both directed by Billy Wilder, *The Magnificent Seven* (1960) and *West Side Story* (1961).

As Maurice listened to Blake mention some of the projects that he was hoping to develop with the Mirisches, he was eager to share his own news. 'I waited until Blake finished, hanging on breathlessly as we sped around curves and over hills.'[1]

'Now, Blake,' said Maurice, finally. 'I've got a story to tell you.'[2] The idea revolved around the exploits of a notorious jewel thief out to steal the biggest diamond in the world. As Maurice went on, Blake grew more and more enthusiastic. This was no poor man's rip-off from previous crime capers, but a picture that had potential for a lot of laughs. Above all, it had a great funny twist, a detective whose wife is the mistress and accomplice of the criminal he has sworn to capture and imprison. When it came to that detective, hailing from the French Sûreté, Maurice was sure it had the potential to be, 'A wonderfully comic character, a pompous but likeable cuckold.'[3] That cuckold would go on to become one of movie history's most celebrated and popular comic creations – Inspector Clouseau.

Blake had a lot to thank Maurice Richlin for. With Stanley Shapiro he had written the sparkling screenplay for his 1959 Cary Grant/Tony Curtis naval comedy *Operation Petticoat*. A big box office hit, it propelled Blake into the top rank of emerging directors. That same year Maurice and Shapiro won an Oscar for their screenplay of the Rock Hudson/Doris Day romantic comedy *Pillow Talk*.

Blake grew up around the movie business. He was born William Blake Crump in Tulsa, Oklahoma, in July 1922. His father left home shortly before the birth and Blake's mother, Lillian, turned the child over to an aunt and uncle to raise. Blake didn't meet his biological father, Donald, until he was 40 years old. Blake always assumed that he was probably dead, having been a phantom for most of his life. The encounter, when it happened, was an odd and unsatisfying experience; the father suddenly wanted to have a relationship – Blake did not, it was too late.

Lillian remarried and moved to Los Angeles when Blake was 3. The man Blake always considered his 'real' father was Jack McEdward, a studio production manager and assistant director. He was the son of J. Gordon Edwards, a notable director of silent pictures, specialising in epics featuring stars like Theda Bara, including the 1917 version of *Cleopatra*.

As an only child, Blake claimed that Lillian and Jack were dysfunctional parents. There was not a lot of love in the household, either they didn't know how to love or could not express it; both had trouble communicating not only with him but with each other. The young Blake found escape at the movies. 'I naturally embraced the Laurel and Hardys, the Keatons and the great comics. I laughed and made my hours there happy. I could take a certain residual of that home with me.'[4]

Graduating from Beverly Hills High School, Blake served in the Coast Guard during the Second World War but was invalided out. After a night of booze-fuelled partying, he thought it would be a good idea to dive into a shallow swimming pool. It resulted in a fractured skull and broken neck and Blake ended up spending five months in traction at the Long Beach Naval Hospital. Chronic back problems were to plague him for the rest of his life, leading sometimes to bouts of suicidal depression.

Something else came out of that traumatising experience.

> Lying in that hospital, I watched them bring these poor bastards out of the Pacific, shot to hell in sea battles, and I looked worse than anybody. 'Jesus,' they would say, 'what happened to you?' I could not say that I dove into a Beverly Hills swimming pool. I would groan and turn away.[5]

One day he woke up and saw the unlikely figure of Eleanor Roosevelt standing at the foot of his bed. She was paying a visit to the hospital. When she asked the inevitable question about what happened to him, the whole ward erupted in laughter. It was perhaps this moment, along with his love for silent movie comedy, that gave birth to a peculiar mix of pain and pratfalls that is the trademark of all Blake Edwards comedies, especially the Pink Panther films.

Thanks to his stepfather, Blake had already begun getting work in the movies, as an extra on the 20th Century Fox lot, or earning a few more bucks delivering pages from the writing block to the sound stages. Then in 1942, Jack McEdward got him a small role in Henry Hathaway's period drama *Ten Gentlemen from West Point*. Blake went on to play bit parts in more than two dozen movies between 1942 and 1948, usually without screen credit. He was an airman in *A Guy Named Joe* (1943) and *Thirty Seconds Over Tokyo* (1944) and a soldier in *The Best Years of Our Lives* (1946). On John Ford's *They Were Expendable* (1945), the director played a trick on the young actor, making him climb up a palm tree on an island where they were shooting. 'I thought it was for a scene,' related Blake. 'But when I looked down, I saw the entire company sailing away for the next location, leaving me stranded up a tree.'[6]

One afternoon Blake went to the cinema with an old school pal, John Champion. It was a Western and Blake sat there in the theatre criticising just about everything about it. By the end both Blake and Champion had reached the conclusion that they could do much better and set about writing their own. The result was a low-budget western called *Panhandle* (1948), which they co-wrote and co-produced for the Poverty Row studio, Monogram, with money from Champion's trust fund. Blake appeared in the role of a gunslinger. It did well enough to encourage them to do another one, *Stampede* (1949). After that both men parted ways but Blake continued writing, mainly undistinguished screenplays, all the time leaning towards directing, realising early on that this was where the control lay. His first film as a director, *Bring Your Smile Along* (1955), was a musical vehicle for the popular singer Frankie Laine. Four more pictures followed in quick succession, neither of them making much impact. It was on television that Blake scored his first big triumph when he created and produced the private detective series *Peter Gunn*. Featuring a classic jazzy theme tune by Henry Mancini, the show ran on NBC and then ABC for three seasons from 1958 to 1961.

The success of *Operation Petticoat* sent ripples out into the Hollywood pool. What impressed Kurt Frings about it more than anything else was the way Blake handled Cary Grant. Frings was Audrey Hepburn's long-time agent and friend and his client was currently fretting over being asked to play Holly Golightly in the screen adaptation of Truman Capote's novella *Breakfast at Tiffany's* (1961). She feared that playing the role of a New York café society girl who lives by socialising with wealthy men was too drastic a career departure. If this young and largely inexperienced director could manage a star of the luminosity of Cary Grant, figured Frings, then he could take on Audrey. Blake got the job. It was another big step up.

Blake was exactly the kind of director the Mirisch brothers were trying to attract to their production company. Walter Mirisch, who first met Blake back in 1948 when the two of them were just starting out in the business at Monogram Studios, even went so far as to call him, 'a spiritual heir' to Billy Wilder. What turned Blake on to the Mirisch brothers was the promise of creative freedom. By inclination, the Mirisches preferred not to interfere with the art of the filmmaker and for the most part let them get on and make the films they wanted to make. The company had a reputation for it. The same largely went for United Artists, with whom the Mirisch brothers had an exclusive distribution deal. That was a rare thing in Hollywood. Once a script, casting and other elements were approved, along with a budget, and someone to make sure it was spent correctly, UA executives pretty much left the filmmaker to his own devices.

Blake was currently making the picture *Days of Wine and Roses* (1962) over at Warners, a powerful and socially conscious film about alcoholism starring Jack Lemmon and Lee Remick. At the same time, he was eager to get the project with Maurice Richlin up and running. 'We started working out the treatment for the still-untitled comedy between shots,' said Maurice.[7] Working with Blake was never a chore, according to Richlin, and both men quickly began to realise that maybe they had something special on their hands. The result was a fourteen-page treatment that set forth many of the plot elements familiar in the finished film, including the characters Inspector Clouseau and Sir Charles Lytton (Whittingham in the treatment), a debonair playboy who leads a secret life as a jewel thief called 'The Phantom'. For years, Clouseau has been hot on the trail of this notorious thief, who always leaves behind a calling card at the scene of his crimes, a white monogrammed glove. Clouseau and his duplicitous wife Simone arrive at a jet-set ski resort in the Alps, where one of the guests is the beautiful exiled Princess Dala, the owner of a magnificent diamond.

Clouseau is certain that the presence of the diamond will be too much of a temptation for 'The Phantom'. Another guest at the resort is Sir Charles, who starts to fall in love with the princess. Complications arise when George, Sir Charles' wayward son from America (relegated to a nephew in the film), arrives on the scene.

Struggling for a title for their picture, Maurice did a little bit of research on diamonds in an issue of *National Geographic* magazine and discovered the common practice that the world's rarest diamonds are given names. Sometimes this is coined after the owner, sometimes the place they were found, such as the 'Star of Africa', or indeed the colour of the diamond, or both, as in the case of the 'Rose of Dubai'. Using that as a guide, Maurice came up with 'The Pink Rajah'. As a movie title, everyone seemed to like it, until it was discovered that a book called 'The White Rajah' had been bought by Columbia Pictures with the intention of bringing it to the screen. Maurice and Blake got thinking again. Both liked the idea of using the colour pink, so that could stay. Pink was funny; they had painted the submarine pink in *Operation Petticoat.* Maybe instead of a place name could they use an animal perhaps. Almost at the same time, Blake and Maurice said, 'The Pink Panther!'

With the story taking shape, Blake formulated a plan to bag a big-time actor to star. By this time the two men were working in offices at the Goldwyn studio and Maurice always drove home in the evening past the Universal lot. Why not pop in and see Cary Grant, who had a small bungalow office there, suggested Blake, and pitch him the story. Maurice thought it was worth a shot, given how they all got along so well on *Operation Petticoat.* Cary was his usual gracious and debonair self when Maurice called round one afternoon. After a few pleasantries, Maurice started his pitch and explained the plot of the film and the character they wanted Cary to play of this jewel thief living on the French Riviera.

Cary stared at Maurice. 'I thought I did that picture,' he said, thinking of Hitchcock's *To Catch A Thief* (1955).

Maurice sensed things were not going well. 'Wait, Wait, Cary. This is about a jewel thief after the most valuable diamond in the world. it's called the…'

'The most valuable diamond, you say.' interrupted Cary. 'How much is it worth?'

Maurice was stumped. He and Blake had not come up with any figure yet. Out of the air Maurice came up with a number. 'Five million dollars, Cary. And the thing is, there is this…'

'Hold it,' said Cary and went to get a large book off a shelf behind his desk. He studiously leafed through it and then looked at Maurice. 'There's no diamond in the world, outside of a museum, that's worth that today.'

'Maybe it's four million dollars, Cary,' said Maurice, trying to salvage things. 'But listen. You see, there is this detective after the jewel thief, and his wife…'

Cary shook his head as he put the book away. It was a polite no thank you.[8]

Years later, it was suggested to Maurice that if they had succeeded in landing Cary Grant, then maybe Inspector Clouseau would have remained in the shadows and not turned into the hit of the film at the hands of Peter Sellers. 'Because Cary would never have allowed another character to take over *his* picture, and I suppose that's true.'[9] The actor who finally played the role of 'The Phantom' was David Niven, a friend of Blake. 'And the finest man it was my good fortune to meet in Hollywood,' said Maurice.[10] When Niven accepted the project, he did rather entertain hopes that it might launch a series of films for him playing the urbane Sir Charles Lytton, very much in the spirit of the Thin Man series. Ironically, of course, it did launch a series, but not for him. 'Niven knew during shooting *Panther* that it was becoming Inspector Clouseau's picture,' confirmed Maurice. 'But he also knew, as a professional, that it was going to be a success because of that.'[11]

At first, Harold Mirisch was not that enthusiastic about the Panther project. 'He didn't want me to do it and he told me so,' recalled Blake. 'He did not understand it. He said, "Can't you come up with something else."'[12] Nonetheless, Blake felt good about the project and wanted to press ahead with it. In a way this was a test; did the Mirisch brothers' claim of allowing their artists to make their own films ring true, or was it all bluster? Getting Niven's signature to play the lead probably helped and the picture was green-lit that summer. Maurice and Blake entered into an agreement to write the screenplay for a combined fee of $150,000: $50,000 for the property and $100,000 for the screenplay.[13]

With Niven in the bag, thoughts turned to the crucial casting of the police inspector. Maurice told Blake about this small British film that he had recently seen called *Only Two Can Play* (1962) starring Peter Sellers as a professionally frustrated librarian who attempts an affair with the wife of a prominent community figure. A big star in his native Britain, Sellers had yet to establish himself on the international stage. Blake, too, had been thinking of casting Sellers but knew the studio would want a bigger marquee name to bounce off Niven. He was proved right when United Artists suggested

Peter Ustinov. 'I thought Ustinov was a fine talent,' said Maurice, 'but I could not see him as the detective. But then I was not financing the film, so what did I know?'[14]

Not content with casting Ustinov, to protect their investment, United Artists wanted more stars and asked Blake and Maurice to go to Paris to see if they could persuade Audrey Hepburn to play the princess. Blake, of course, had directed Audrey not long before in *Breakfast at Tiffany's*. The plan was to get as much of the script finished before meeting the actress. Maurice pondered how much could be realistically done on a plane. Blake said they were not flying; United Artists had booked them passage on the ocean liner SS *France* sailing from New York. They had four days on board to write enough material to entice Audrey to say yes.

By chance, some of Blake's friends were on board, including Henry Mancini and his wife Ginny. Despite the social distractions, eighty-seven pages of the script were completed. According to Mancini, Blake and Maurice locked themselves in their cabin all day to write, 'emerging at night for dinner'.[15]

In Paris, Blake and Maurice took rooms at the George V Hotel and made plans to meet with Audrey after she had found time to look over what they had written. Audrey was currently playing opposite William Holden in a comedy called *Paris When it Sizzles*, directed by another old friend of Blake, Richard Quine.

At the weekend Blake and Maurice drove to the outskirts of Paris to the home Audrey was renting. They had a good lunch and Audrey was a delightful host. But she did not want to make their movie. She liked the script well enough. 'You see, Blake,' she said. 'There's one thing in films or on stage that I can't do at all well – and that is a drunk scene.'[16] There was such a scene planned for the picture, where Sir Charles gets the princess drunk on champagne.

Disappointed, Blake and Maurice were invited to come down to Monte Carlo and stay at the Hotel de Paris where Harold Mirisch was holidaying with his family. Harold even asked the boys to stay on and finish the script there, but both of them wanted to get back to the States. They caught another ship, this time the famous *Queen Mary*, and by the time it sailed into New York *The Pink Panther* was finished. Incredibly, it had taken Blake and Maurice just eight days, while crossing the Atlantic each way.

With the script complete, and a budget set at $3 million, the rest of the cast fell into place. Ava Gardner signed on to play Simone, the inspector's wife. Several stars were talked about for the role of the princess including Nancy Kwan and Cyd Charisse before Claudia Cardinale was chosen. 1963 was to prove a breakthrough year for the young Italian actress, besides the release of *The Pink Panther* she also appeared in Fellini's *8½* and Luchino Visconti's *The Leopard.*

For Sir Charles' brash American nephew George, keen to take over the family thieving business, Blake turned to Robert Wagner, whose then wife Marion Marshall the director knew well. 'Blake thought that I would be just right for that character,' says Wagner, 'and I was so happy to be involved in that picture. It turned out to be one of the highlights, if not the highlight, of my career.'[17]

With production due to begin that November 1962 at the Cinecittà Studios in Rome, things began to unravel as far as Ava Gardner was concerned. She had taken a lot of persuasion to leave Madrid, where she now lived, to film *The Pink Panther* in Italy. Tasked with the job of delivering Miss Gardner was *Panther*'s producer Martin Jurow. 'I flew to Madrid to apply some friendly persuasion. I wound up being so friendly that I bought dinner for her and fourteen of her closest friends.'[18] Negotiations took place over Ava's not inconsiderable salary, $400,000 according to a report in *Variety*, and she agreed to dutifully arrive for work. No sooner had Miss Gardner stepped off the plane she started making demands, such as an all-expenses-paid private villa, her own chauffeur, and sundry other assistants. According to Jurow she was rude and even made the ridiculous demand that the entire production move to her beloved Madrid and shoot there instead. It was all too much, and just two weeks before the start of shooting the decision was made to discharge her. Jurow was the one despatched to break the news and work out a settlement of her contract.

Robert Wagner, however, offers another explanation for the departure of Ava Gardner; that the paparazzi, then rampant in Rome, drove her crazy from the minute she arrived and she had to step away from it all. Whatever the truth, the important role of Mrs Clouseau needed to be filled – and fast. It was offered to Janet Leigh. Recently married, to stockbroker Robert Brandt, Janet didn't fancy the prospect of being away from her new husband for several months working in Europe, so politely declined.

It was Charles K. Feldman who recommended his client and lover Capucine, a former French fashion model that the agent and producer spotted in 1957 modelling in New York. Feldman put her under contract and brought her to Hollywood to learn English and study acting. The casting of Capucine did not sit well with Ustinov, who was expecting to play opposite the far more experienced and established Ava Gardner. 'I knew Capucine and I had no great faith in her acting abilities,' Ustinov later stated. 'So, I said no.'[19] Ustinov did more than just say no, he walked off the picture.

The way Blake explained matters to Maurice, Ustinov had taken on the role of Inspector Clouseau rather reluctantly in the first place. The script did not meet with his approval and he had voiced an intention to rewrite parts of it. Something else that must have alarmed Ustinov was Blake's working methods. Blake liked a loose set, a fun atmosphere and encouraged his actors to improvise. Robert Wagner remembers that:

> There was a little bit of disagreement on Ustinov's part about doing the script, because a lot of it was going to be improvisational and he felt that it should be on the page. So, he and Blake had a bit of a discrepancy about that, not much, but Blake said, ok, let us forget it, and so Peter Ustinov went on his way.[20]

That did not stop the Mirisch brothers suing the actor, seeking a reported $175,000 in damages.[21] Harold Mirisch declared that commitments to starring roles needed to be honoured, lest the motion picture industry become 'seriously impaired' by the whim of actors. The case dragged on for a long time. 'When the picture came out,' said Walter Mirisch, 'and it was a huge success, I remember a lawyer saying to me, can you prove any damages? We were not damaged, we were helped.'[22] Indeed, both parties ended up winning. Peter Sellers took over as Clouseau while Ustinov stepped into a role that Sellers had recently vacated, that of a small-time hustler in the crime caper *Topkapi* (1964). Ustinov's performance earned him an Oscar for best-supporting actor.

With just days before the start of shooting Blake did not waste any time finding Ustinov's replacement. According to Wagner, Blake wanted Peter Sellers as Clouseau from the beginning, having seen him in *I'm All Right Jack* and *The Mouse That Roared*, both released in 1959.

> He always thought he was the man to play the part. So, when Ustinov left Blake was on the telephone with Peter Sellers. And thank God because nobody could have been better in *The Pink Panther* than Peter Sellers. He was so perfect for the role. Now you cannot think of anybody else playing Clouseau.[23]

Martin Jurow was sent to London to get Sellers. With time running out, Jurow could not afford to take no for an answer and planned a little deception. Armed with the knowledge that Sellers fell in love with his co-star Sophia Loren while making *The Millionairess* (1960), Jurow informed the actor, 'Peter, she's waiting for you.' Loren lived in Rome. 'Sellers never saw her once,' revealed Jurow. 'Whenever she was in residence in Rome, she was faithful to Carlo Ponti.'[24]

Jurow need not have worried, Sellers jumped at the opportunity to appear in *The Pink Panther*. Among the first people he called after signing on to do the film was one of his closest friends, the comic actor Graham Stark. Both had met towards the end of the war when they were in the RAF and had remained buddies ever since. 'Guess what,' said Sellers. 'I'm going to Rome and I'm going to get £80,000 for five weeks' work.'

Stark grabbed a pencil and a scrap of paper and did some quick calculations. 'I've worked it out that you're going to get something like £2,500 every day!'

'Jesus Christ!' Sellers responded.[25]

Peter Sellers came from a show business background; his mother Peg was in the music hall and his father Bill was a pianist. As a young child he spent a lot of his time in the back seat of the family car, going from town to town, and staying in miserable theatrical boarding houses as his parents toured the country's vaudeville circuit, living out of suitcases. While his parents performed on stage the infant Peter was left, or abandoned as he came to realise it, in an empty bedroom in an unfamiliar house filled with dreaded landladies and complete strangers.

Sellers was born on 8 September 1925 in Southsea, near Portsmouth. He was christened Peter in memory of his stillborn older brother. At two weeks old Sellers made his professional debut when Bill proudly held him aloft on the stage of the King's Theatre in Portsmouth and the audience sang 'For He's a Jolly Good Fellow'. At the age of 3 he was part of his parents' act, dressed in white tie and tails; Bill had taught him to sing the old music hall classic 'My Old Dutch'. He attended dancing lessons in Southsea before enrolling in St Aloysius' Boarding and Day School for Boys in Highgate when the family moved up to London.

By this time Peg and Bill had stepped back from full-time performing, although the lure of the theatre never left them. For Peg, this passion was transferred to Peter and a determination that her only child succeed in show business. Consequently, the young Peter was controlled, obsessed over, mollycoddled, and smothered.

For a while it seemed that Sellers would make his career as a professional musician. By his teens he played the drums in local jazz bands and learned to play the banjo and ukulele. Just after his 18th birthday, he was drafted into the Royal Air Force and for the last two years of the war performed in concert parties and in ENSA, entertaining the troops overseas.

After returning home from the war Sellers tried to get work with the BBC but kept failing at the audition stage. At the time his act revolved around impersonations, mainly of movie stars and radio personalities. He heard about a new radio programme called *Show Time* which was putting on a lot of new people and decided to call the producer, Roy Speer. Posing as Kenneth Horne, a popular radio star of the day, Sellers got past the secretary and found himself speaking with Speer, who began, 'Hello Kenneth, what can I do for you?' Continuing with the deception Sellers, as Horne, mentioned having seen this great new comic in cabaret the other night called Peter Sellers and that Speer should put him on his new show. As Speer began to offer his gratitude for the tip, Sellers revealed himself, confessing that this had been the only way to reach the producer and could he have a date on his show. 'You cheeky young sod,' said Speer. 'What do you do?' Sellers replied, 'Well, obviously I do impressions.' Sellers got the gig and ended up with his first write-up in the press. This led to him becoming a sought-after radio personality.

Sellers never lost this gift for mimicry. During the filming of *A Shot in The Dark* Sellers stayed at the Dorchester. One morning he was coming down in the lift with composer Henry Mancini. It stopped and two Arab gentlemen got in, both in deep conversation all the way down to the lobby. As Mancini recalled:

> The minute they were out of earshot, out of Peter's mouth came the exact voices of these two men talking to each other. Not just the accents – Peter was a genius with accents – but the actual voices. I looked around, thinking the two must have come back, but it was Peter.[26]

Sellers really established himself on *The Goon Show*, playing a zany collection of radio characters alongside Spike Milligan and Harry Secombe. It ran from 1951 to 1960 and many times Sellers was to call working on the show the happiest time of his professional life. By the time *The Goons* was no more Sellers had already made a successful move into pictures with the Ealing classic *The Ladykillers* (1955), *I'm All Right Jack* and *The Mouse*

That Roared (both 1959), which was a modest success in the US. In 1960, he gained more attention with his role in *The Millionairess*. And in 1962 Sellers worked for the first time with Stanley Kubrick playing a small but important role in the controversial *Lolita*. For the most part though, Sellers was stuck making modest British comedies. So, the offer to do *The Pink Panther* came at the perfect time as he had resolved to do no more 'little English' pictures and to focus more on international projects.

The character of Inspector Clouseau began to take shape in Sellers' mind on the flight across to Rome, or so he would later claim. Usually, it took the actor much longer to find himself in a role, this time the pieces appeared to fall quickly into place. They needed to do, of course, he would be on set filming in a matter of days. The physical appearance of Clouseau was the first thing that came together and the main inspiration, so said Sellers, was an image from the front of a box of matches. That image belonged to Captain Webb, a true British hero, the first person to swim the English Channel, unaided, in 1875. There he stood, on this box of matches, in all his Victorian pomp and splendour in front of the White Cliffs of Dover, wearing a short-sleeved bathing suit and an impressive moustache. So, Clouseau would sport a moustache. As for the rest of him, there was a Burberry trench coat that Sellers had brought along with him to combat the chills of a wintry Rome and the actor's own sleek frame. Physically there was very little of the baby fat that had been evident in the younger Sellers, the result of taking slimming pills for over a year. Henceforth, Sellers would fight an almost constant battle over his weight as his stature as a star ascended.

As for Clouseau's personality, Sellers felt that the script presented him as too much of a clueless idiot. In Sellers' mind, Clouseau was a man who believed desperately that he is a master detective and as such he intended to play the role with dignity intact. 'Even when he comes a cropper, he must pick himself up with that notion intact,' said Sellers.[27] This was one of the reasons why the character worked so well and caught the public's imagination. There are people like Clouseau all over the world. As far as Sellers was concerned, a little forgivable vanity would only serve to humanise Clouseau in the eyes of the audience, 'and make him kind of touching'.[28]

Blake Edwards was to seize on that personality trait, and it became the biggest key to the Clouseau character, this ability never to give up. Not for one moment does Clouseau imagine that he will fail in whatever task he has been asked to perform. Of course, this is one of the reasons why Clouseau is so funny, we laugh at his pomposity. However, the real tragedy is that deep down Clouseau knows he is an idiot. Everyone around him does too, and Clouseau either can't see it or tries desperately not to notice. Instead, after each gaffe, his built-in defence mechanism comes into operation. If he walks into a wall instead of through an open door, he immediately attempts to regain his dignity by claiming that the architect of the building ought to be investigated. When he falls down a flight of stairs into a room full of people, he pretends that it was some form of exercise. Or when leaving a room, he walks instead into a closet he emerges seconds later to announce, 'Most ingenious. The old closet ploy. I really must congratulate you. If there's one thing I do enjoy, it's a good closet ploy.'

The final piece of the Clouseau puzzle was the accent. In this the first *Panther* film there is nothing very extraordinary about it. Indeed, it is no different than most English-speaking actors putting on a slight comic French accent. Only in later instalments did the Sellers vocal gymnastics reach ludicrous proportions. Indeed, so famous did the Clouseau accent become that in 2004 an expert in linguistics at the California State University, Fullerton, wrote a paper about it.

Sellers arrived in Rome with just three days to prepare for his first day on the set. Waiting for him at the airport was Blake Edwards. The two men had never met before and during the long drive into the city and the Excelsior Hotel, on the fashionable Via Veneto, both 'discovered each other, so to speak', in the words of Blake.[29] The biggest discovery was a shared love for silent comics like Laurel and Hardy, Chaplin and Buster Keaton, exponents of pure slapstick. At his home in California Blake owned a large collection of old 16 mm silent comedies and often, as he called it, 'refreshed' himself with them. He watched them with no other purpose other than enjoyment, but always found little things later that he could adapt and use. Stuntman Joe Dunne, who doubled for Sellers in the later *Panther* films, recalls visiting the star's London flat and noticing on the wall a framed photograph of Stan Laurel. Whenever Sellers was in Los Angeles, he always made a point of going to visit Stan Laurel, then in the twilight of his years, at his home.

The accident-prone Clouseau can certainly trace his antecedents back to those silent slapstick comedy shorts. Sellers, however, also drew upon another comedy hero, Jacques Tati and his creation, Mr Hulot. Like Mr Hulot, Clouseau appears to be unable to cope in a world where everything seems to be against him. He cannot open a door without the knob coming off in his hand or get out of a taxi without falling into an ornamental pond.

For Blake and Sellers that car ride was a real meeting of minds. 'We found that we could work together the moment we met,' Blake later claimed.[30] It was the start of one of the most creative professional relationships in movie history, and one of the most incendiary. For years, Blake had wanted to revive the neglected tradition of slapstick but never found the right vehicle or collaborator. 'Then along came Peter, a walking storehouse of madness, a man with an almost surrealist approach to the insanity of things, and we found an immediate affinity.'[31]

And along came Clouseau, too, the perfect foil, the perfect host. For Blake, slapstick, like all forms of comedy, is born of character:

> If the character exemplifies some kind of authority that you or I would like to laugh at, and if we can present it in the kind of violent, physical action of slipping on a banana or falling into a manhole, the better the character is defined, the funnier it will be.[32]

Clouseau was the instrument with which Blake would bring his beloved slapstick back to the American cinema.

Without sufficient time to rewrite the script, Blake and Sellers ended up improvising quite a bit of the material revolving around Clouseau. Each would take what was written on the page, then ad-lib and work around it. Blake suggested something, then Sellers, and it built and built until it almost had a life of its own. Sellers came in every day with a whole bunch of ideas, and he and Blake would sift through them. Blake was always on hand to pull Sellers back a little bit if he went too over the top. 'It was a terrific match between Peter and Blake,' says Wagner. 'They got along so beautifully. It was a romance. The chemistry between them was great. Just everything worked, everything fell into place.'[33]

It was Sellers that suggested making Clouseau less of a fool and more of a physical clown, an aspect of the character that reached its zenith in the '70s' films but is largely absent in Blake and Maurice Richlin's screenplay. On the page the Inspector is very much a routine sort of detective; when reading the original script it is obvious that much of the Clouseau character we know and love today was created by Sellers and Blake on a daily basis throughout shooting. In the script Clouseau is not really that accident prone, nor causes mayhem wherever he goes. A perfect example is the scene where Clouseau and Simone first arrive at their hotel in the ski resort and observe Sir Charles Lytton being brought in on a stretcher after an accident on the slopes. In the script, Clouseau simply watches as Lytton's entourage pass by. In the film, Clouseau enters the lobby, unaware of Sir Charles on the stretcher, walks straight into it and they all crash to the floor.

There is an element of a Whitehall farce in the script, which does transfer to the film version, of people hiding under beds or in wardrobes, running in and out of bedrooms. For the scene where Clouseau attempts to seduce his bored wife, Sellers used the memory of one of his earliest sexual experiences, when he was in the RAF and invited to the bedroom of a girl that he had met at a concert party. He arrived dressed in his pyjamas and wearing a dressing gown, then proceeded to get into bed without removing a stitch of clothing. Sellers remembered this faux pas and came up with the gag of Clouseau vainly trying to get out of his clothes as his wife grows ever more exasperated. 'It made a good gag,' said Sellers, 'and consolidated the conviction I had about Clouseau that, in all circumstances, whatever boob he'd made, the man must keep his dignity – which gave him a certain pathetic charm.'[34] This gag was repeated later in the series when Clouseau is about to bed Lesley-Anne Down's Russian assassin and, undressing, has problems unzipping his fly and removing his tie, which ends up round his forehead, like an Apache headband. Clouseau does not appear to have much luck with the opposite sex and this first entry in the series is the only one in which he is married. Even then his attempts to seduce his wife are continually thwarted, both by her indifference and outside forces.

As this improvisation between director and actor continued and grew, Clouseau as a character took on a whole new life and it became patently clear to everyone, especially David Niven, that Sellers was stealing the show. 'Blake was very smart,' recalled Walter Mirisch, 'and realised what was happening and instead of fighting it, he encouraged it.'[35] Maurice Richlin recalls Niven coming out of a screening room at Cinecittà studios and commenting, 'It's a very funny movie, but it's not mine, it's Peter's.'[36]

This was picked up in Penelope Gilliatt's review of the film in the *Observer*:

> Sir Charles has the basis of being a marvellous send up of all the classy cads in fiction, but neither the star nor the director seems to have quite the energy to do it – it's the sight gags that work best, and they all belong to Sellers as the hopelessly inefficient detective.

Years later, at one of the Academy Award shows, Niven was making a guest appearance. Henry Mancini was conducting the orchestra and had decided to use *The Pink Panther* theme as Niven's walk-on music. After rehearsals, Mancini was told that Niven wanted to see him in his dressing room. 'Hank,' said Niven. 'As much as I love *The Pink Panther* movie, I don't think I can quite claim that as my music.' Mancini had to agree with him. 'How about *Around the World In 80 Days*.' Niven smiled and that is what they ended up doing.[37]

Robert Wagner, of course, was observing all this unfold at first-hand. He was on the set the day of the now classic scene where Sellers, in his office at police headquarters, spins a large globe, casually places his hand on it and does a pratfall out of frame. 'And from then on you just had a feeling that this was going to be a hit.'[38] Maurice was to recall years later that Blake told him when Sellers invented that bit of comedy business with the globe, he knew the film was going to work. Again, as written in the script, it was a very simple scene, intended to introduce Clouseau to the audience. There has been another robbery, and the Phantom's female accomplice has got away. A determined Clouseau demands that this woman be apprehended, oblivious to the fact she is his own wife. Keen to bring the scene alive, Blake spied a big globe on the set, and together with Sellers came up with the spinning globe fall. The character of Clouseau had been established in his very first scene in the picture.

Wagner had never met Sellers before beginning work on the picture but admired him as a comic actor. Unsure what to really expect, the two men got on well and became lifelong friends. 'I had great compassion for Peter and he was a very positive man in my life, very helpful to me. I had great times with him.'[39]

On the set, Wagner and Sellers often talked. One day Wagner was taken aback when Sellers revealed his predilection for taking isobutyl nitrate during sex. The drug, he said, extends the orgasm. Wagner voiced concerns about the side effects of taking it, that overuse might lead to coronary issues. It was a warning Sellers should have paid heed to.

Meanwhile, Wagner was enjoying playing the role of George and working for Blake. 'He was terrific. Blake was very inventive and creative. He had a concept about what the film should be.'[40] For one scene Wagner was required to hide fully clothed in Capucine's bath. Instead of normal soapy foam a longer-lasting industrial-strength foaming agent was used. The results for Wagner were to be traumatic. 'This stuff burned and lacerated my corneas and I was blind for about three weeks.'[41] Capucine was quite badly burnt, too, but because Wagner had to submerge fully under the water, take after take, he came out of it far worse. His mood worsened when talk emerged from the suits back in Hollywood about replacing him. 'But everyone on the film stood by me and Blake said no, I want him, so they rearranged the schedule and Blake shot around me until I recovered.'[42]

In January production moved to Cortina d'Ampezzo, a ski resort in the Italian Alps, a playground for the rich and famous. Blake and Maurice Richlin deliberately set their story in an impossibly glamourous and sophisticated world, wonderfully captured by the camera of Philip H. Lathrop who had collaborated with Blake on *Breakfast at Tiffany's* and *Days of Wine and Roses*. Every frame of the film looks gorgeous, the production design is lush and it is no surprise to learn that both Capucine and Claudia Cardinale were dressed by Yves Saint Laurent. This was the French designer's first movie project.

One weekend afternoon the skies in Cortina were a brilliant crisp blue and Niven suggested to Wagner they share a lunch up in the mountains. Dressed in only casual wear, up they went in the chair lift about 10,000 feet. Soon after arriving the weather seemed to be changing but they persevered with lunch. Finally, the bitter cold became too much to bear. Niven nudged Wagner, 'Bob, my unit is frozen. We have got to get down.' Both took the chair lift back, with Niven visibly uncomfortable in his nether regions. 'I can't stand it Bob, it's frozen. It's frozen solid.'

At the bottom, Niven led Wagner into the hotel and made straight for the bar ordering three shots of brandy. Wagner then followed Niven into the men's toilet where he immediately unzipped his pants. Just about to pop it in the brandy snifter to warm up, with Wagner on the floor in hysterics, a man entered the bathroom and saw the two of them. 'What is going on here?' he asked. Niven looked at the stranger and said, 'I always give it a little drink now and then.'[43] For Wagner, Niven epitomised the perfect English gentleman and, like Sellers, he became another lifelong friend. 'He was a wonderful man and I loved him very much.'[44]

Niven made a positive impression on the cast. Claudia Cardinale was to remember him as, 'A perfect gentleman every woman would want to be with. He would open doors, walk a step behind you and offer his arm at every opportunity to help you out.'[45] As for Sellers, Claudine revealed he was fun to work with, but off the set things were very different, that he was uncommunicative and kept to himself. 'He was a very sad person, very serious, very unhappy, a lonely man. He never relaxed.'[46] This character flaw persisted throughout his life. Sellers was the kind of person who could never relax, just put his feet up and take things easy. For short periods perhaps, but then he would find ways to cause chaos or conflict. A good example was when he was making the film *Ghost in the Noonday Sun* (1974) in Cyprus and the production had rented a villa for him. His secretary for most of the 70s, Susan Wood, remembers it as being beautiful:

> And when we first arrived Peter was like, this is so lovely. It's so gorgeous, the garden, the pool. Then a couple of days later he'd be cursing it, I don't like this and I don't like that. And there was no rhyme nor reason to his likes and dislikes. It was all inside his head.[47]

Besides Cortina, Rome, and a few days' location work in Paris, Blake shot in Rocca di Papa, a small and picturesque town several miles southeast of Rome. This was the site of the climactic car chase. After a lavish fancy dress party, during which Princess Dala's diamond is stolen, Sir Charles and George escape in gorilla costumes with Clouseau, resplendent in a suit of armour, and the police in hot pursuit; not forgetting two constables trying to catch up dressed as a pantomime horse. The cars speed through the ancient streets and back and forth across the town square. This scene perfectly encapsulates Blake's working method. As a director he always had the scene mapped out in his head but was loose enough to just allow things to happen. While setting up a shot, Blake had spotted an old man sitting quietly in the piazza idly watching the crew busily at work, wondering what was going on. Out of that came the idea of an elderly gentleman outside a trattoria who pulls up a chair to watch all the cars zooming up and down the street and ultimately piling up into each other.

Principal photography on *The Pink Panther* concluded in mid-March 1963. For Wagner, the film remains a cherished memory, something he feels fortunate to have been part of:

> Being with David Niven, who was a marvellous man. Capucine was wonderful. And Claudia. We all had a tremendous time – we were all very close. Blake kind of brought everybody together. We all had great affection for each other. It was one of the greatest experiences I have ever had. We all stayed very close.[48]

For Sellers, too, it had been one of the happiest pictures he had ever worked on, and a therapy of sorts. Back home in England his personal life was slowly disintegrating, as he was in the process of divorcing his first wife, Anne. So why, when the film was in the can, did Sellers suddenly and viciously turn against it? Getting in touch with the Mirisch brothers, Sellers said he thought the film was going to be a disaster. This was the first real warning sign for Blake of Sellers' own peculiar brand of madness, his unpredictability and capacity for deep mood swings. As Blake was to discover, this attitude to his work was not an uncommon occurrence after Sellers finished a picture, but the director wanted nothing to do with any kind of negativity and totally disengaged from Sellers as he entered post-production. 'Fuck him,' Blake thought, 'I'm never going to see him again.'

Back when Blake and Maurice were first putting the script together, the idea of a diamond that was going to be called the Pink Panther seemed to lend itself to having some kind of animated animal character. Handling second unit duties on the film was Blake's uncle, Owen Crump, a writer, and a director who had worked at Warner Bros. He knew someone called David H. DePatie, then executive in charge of the studio's cartoon division. By the early '60s Warner's cartoon department was in steep decline and eventually shut down completely in 1963. Recognising that the writing was on the wall, DePatie had gone into business with Friz Freleng to create their own independent animation studio: DePatie–Freleng Enterprises. Freleng, along with Chuck Jones and Tex Avery, was a primal force in the history of Warner Bros cartoons working on the studio's Looney Tunes and Merrie Melodies series that featured the likes of Bugs Bunny, Sylvester and Tweety, Porky Pig and Speedy Gonzalez.

DePatie and Freleng managed to make a deal with the head of the Warner studio, Jack Warner, to rent the now defunct animation department. Everything was still intact, the cameras and equipment, all the supplies, it was just the way it had been left; paper and pencils even lay untouched on the work boards. Depatie and Freleng were in business. For the first few months the company got by mainly doing animation for television commercials. Then everything changed. One afternoon DePatie was in his office when the phone rang. It was Blake – could DePatie come over and see him? Blake handed over the script for *The Pink Panther*, asked DePatie to go away and read it and then get back to him. DePatie thought the story had all the makings of a hit and accompanied by Freleng returned to Blake's office full of enthusiasm. Blake explained that although the movie was going to be live action, he wanted to somehow use this animated Pink Panther character. DePatie and Freleng's job was to come up with some concept ideas.

Back at the office the two men pooled together some of their best character designers, including their top layout artist Hawley Pratt. Over the next week they worked on close to a hundred drawings and different variations about what a Pink Panther would look like. Those drawings were taken over to Blake's house one Sunday afternoon and the director laid them all out on his living room floor. Walking around, and up and down, studying each picture carefully, Blake made his choice. 'That's the one I want.' In that moment, one of the world's most famous cartoon characters was born.

According to DePatie, the artist that made the biggest contribution to the *Pink Panther*, more even than Freleng, was Hawley Pratt. It was his design that Blake picked that day. However, the director still had no clear idea of what to do with the cartoon feline when he flew off with the cast and crew to Rome. All he did with the character was put it on his production letterhead and on business cards. DePatie and Freleng had no clue either where the character was going to go from there either and went back to their television commercials. A few months passed by and then Blake got in touch again. 'I'm back,' he told Depatie. 'I've got the movie in the can and I know what I want to do. Come over.'

Blake's concept was to use the Pink Panther character as the star of an animated main title sequence. Blake showed them some of the dailies and Freleng set to work on a storyboard. Blake loved it and didn't change a thing. As it stands, the film opens with Princess Dala as a young child receiving the famed Pink Panther diamond from her father. He tells her that it has an unusual flaw and that one can look deeply into the stone and see what appears to be a leaping panther. The camera then moves slowly into the centre of the stone to reveal a panther, but this is no wild animal, rather a sophisticated creature, with a gold cigarette holder.

However, putting together a fully animated main title was not going to come cheap and the Mirisch brothers had already thrown a lot of money into the production. Far from reeling at the thought of spending more cash, they liked the idea and DePatie and Freleng were given the green light. The process itself took two months.

From the earliest previews the audience reaction to the title sequence was extraordinary, nothing quite like it had been seen before. According to DePatie, at one preview at the Westwood Village Theatre in Los Angeles, when the title sequence ended, they had to switch off the projector and turn on the house lights, 'because people were just going really crazy about it'.[49]

Accompanying that marvellous animated opening was a theme tune that itself was to make movie history. Blake only ever had one person in mind to write the score for *The Pink Panther*, and that was Henry Mancini. By 1963, after collaborating on films like *Breakfast at Tiffany's* and *Days of Wine and Roses*, they were already established as a winning team. It was luck that first brought them together, a chance encounter back in 1958 at Universal Studios. Mancini had just had his hair cut at the barber shop on the lot and, walking out, just happened to pass Blake. They started to chat. Blake said he was doing a new TV series called *Peter Gunn* and did Mancini fancy writing the music. They ended up working on over twenty pictures together. Theirs was like the relationship Steven Spielberg was to enjoy with John Williams. 'My dad had a very special relationship with Blake,' says Mancini's daughter, Monica, who is an accomplished singer. 'They understood each other and knew how to navigate around each other because Blake could be difficult to work with.'[50]

Right at the beginning, during *Peter Gunn*, the ground rules of their working relationship were laid out, as Monica recalls:

> Blake was a very hands-on director and quite controlling. The first time he went in to see dad when he was doing some scoring for *Peter Gunn* Blake said, 'Hank, I think you should put a little bongos here,' and dad just kind of rolled his eyes and gave him a look. And Blake got it in that moment, to just leave him alone and trust him, and not interfere in his musical choices at all. So, they laid down their territory early on and Blake had total trust in him.[51]

Mancini's work on *The Pink Panther* began when Blake was still shooting in Rome. Blake had created a scene to showcase the talents of American singer Fran Jeffries, then well-known on the cabaret and Las Vegas circuit. Dressed in a black cat-suit she was to seductively slither her way around an Alpine ski chalet singing a song during a party scene. Blake wanted Mancini to come out to Rome and provide the music. 'I boarded a plane,' Mancini recalled, 'and wrote the basic melody on the back of a menu during that flight.'[52]

Blake wanted the song to be in Italian. One of the biggest international hits of recent years had been 'Nel blu, dipinto di blu,' more commonly known as *Volare*, recorded by Italian singer-songwriter Domenico Modugno. Mancini contacted the lyricist for *Volare*, Franco Migliacci, and asked him to provide some Italian lyrics for the song he had written for the film. Mancini's melody had a pleasing samba rhythm to it and the song became known as *Meglio Stasera.* Johnny Mercer provided lyrics for the English version, *It Had Better Be Tonight.*

While all this was going on Fran Jeffries was in hospital with such a bad case of flu that she literally could not talk, let alone sing. Mancini, accompanied by Sellers, took a taxi to visit and cheer her up. It was in her hospital bed that Fran learnt the song, so as soon as she came out, she was ready to record it.

Back in Los Angeles, Mancini began work proper on the main score. Reading the script, he was initially drawn to David Niven's jewel thief, thinking what an interesting character he would be to compose music around. Here was a man, as personified by Niven, who was suave and sophisticated, with a lot of class. As a thief, he slinks or creeps around in the dark and Mancini started to write a theme just for him. It was one of the few occasions he ever wrote a theme before seeing the finished film.

Pleased with the result, everything changed when Blake told Mancini of his plan to employ an animated opening to the picture featuring a pink panther. Returning to his theme for Niven's jewel thief, Mancini thought it would work equally well for this cartoon panther. That proved to be something of an understatement. The melody has since become one of cinema's most beloved and recognized title themes. Mancini's concept was for the theme to have a swinging jazz style and he brought in Plas Johnson, a jazz tenor saxophonist, to be the soloist on the recording; Johnson had played on the *Peter Gunn* theme. As for Mancini's jazz-inflected score, it was nominated for an Oscar and later ranked No. 20 on 'One Hundred Years of Film Scores', the American Film Institute's 2005 list of the twenty-five greatest film scores of all time.

Graham Stark was relaxing at home when the phone rang. It was Sellers. 'I'm back,' went the voice. 'Had a great time. Come and see the film tonight.' There was going to be a special screening of *The Pink Panther* for a small invited audience:

> I went down to this little preview theatre in the West End and they were all there, Niven, Capucine, Claudia Cardinale, and Peter walked on the screen and you never looked at anyone else. It was in the pocket. Roars of applause. Afterwards we walked across Soho Square and I remember Sellers stopped me and asked, 'Go on, what do you reckon?' I said, 'Peter, you bastard, you've fucking done it.'[53]

Opening in time for the Christmas holidays in Italy, *The Pink Panther* arrived in British cinemas in January 1964 and went on to become the sixth most popular film at the UK box office that year, beaten only by *Goldfinger*, *A Hard Day's Night*, *Zulu*, the Norman Wisdom comedy *A Stitch in Time* and Cliff Richard's *It's a Wonderful Life*. Sellers was ranked the second most popular star, after Sean Connery, thanks to *The Pink Panther* and his other successful film of 1964, *Dr. Strangelove*.

For the New York opening in March 1964, United Artists secured the Radio City Music Hall, perhaps the most prestigious movie theatre in the United States at the time. When Robert Wagner first caught a performance, it did not take him long to realise its potential. 'I was thrilled when I first saw the film. The whole thing worked perfectly, everything came together and that does not happen often. The reaction to the film was terrific. And it was obvious to me that it was going to be a franchise.'[54]

Reviews, however, were mixed on both sides of the Atlantic. America's *Time* magazine thought the whole thing had a, 'pervasive air of desperation', while Bosley Crowther of *The New York Times* called the script a 'basically unoriginal and largely witless piece of farce carpentry that has to be pushed and heaved at stoutly in order to keep on the move.' *Variety* was much more positive, calling the film, 'intensely funny', and the *Hollywood Reporter* gave it a thumbs up, too. Britain's *Sunday Express* dismissed the picture as, 'feeble', and the *Daily Telegraph* felt that the, 'animated credit titles provide the most satisfying sequence'. *The Times*, however, said, 'The film is so smooth and glossy, a first-rate professional job in every department, that one can just relax and enjoy it, like a cinematic bubble-bath.' And *Films and Filming* wrote that it was 'that rare thing, a thoroughly agreeable entertainment', and that the movie was one of the best things Sellers had yet done, 'one really does tend to forget how good he can be'.

One thing all critics certainly seemed to agree over was the excellence of Sellers' performance. In her review for *The Observer*, Penelope Gilliatt called it, 'one of the most delicate studies in accident-proneness since the silents'. While *The Guardian* hailed *The Pink Panther* as, 'A triumph for Sellers at the expense of the rest of the film, the success of which becomes over-dependent on his presence.' Alexander Walker of the *Evening Standard*, already a great admirer of the Sellers talent, wrote that this performance 'puts him into a select new class. He joins the comics of the great silent films in raising accident-proneness to a high art.'

The passing of years has treated the original *Pink Panther* well. Today it is viewed as a comedy classic. In 2010, it was selected for preservation in the United States National Film Registry by the Library of Congress for being, 'culturally, historically, or aesthetically significant'.

Looking back on it today, one of the most interesting things to say about *The Pink Panther* was that even before it opened in cinemas cameras were turning on the second instalment. And how that sequel came about is an intriguing tale.

Chapter 2

A SHOT IN THE DARK

A Shot in the Dark is not really a sequel to *The Pink Panther*, the Pink Panther jewel is nowhere to be seen, and neither is The Phantom. No, *A Shot in the Dark* is the further adventures of Inspector Clouseau. And there is a very good reason for that.

L'Idiote (*The Idiot*) was a successful French farce by Marcel Achard that played in Paris from 1960 to 1962. The plot centres on a bumbling French Examining Magistrate by the name of Paul Sevigne, who is investigating his first case, a murder at the residence of an aristocratic family. Josefa, the chambermaid, has been discovered unconscious in her bedroom next to the dead body of her lover, with the gun that killed him by her side. There seems little doubt she is the murderer. Sevigne, however, is adamant she did not commit the crime and plans to unravel the mystery.

Novelist and screenwriter Harry Kurnitz adapted the story for an American audience under the new title of *A Shot in the Dark*. Opening in October 1961 at the Booth Theatre on Broadway, it played for over a year before going on a national tour. The part of Paul Sevigne was played by future *Star Trek* actor William Shatner, while Julie Harris was cast as Josefa the maid. As the play unfolds Sevigne discovers that the real murderer is the family patriarch, wealthy bank boss, Benjamin Beaurevers. Originally cast as Beaurevers was film and stage actor Donald Cook. Unfortunately, Cook suffered a fatal heart attack during the pre-Broadway try outs, less than a week after his 60th birthday. He was found on the floor of his hotel room after failing to appear for that day's matinee performance. Rushed in at short notice was Walter Matthau, who had just two days to learn and rehearse the part before taking over. 'I spoke in an exaggerated English accent,' he later joked. 'And I walked like a combination of Charles de Gaulle and my mother having desperately to go to the bathroom.'[1] For Matthau the play was something of a personal triumph, picking up a Tony award for best actor.

For some time, Harold Mirisch had been talking to the Russian-born director Anatole Litvak about doing a film for them. When Litvak saw the Broadway production of *A Shot in the Dark* it seemed to him that this was the right vehicle. The three Mirisch brothers went to see the play, liked it, and bought the rights. Litvak brought in Alec Coppel to write the screenplay. Coppel was an accomplished writer specialising in light thrillers, mysteries, and sex comedies (he wrote *Vertigo* for Hitchcock), so was perfect for the job. According to Coppel's son Chris, although his father wrote a draft screenplay, his heart just was not in it.

> He thought the whole premise of a bumbling French detective was weak and unrealistic. He felt the level of slapstick they wanted in the script was almost childish and would not work on the big screen. He felt that the film would be a complete disaster and did not really want anything to do with it. When he went to see the final film (with me) he laughed until he cried. He openly admitted (often) that he had got that one badly wrong.[2]

Meanwhile, Litvak had persuaded Walter Matthau to reprise his stage role. With Shatner and Julie Harris not considered well-known enough to carry a big studio film, Peter Sellers was brought in to play Sevigne. Talks also began about Sophia Loren playing the accused maid. However, when her husband Carlo Ponti read Coppel's script he advised his wife to drop out. The Mirisch brothers, equally disappointed with the adaptation, sent it to Norman Krasna for rewrites. Krasna specialised in screwball comedies, although his most famous credit was the perennial holiday favourite *White Christmas* (1954). When the new pages came back the Mirisch brothers still felt it was a bit flat.

Further bad news arrived when Litvak decided to leave the project. This was partly due to Sophia Loren withdrawing, but also undoubtedly his testy relationship with Sellers. Unhappy with the script Sellers was trying everything to get out of his contract. Behind the back of Litvak and the Mirisch brothers, Sellers had been bombarding Blake Edwards with desperate pleas to step in and save the film. Blake refused each time, but Sellers would not be rebuked and kept pestering him. Finally, Blake agreed to read the script and didn't like it, turning the offer down once again. Litvak's decision to walk obviously changed matters and Sellers urged the Mirisch brothers to put a call through to Blake.

At the time Blake was working on another project for the Mirisch company, a comedy war drama called *What Did You Do in the War, Daddy?* It was a collaboration with a rising young New York writer called William Peter Blatty. One day at lunch Blake explained to Blatty that he had been asked to take over on another film, 'And I won't do it unless you write it.'[3] Blake gave Batty the script, which he read that evening to see if he could do anything with it. 'It wasn't a straight comedy at that point,' Blatty recalled, 'more of a thriller, really, and apparently Peter Sellers had just had a huge fight with the original director.'[4] Blatty came up with an idea that took the story in a completely new direction. Quickly he typed out a page-and-a-half scenario and gave it to Blake. Blatty proposed that more dead bodies keep being found in the Beaurevers' mansion. The clever twist is that each new murder has been carried out by a different killer for a different motive. Of course, the poor maid is blamed for all of them, meaning that Paul Sevigne's protestations of her innocence makes him look even more foolish. Then came the bombshell, for all that to work, said Blatty, Sellers had to play the detective as Clouseau. Blake said the actor would never agree.

After *The Pink Panther* was in the can there was no real notion or desire from anyone to make another movie or turn it into a series. However, Blatty's suggestion found favour with Sellers, as well as the Mirisch brothers. *A Shot in the Dark* had become the follow-up to *The Pink Panther* by default, and Paul Sevigne was now Inspector Jacques Clouseau.

One casualty of the change was Walter Matthau. After Blake and Blatty's rewrite the screenplay bore so little resemblance to either Kurnitz's play or the Coppel/Krasna versions that he felt obliged to leave the picture. He was replaced by George Sanders, an actor who was the very definition of class and debonair manners, very much in the David Niven mould. The character's name was also changed to Benjamin Ballon. Someone else who lost out was Maurice Richlin. He had rather hoped that if more *Panther* films were going to be made it would be he and Blake that would be working on them together. This was not to be.

Principal photography on *A Shot in the Dark* got underway in November 1963 at the MGM British Studios, Borehamwood, near London. Sellers had bought property near King's Langley, Hertfordshire, that boasted a seven-acre park, tennis court, swimming pool, paddocks and two Tudor barns among its assets. Sellers quickly restored the barns to house his drum kit, model railway set and a home cinema. The house was just a swift half hour drive to the studios, but Sellers still managed to persuade United Artists to put him up at the Dorchester for the entire duration of the shoot. 'He was given superstar treatment,' recalled his son Michael Sellers, 'occupying the elegant Oliver Messel suite, with its crystal glass chandeliers, chintz curtains, garden murals and original oil paintings. There was also a garden terrace reached through French doors.'[5] Sellers was adept at getting film companies to cough up for sometimes unwarranted expenses. On another picture, *The World of Henry Orient* (1964), again for United Artists, Sellers was in New York on promotion duties and put up at the Regency Hotel on Park Avenue. At 2.30 in the morning, United Artist executive David Picker was awoken by a phone call from the film's frantic producer Jerome Hellman. 'We've got a problem with Peter Sellers.' It turned out that Sellers wanted out of the hotel, complaining that his room had a poltergeist in it. 'What the hell, is he crazy?' asked Picker. Sellers was moved into a more expensive room at the Waldorf.[6]

Sellers certainly had a thing about poltergeists. During the filming of *A Shot in the Dark* Blatty was to recall Sellers telling him that he had left a previous home because of a disruptive spirit. As Sellers described it, he was sitting on the edge of his bed after waking up one morning to see both of his socks levitate up to the level of his eyes. 'I decided I'd had enough of all the knockings and rappings and footsteps in the middle of the night in an empty house.'[7] Blatty wasn't quite sure what to make of it. Of course, in a few years' time the writer would delve into the supernatural himself when he wrote the novel *The Exorcist*.

It appears that Sellers did go back to his country home at weekends. Elke Sommer recalls being invited there for one particularly memorable lunch. The German actress had been cast as the maid, here called Maria Gambrelli, after both Shirley MacLaine and Austrian actress Romy Schneider were briefly considered. Elke had already appeared opposite Richard Todd in *Why Bother to Knock* (1961) and Paul Newman in *The Prize* (1963), and was well on her way to becoming one of the sex symbols of European cinema. Even so, she arrived in England with her mother, who was to stay for most of the shoot. Both Elke and her mother travelled up together to Sellers' country house, where he now lived on his own, after he and his wife Anne had divorced. Elke remembers: '

> He was so happy we came. He prepared a wonderful luncheon. Then we went horseback riding. My mum stayed in the house. He did everything to make us comfortable. He played some

> music from *The Millionairess* film and showed us some clips. I think he was very much in love with Sophia Loren. He told me that she had promised to stay with him. But then when the movie was finished, she went back to her husband Carlo Ponti. Sophia really led him on. And that broke his heart. It really broke his heart.[8]

Because Elke had a prior engagement that evening, at five o'clock she announced that both she and her mother had to leave. 'And he was so sad, he said, "Really, can't you stay for dinner, please, stay for dinner." "I can't Peter," I said. "I thought it was only for the afternoon." We drove away and I turned around and waved goodbye and he was this lonely figure in front of that beautiful cottage and he waved and waved and waved until we were gone.'[9]

Elke claims that she and Peter were on a very similar wavelength during production:

> I was watching one of the office scenes being filmed, when Peter plays with this big globe and gets his hand stuck. He rehearsed it and I said, 'Oh Jesus, you've got Africa all over your hand,' and he took that and used it in his dialogue, he thought it was funnier than hell.[10]

Someone else watching this classic scene unfold was Terry Ackland-Snow, a young draughtsman working on the film . 'Each take just made it funnier, till the final one when the timing was spot on.'[11]

Elke recalls a scene in which Clouseau and Maria are stranded in their car in a traffic jam:

> There was supposed to be this big bus next to us with people looking out and staring at us. And I screamed and I bit Peter in the shoulder, and he had very hairy shoulders, so then I got a hair stuck between my teeth. That was all unscripted, it just happened.[12]

Clouseau and Maria are returning from a nudist camp, where another dead body has turned up. Convinced of Maria's innocence, Clouseau insists she is released from custody every time there is a murder, in the hope she will lead him to the real killer. The only flaw in the plan is that each time a fresh dead body appears Maria is always in the vicinity. Clouseau's colleagues can't understand why he is so convinced Maria is not the murderer. Of course, we know it is because he is infatuated with her and wants to get her into bed. In the new film, Clouseau is now a bachelor. Mrs Clouseau is no more. She doesn't even warrant a mention.

The nudist camp scene is a highlight of the picture. 'It was so much fun,' recalls Elke. 'We laughed ourselves silly.'[13] Following a lead, Clouseau stumbles upon the nudist camp and gets into an argument with the cloakroom attendant who tells him, police officer or not, to remove his clothes if he wants to enter. The attendant, resplendent with a beatnik beard and strumming a guitar, was played by one of Sellers' closest friends, the actor/writer Bryan Forbes. It was just a cameo and Forbes delighted in going by the name of Turk Thrust in the credits.

Turk Thrust was in fact a Sellers invention. A few months previously Sellers and Forbes, along with Forbes' wife Nanette Newman, were spotted at Heathrow airport going on a trip to Paris by a journalist from the *Daily Sketch* newspaper. The reporter asked what the purpose of their trip was. Sellers announced that he and Forbes were on their way to sign up a new singing sensation. The reporter began feverishly scribbling in his notebook, delighted by this scoop. He asked for a name. 'Turk Thrust,' said Sellers. 'Are you going to manage him?' asked the reporter, completely taken in. 'We hope to,' continued Sellers. 'He is going to be big, really big. Bigger than Freda Clench.'

The reporter still hadn't sussed it; instead, he thanked Sellers for this exclusive piece of showbiz news and let them catch their flight. Sellers and Forbes returned to London a few days later to find the piece had made it to print.

After this, Sellers was determined to keep the legend of Turk Thrust alive. He and Forbes produced a fake LP entitled 'Turk Thrust's Greatest Hits,' with a suitably garish cover. Then Forbes made his cameo appearance in *A Shot in the Dark*. For a while Sellers considered finding an unknown singer and grooming him as Turk Thrust but his interest waned and that was the end of Mr Thrust.

Finally allowed into the nudist camp, Clouseau wanders around with a guitar covering his modesty. The whole sequence was a little risqué for a family comedy at the time. Indeed, one of the more contentious bits of dialogue was cut. Clouseau bumps into a blonde female nudist, who scolds him. 'Monsieur, you are no gentleman.' Clouseau sneaks a downward glance, then replies, 'And you, madam, are no blonde.'

Another classic scene is the billiard game during which Clouseau interrogates Mr Ballon, while demolishing his collection of snooker cues and tearing the table's green baize. Elke remembers being on the set and watching that being filmed. 'I think it took two days, with all the preparation and the baize ripping. I almost killed myself laughing.'[14] If Elke was not in a particular scene or had time off, she liked to stay around the studio to observe things. 'I always watched in the background and thought, maybe you will learn, you are so young, you have so much still ahead of you. And it helped me tremendously.'[15]

A Shot in the Dark reinvents the world of Jacques Clouseau, not least in the introduction of two new regular characters that in their own way are just as iconic as the Inspector. First there is Cato, Clouseau's Japanese manservant, an invention of Blake. Based at the Dorchester during pre-production, Blake must have interviewed every Chinese or Japanese actor then living in London, of which there were not many at all. Among this small number was Burt Kwouk. He came along, recalls having a nice chat with Blake and then about a week later hearing that he had got the part.

At first Burt was of a mind to turn the job down. Reading the script, he found this character he was being asked to play hardly made an appearance, and scarcely said a word. Burt rang his agent with the intention of telling him he did not want to do it. Then he thought about it again, after all it was a few weeks' work and the money was good, so he did it.

Burt Kwouk was born in Warrington, Lancashire (now in Cheshire) in July 1930, but as a baby was taken back to the family home in Shanghai. There he remained until he was 17, when his parents sent him to the US to study politics and economics. After graduating Kwouk returned briefly to Shanghai before taking advantage of his dual nationality and returning to Britain, where he took various menial jobs before trying his hand at acting. Back in the late '50s and early '60s the only roles Kwouk was deemed suitable for were based on his oriental looks. An early television appearance was in an episode of *Hancock's Half Hour* where Kwouk informs Hancock he has won a lifetime's supply of rice in a newspaper competition. In 1958 he appeared in *The Inn of the Sixth Happiness* starring Ingrid Bergman and then a couple of China-set Hammer films, *The Terror of the Tongs* and *Visa to Canton* (both 1961). In the same year he landed the role of Cato, Kwouk also appeared as a Chinese scientist in the James Bond classic *Goldfinger*.

Burt Kwouk developed a good working relationship with Sellers on the set almost at once. 'I never really saw anything of the dark side of

Peter. For me it was the light side that I knew and liked to remember.'[16] Of course, there were some days when Burt liked him better than other days. But overall, he never found the actor difficult or challenging. There was a chemistry between them that just seemed to work.

On this one occasion Kwouk couldn't get a bit of business right, got despondent and went and sat in a quiet corner of the studio. Sellers came over and put a calming hand on his shoulder. 'That's all right Burt, none of us can do it.' As Kwouk got to know Sellers more over the years he came to realise just how unusual this was, that normally he wasn't aware of other people's problems. 'Often he wouldn't have noticed, but he did on this occasion.'[17]

Sellers never told Kwouk what to do in a particular scene. Instead, he would say, 'That's not very funny,' and Kwouk would have to find out for himself how to make it funnier. 'And it was much better for me to discover it that way, much more effective. He didn't impose his ideas on me of how to make something funny.'[18]

Cato's main function in the Clouseau household, it appears, is to ambush his employer with kung fu attacks at the most unexpected moments and from the most unsuspected places. Clouseau came up with this bizarre plan in order to keep his wits about him and his fighting skills sharp. In *A Shot in the Dark*, Cato's first appearance carries an element of mystery, who is this person, some deadly assassin sent to kill Clouseau? Then, just as Clouseau puts a stranglehold on his assailant, the phone rings and Cato picks it up. 'Inspector Clouseau's residence,' he asks. These fights were to become a fondly awaited staple ingredient in subsequent *Panther* instalments, increasing in their ludicrous nature each time until they almost resembled a cartoon. 'I did my own stunts in the early days,' Kwouk recalls. 'But as I got older I did less and less. I could fall just as fast; it just took me longer to get up. And Peter loved doing those fights. But you must realise that neither Cato nor Clouseau were very good at martial arts. We are a couple of lunatics who think we are great; in fact, all we do is smash up the house we live in.'[19]

What many people did not know was that Sellers was already proficient in judo. He had been taking lessons since the late 1950s and belonged to the London Judo Society. He even gave them a trophy in 1962, called the Peter Sellers Junior Inter-Club Team Trophy, which they could compete for every year. At one point he was appointed the society's vice-president. On the set of *The Pink Panther Strikes Again* in 1976, Cyd Child, a judo expert working on the film, got chatting with Sellers about martial arts. 'And he was quite thrilled when I told him the Judo Society were still competing for his trophy.'[20]

The second new character is Chief Inspector Dreyfus, Clouseau's increasingly exasperated boss, played so expertly by Herbert Lom. Both Sellers and Lom had previously worked together on the Ealing classic *The Ladykillers*, when Sellers was on the cusp of becoming quite famous. He had done *The Goon Show* and was beginning to make films, although *The Ladykillers* was his first picture of any real distinction. Michael Birkett was a lowly third assistant director on the film and found himself particularly drawn to the young Sellers. 'We all thought he was a star in the making. No doubt about it.'[21]

Sellers himself remained unconvinced and desperately anxious during the production of *The Ladykillers*, repeatedly asking Michael Balcon, the head of Ealing, 'Is it alright? Am I any good?' There were early signs, too, of the behavioural problems that were to plague Sellers' life. Birkett recalls that Sellers had just bought his first Rolls-Royce, albeit second-hand:

> After a few days we noticed he was looking very carefully at the paintwork, and had decided that it was not up to scratch. He used to stick little bits of sticky tape anywhere on the paintwork where he thought it was imperfect. We all thought this was neurotic to a degree, and we said, 'Peter, you'll go bananas if you carry on like this.' But he told us that he was going to write to Rolls Royce saying, now look here. We tried to persuade him to be more rational, but he was not.[22]

As a joke, Lom painted a fake scratch the whole length of the car. Sellers blew a fuse when he saw it but on closer inspection discovered the truth and Lom owned up. A few days later Lom was driving home from the studio when an overpowering stench of fish hit his nostrils. Unable to fathom where on earth the smell was coming from, he eventually had to take the car into a garage to be looked at. A mechanic opened the bonnet and there, securely fastened with wire under the engine, were some kippers. 'Every time I had started that engine the kippers had been grilling. Peter's revenge.'[23]

For most of his career, Herbert Lom had largely played shady characters, hoodlums, and villains, due in part to his foreign and exotic features; he was born in Prague, Czechoslovakia, in 1917. Even in *The Ladykillers* he was the only main character you were not supposed to find funny, with his severe crew cut and flick knife. And so, he was pleasantly surprised to be offered, quite out of the blue, a comedy. A message had come through to have lunch at the Dorchester with Blake Edwards, a director he had never met before or knew much about. One assumes it may very well have been Sellers who suggested Lom to Blake, as the two had remained friends since *The Ladykillers*. During lunch, Blake pointed out that he had seen the actor play many roles, usually as the heavy. 'But I think you're a funny man.' At first, Lom did not know whether to take that as a compliment or not. Blake explained that he did not want a comedian or a comic actor to be Dreyfus, someone who would only play him for laughs. Instead, he wanted a dramatic actor to come in and play it dead straight, as a counterpoint to Clouseau's clowning.

Lom was to call getting the role of Dreyfus, 'a godsend', the chance to finally try his hand at comedy. Ironically, though, it did become both a blessing and a curse. 'People started to associate me with Dreyfus and I lost a number of dramatic parts because of it.'[24]

When we first see Dreyfus, he is already virtually on the brink of a nervous breakdown because of having to deal with Clouseau, as he states: 'Give me ten men like Clouseau and I could destroy the world.' He has even begun to develop a nervous twitch in his eye. That twitch was not in the original script and came about during a scene in Dreyfus' office. As usual, Dreyfus is reprimanding the Inspector and, in a bid to be encouraging, Sellers adlibbed a little wink. Instinctively, Lom gave a wink back and kept on for several seconds. Watching from the sidelines, Blake told the actor to keep it in. This twitch was to become the character's trademark and something of a millstone around Lom's neck. Whenever the writers were at a loose end for a quick laugh, they always pressed the actor to, 'Do your eye thing.' To which Lom invariably replied, 'I am not going to wink. You write a good scene and I won't have to wink.'[25] As it was, that twitch became just as exaggerated as Clouseau's French accent.

It is in *A Shot in the Dark* that Sellers begins to strangle the French language. The story goes that about halfway through filming Sellers hopped over to Paris for the weekend. 'He just disappeared,' recalled Blake. 'We didn't know where he was. He came back and when I was just about ready to chew his ass, which happened quite frequently, he said, "I ran into a concierge in Paris who talked like this." I said, "We've got to use it."'[26] Sellers had observed how this concierge dealt with American tourists at the hotel, talking to them in a strange accent that wasn't French but sounded French to an English-speaker. Another story regarding the origin of the accent came from Max Geldray, a jazz harmonica player that had provided musical interludes for *The Goon Show*. He always claimed that Sellers told him that he lifted the accent from one of Princess Margaret's hairdressers.

Whatever the truth, it began to be incorporated into Clouseau's speech pattern. Sellers even started going through the script looking for words he could play with, such as 'officer of the leu' instead of 'law.' Pretty soon these mispronunciations were causing the cast and crew, along with Sellers himself, to corpse on the set. In the scene where Clouseau assembles the entire Ballon household to reveal, in true detective fashion, who the killer is, he talks about 'murths' flying out of the cupboard when he searched Maria's room. Sanders' Benjamin Ballon says 'moths', correcting him, to which Clouseau answers, 'That was what I said, murths.' This was enough for Sellers to collapse into the giggles and it carried on into the next few takes. It was Friday afternoon; time was running out to get the scene in the can. Blake took his wallet out, pulled out some notes and put them in the centre of the room. 'The next guy who laughs doubles that, and it's beer money for the crew.' As everyone got ready for the next take, Sellers caught sight of Sanders practicing not to laugh in front of a mirror and that set him off again. Blake called it a day. The shot was finished the following Monday.

There is another version of this story, that it was Sanders' suggestion that each person who corpsed put £5 in a kitty. By the end of the day, when the money was counted it came to the princely sum of £200. Driving to the studio each morning Sanders had noticed a dilapidated farm that looked after old horses. It was his idea the money be sent there.

A Shot in the Dark was the first film Blake made in Britain and he enjoyed the experience much better than his ordeal shooting *The Pink Panther* at Rome's Cinecittà, which he described as, 'quite terrible. Outmoded equipment, confusion, and bad management. I even had a strike on the set with fights. Maybe I had too many Americans on the crew and they resented it.'[27] Blake surrounded himself with a first-rate crew. 'He wouldn't have idiots,' says Brian W. Cook, the film's third assistant director. 'Blake wanted the best.'[28] The cinematographer was the highly respected Christopher Challis. The editor was Bert Bates, who already had a slew of prestigious pictures behind him. Derek Cracknell was the assistant director, brought onto the film personally by Sellers. This was Cracknell's first big international movie and an important break in his career; he later worked on Bond pictures and for Stanley Kubrick. John Jordan was the focus puller, later a distinguished aerial cameraman who tragically lost his life working on the film *Catch 22* (1970). Blake also brought along his small regular team from the States, notably Dick Crockett, a former stunt performer who was with the director for many years.

Starting his career proper on the film was Brian W. Cook. He had started in the business working on the model unit for the Mirisch company's war film *633 Squadron* (1964) shot at Borehamwood. Brian liked the Mirisch brothers a lot. 'They were terrific, easy to work with and charming. They did not get too involved really; they had people there looking after things for them.'[29] Following *633 Squadron*, Brian went straight into *A Shot in the Dark*, where he really started to learn how the movie business operated. Brian went on to enjoy a highly successful career in movies, rising to producer and director, and working with the likes of Kubrick and Michael Cimino. Looking back on *A Shot in the Dark*, he recalls that most of the sets were built on the studio lot, the nudist camp, for instance, and large sections of the Ballon family mansion. 'It was a very controlled set, something that Blake always liked.'[30] There was very little location shooting, save for some exteriors at a stately home called Luton Hoo in Hertfordshire; a place Brian returned to for Kubrick's *Eyes Wide Shut* (1999).

Brian noticed how well Sellers seemed to get on with the crew. 'He was never any trouble with them. And he was a very generous guy, giving them drinks and gifts.'[31] As for Blake, Brian found him to be easy going. 'He used to have a pool table on the set and played on it between takes. He was great to work with.'[32]

A Shot in the Dark very much follows the slapstick, farcical, wild, pratfall comedy of its predecessor. If anything, Blake told reporters, they had gone even broader this time. He also cheerfully admitted to the classification of 'black comedy.' There are numerous murders in the film, and quite brutal at that, shootings, poisonings and death by garden shears. Blake compared this kind of comedy-making to walking a tightrope — fall off and you're dead. In drama, it's much easier to correct oneself if you make a false step, but in comedy, the main function is to make people laugh and if you fail at that, you're finished. All the time you have to stay just on this side of believability.

A lot of this Blake would accomplish on just instinct, but this new-found affinity with Sellers provided a natural system of checks and balances. If both thought an idea was funny all was well. If one was doubtful then the other felt they ought to re-examine the idea. Of course, this was when they were working well together. Curiously, Blake said that Sellers was able to step outside of himself while he was working and see what he was doing. Sometimes, in the middle of a scene, Sellers would break up and start laughing and Blake would say, 'what is going on?' and Sellers would reply, 'can you imagine this? Look at this idiot.' Sellers was talking about himself, like it was another person.

It was Sellers' idea that Clouseau should have an assistant in the new film – enter Hercule, and it was also his suggestion that his friend Graham Stark play him. Blake had no idea who Stark was and had to look at a copy of *Spotlight*, the actor's directory. *Spotlight* was a book that came out once a year where actors provided an up-to-date résumé of their credits along with a contemporary photograph. For that particular year, by chance, Stark had chosen a photograph of himself dressed as a French Gendarme, taken on a recent film, for no other reason than he thought he looked quite dashing in the hat. Blake saw the photograph and surmised that since Stark was already dressed for the part, he might as well get the job. Stark signed the contract within the week. It was the actor's first introduction to Blake and he would appear in all subsequent *Panther* films, in various roles, and in the non-*Panther* Blake films, *Victor/Victoria* (1982) and *Blind Date* (1987). Clouseau and Hercule make an amusing double act. In one scene Clouseau reprimands Hercule for his theories on the murder case, 'We must have the facts Hercule,' he admonishes. After the film came out Stark got into a cab one day, gave directions, only for the driver to take one look at him and say, 'I got the facts Hercule.' The driver explained that the line had been adopted by cabbies across London when they radioed into base for instructions or talked to each other on the radio.

Stark immediately liked Blake's way of working, by creating a fun atmosphere on set. 'And he never imposed himself on any of the actors. You were always invited to contribute what you liked to a scene, providing it was funny.'[33] A good example of this happened in the scene where Clouseau and Hercule have trouble synchronising their watches. Sellers and Stark forewent the need to do any rehearsal, they knew each other so well they ad-libbed the whole thing.

On the set there was always room for that kind of expression. 'Blake encouraged us to improvise,' confirms Elke Sommer.[34] She also recalls that Sellers and Blake always went to rushes together every day and can't recall any major re-shoots. 'Blake preferred short takes. The less the better.'[35] The whole experience turned out to be an enjoyable one for Elke, and she found Blake both courteous and nice, 'but not especially friendly'.[36] Often Blake, Sellers and Elke would go out to dinner together. 'Blake was very professional, but not warm hearted. Not as warm hearted as Peter was.'[37] Elke did get to like Sellers enormously. Of course, she respected his talent. 'He was a genius.'[38] But she sensed that he wanted more than just a professional relationship with her. Very early on in the shoot, Sellers presented Elke with an expensive gold pin in the shape of a flower, the petals were made from very fine gold mesh and there were beautiful blue sapphires that shook on their little stem:

> Peter was very lonely. He wanted to get married. He was looking for a wife and I think he had his eyes on me. I adored him but not that way. There was this sadness that Peter had which he very rarely showed to other people, but he showed it to me.[39]

In the last few weeks of shooting Sellers told Elke that his astrologer had said he was going to meet someone special very soon. Sellers often went to see an astrologer called Maurice Woodruff, who wrote for several newspapers and had many celebrity clients. Adding to the mystery, this person would have the initials BE. Just a few days later Sellers saw in an evening paper that a young Swedish actress had arrived in London to start work on a new film. Her name was Britt Ekland. What is more, she was staying at the Dorchester. Sellers invited Britt to his suite for drinks and then got his loyal chauffeur Bert Mortimer to drive them to the Odeon Leicester Square to catch the evening performance of *The Pink Panther*, which had just opened. They were ushered into their seats by the manager who gave them the full VIP treatment. Britt was to remember enjoying the film and laughing a lot, and realising for the first time just how famous this Peter Sellers really was.

In the morning she woke up in her room and at the bottom of her bed were huge bouquets of flowers, orchids and freesias, lilies and roses. She noticed a little card with them. It read simply: 'Hope you slept well, Inspector Clouseau.' They would be married barely ten days later.

As Sellers wooed Britt during those last weeks of shooting, there was a deterioration in his relationship with Blake Edwards. Both had worked well together on *The Pink Panther*, and for most of the filming on *A Shot in the Dark* things went along fine. 'Peter got on with Blake well, at the beginning,' Elke recalls. 'I would not say fabulously. I would not say it was a deep friendship, but they got along well.'[40] Then the shit hit the fan. 'Sellers became a monster,' Blake later claimed. 'He just got bored with the part and became angry, sullen and unprofessional. He wouldn't show up for work and began looking for anyone and everyone to blame, never for a moment stopping to see whether or not he should blame himself.'[41]. By the end of filming Blake and Sellers had ceased communication altogether, save for little notes slipped underneath each other's door.

Writing in his memoirs, Henry Mancini heard about the stories of Blake and Sellers not getting on but never saw it first-hand. Indeed, when Sellers went out for dinner with Mancini and his wife, he was always good company. 'But there were many instances when Blake came to me after the day's work or after a screening and I would say, "How did it go?" and he would say, "Don't ask."'[42] These clashes with Sellers almost certainly affected Blake's health. For years he had suffered from back issues relating to his swimming pool accident, a major contributory factor to why he had bouts of depression all his life. 'And when things grew tense with Peter on the set, he would be in physical pain,' said Mancini.[43]

The fault of this breakdown between actor and director does not lie completely at Sellers' door. Blake too was pretty neurotic and disturbed, and both complex artists had precise views on comedy. It was inevitable that they would clash. Both were driven by ego and a need to be right and to win the argument. Blake has said that when they got on well, Sellers was enormously inventive. But when times were bad, they differed often. 'Then it was imperative that I, as director, prevailed.'[44] Elke saw things a little differently. 'Peter could be stubborn. He knew what he wanted to do and sometimes Blake wanted him to do something else and then they would discuss it and that was not so amicable. But Peter mostly won. It was his Clouseau. He was Clouseau.'[45]

With *The Pink Panther* breaking international box office records, *A Shot in the Dark* was rushed into American cinemas for the summer of 1964, just a few short months after the original. British audiences had to wait until January 1965 for the London premiere. Again, the film features another clever and amusing animated opening titles sequence produced by DePatie-Freleng. With the Pink Panther absent from the storyline, the feline star is nowhere to be seen, instead we have an animated Inspector Clouseau. Gone, too, is *The Pink Panther* theme. In its place Henry Mancini provides a much more rock tempo title tune (almost a pastiche of his *Peter Gunn* theme), featuring electric guitar, heavy bass and an unusual sound that was provided by an antique Indian pump organ that the composer saw in the window of a shop in London. 'I think that's one of the coolest themes dad came up with,' says Monica Mancini, 'He always liked to experiment with different instruments and sounds.'[46]

Mancini rarely, if ever, visited any of the *Panther* sets. He read the script, watched the dailies, and saw what needed to be done. It worked because

Mancini and Blake had very similar comic sensibilities, they laughed at pretty much the same things. Monica Mancini recalls:

> Dad just loved working with Blake on the *Panther* films because he really loved Peter Sellers and he loved slapstick, that kind of physical comedy. When he was working on the *Panther* films he used to write at home. He had a home office studio and he'd have his little moviola and so he would watch the film and you could hear him laughing downstairs at this stuff. So, he really had a blast.[47]

Part of the US publicity campaign saw Sellers given the honour of placing his hands and feet into cement on the forecourt outside Grauman's Chinese Theatre. He smiled dutifully at the hordes of press, even though just a few weeks before he had ordered that *A Shot in the Dark* never see daylight. Sellers had seen the film at a private screening in Los Angeles and disliked it so much he did not want it released. According to Walter Mirisch, Sellers made an extraordinary offer. 'He said that if we would agree not to release the picture, he would refund the entire cost of the picture to us, over a period of years, because he didn't want the picture to be shown. We respectfully declined.'[48]

This was to be a pattern Sellers followed for the rest of his career. 'He worried about everything,' said Blake. 'There wasn't a movie Sellers made, except maybe for *Being There*, that he didn't think was a total disaster by the time it was finished. He'd want to buy it and chuck it out.'[49]

Despite wanting *A Shot in the Dark* killed off, Sellers gave a party at the Beverly Hills Hotel to celebrate the film's impending release. It was the usual Hollywood-type party. It did have one significance, however, as it was where Blake met Julie Andrews for the very first time. It was not at all a momentous first encounter, it was cursory at best, they exchanged a few brief pleasantries and that was all. Over the next few years, they would bump into each other again at the odd showbiz function before fate was to lend a hand and bring them together.

A Shot in the Dark outperformed *The Pink Panther* at the box office. Again, the public's reaction to the film was one of sheer enthusiasm. William Peter Blatty recalled attending a sneak preview in Westwood, California. 'And you couldn't even hear the dialogue the audience was laughing so loud. My stomach hurt from laughing. It was amazing.'[50] When Maurice Richlin caught a performance, he loved it. 'I personally think it was the funniest of all.'[51]

Not all the critics agreed. Although this was only the second film in the franchise, the slapstick elements were starting to veer towards the level of a cartoon. Clouseau had become a character where the simple procedure of walking through a door ends up with him bashing into the wall, or catching his coat on fire when he lights a cigarette. The critic of *The Times* claimed that Blake had pushed Clouseau, 'right over the edge into caricature'. Philip K. Scheuer of the *Los Angeles Times* wrote that the film, 'is all variations of falling down and going boom … I will not say "ad nauseum" because Sellers is a clever comedian and never that painful to take. But enough is enough already.' The *Monthly Film Bulletin* agreed, 'Where *The Pink Panther* had style and a certain subtlety, its successor … can substitute only slapstick of the crudest kind.' For Bosley Crowther of *The New York Times* Sellers was something of a redeeming feature. 'It is mad, but the wonderful dexterity and the air of perpetually buttressed dignity with which Mr Sellers plays his role make what could quickly be monotonous enjoyable to the end.'

The numerous critics that did like the film proved to be on the right side of history. Along with the first *Pink Panther*, *A Shot in the Dark* is today considered a comedy classic. In 2006 *Premiere* magazine voted it one of 'The 50 Greatest Comedies of All Time.' In the same year the film ranked 38th in Channel 4's 50 Greatest Comedy Films poll.

With two hit films on their hands, it was inevitable that the Mirisch brothers and United Artists wanted to keep the *Panther*/Clouseau bandwagon rolling. There was just the small matter of their star having almost died from a massive heart attack a couple of months prior to the US opening of *A Shot in the Dark*. Robert Wagner's dire warning about Sellers taking isobutyl nitrate had proved disastrously correct. During a night of passion with his young bride Sellers took the stuff and afterwards felt a burning sensation in his chest. He was checked out by his doctor and told to rest and not exert himself. Two days later his heart stopped beating for a minute-and-a-half. His doctor managed to get it working again and Sellers was rushed to the intensive care unit at the Cedars of Lebanon hospital in Los Angeles. Seven more times that day Sellers' heart stopped. He was for all intents and purposes a dead man, and yet he survived, emerging from the hospital in a wheelchair almost a month later. From that moment on Sellers knew he was living on borrowed time and must have feared that his fragile heart might give out again at any moment. Graham Stark was to say that after the heart attack, 'Peter was a different man.'[52]

Ironically, Sellers had been working on another film for the Mirisch company, *Kiss Me Stupid*, directed by Billy Wilder. Predictably, Sellers and Wilder did not get on; their working methods being so diametrically opposed, Sellers the intuitive genius, Wilder the by-the-numbers dictate. When Sellers had his heart attack three weeks into the shoot, the more pessimistic commentators wondered if this was simply a ploy to get out of the movie. Of concern to the Mirisch brothers, did Sellers' health put in jeopardy more Clouseau films? Would they be able to get insurance on him? In the end that did not prove to be an issue, Sellers was soon back at work making movies. The real problem was that neither Sellers nor Blake could face the prospect of working together again. *The Pink Panther* franchise looked dead in the water.

Chapter 3

INSPECTOR CLOUSEAU

The opening animated title sequence to *The Pink Panther* had created such a stir among critics and audiences that David H. DePatie began to think there could be a future for the character, maybe even as the star of his own cartoon series. He discussed the possibility with Freleng, who did not share his enthusiasm, convinced that it had just been a glorious one-off. Keen to pursue it further, DePatie met with Harold Mirisch and got a far more positive response. So positive in fact, that the Mirisch brothers approached United Artists and got the idea green lit. DePatie and Freleng, along with Blake Edwards and the Mirisch brothers, were all partners in the enterprise. The result was *The Pink Phink*, a six-minute short that saw our feline hero compete with the plans of a decorator to paint a house either blue or pink. The poor worker, a little white moustachioed man (some said a caricature of Friz Freleng himself), became a recurring character in subsequent shorts, often the foil to the Panther's latest antics.

Released in December 1964, supporting the James Bond film *Goldfinger* on its original Christmas release in the US, *The Pink Phink* went on to win an Academy Award, marking the first occasion that a studio won an Oscar with its debut animated short. By then, United Artists had asked DePatie and Freleng to produce more, which they did in quick succession, around eight to twelve per year. In total, around a hundred *Pink Panther* shorts were made for theatrical release, playing as the support to the main feature. All of them utilised the distinctive theme music composed by Henry Mancini. It was the first time an animated character created for a title sequence became a star in its own right.

No one was more astonished by their success than Blake Edwards, who like Freleng, thought the Panther had worked fine for his film but nothing beyond that. 'I had no idea that it would take off like that. That it would have that kind of a life of its own.'[1]

The director on most of these shorts was Hawley Pratt, who had worked on the Panther's original design. Back in the 1930s, Pratt was one of the first animators at the Walt Disney studios before leaving to work with Freleng at Warner Bros. Supervising the storylines was the Scottish-born John Dunn, another story sketch artist who began his career at Disney before moving to Warner's. One of the problems the animators faced was whether to give the Panther a voice. In the end the decision was made to keep the character silent. However, he does speak in two of the original shorts, *Pink Ice* and *Sink Pink*, both 1965. The comedian and impressionist Rich Little provided the voice, modelling it on David Niven. Ironically, years later Little would dub Niven's voice for *Trail of the Pink Panther* and *Curse of the Pink Panther*, due to the actor's ill health.

The *Panther* cartoons became such a hit that DePatie and Freleng were asked to make another series of shorts, this time based on Inspector Clouseau himself and called simply *The Inspector*. The cartoon figure was very much modelled on Sellers and the animation style copied the style employed for the main titles of *A Shot in the Dark*. The title music was also based on the theme Henry Mancini provided for that film. The Inspector reports to a perpetually ill-tempered Commissioner, a character obviously based on Herbert Lom's Commissioner Dreyfus. He even has an assistant, sergeant Deux-Deux, based on the character of Hercule, played by Graham Stark in *A Shot in the Dark*. Although for some reason Deux-Deux is Spanish and often replies to the Inspector saying 'Sí,' only to be admonished for not saying 'Oui.' Both the Inspector and Deux-Deux were voiced by the television and stage actor Pat Harrington Jr.

In all thirty-four theatrical cartoon shorts of *The Inspector* were released through United Artists between 1965 and 1969. However, even more successful than the *Panther* and *Inspector* shorts was their move into television. *The Pink Panther Show* made its debut in September 1969 on Saturday mornings on the American network NBC. It was an instant triumph, going on to play in forty-one countries. The thirty-minute show featured the *Pink Panther* and *Inspector* theatrical shorts produced by DePatie and Freleng. Henry Mancini's *Pink Panther Theme* was also used extensively in the series. The memorable opening title sequence showed a boy driving a futuristic Pink Panther-mobile, a real vehicle created by renowned car stylist Bob Reisner that was 26-feet long. The car drives up to the famous Grauman's Chinese Theatre in Hollywood where the back opens and an animated Panther and Clouseau climb out. The show ran until 1978, and went on to feature new *Panther* cartoons and other animated characters.

Back when the Pink Panther and Inspector Clouseau first became the stars of their own successful theatrical cartoon shorts, it seemed like an obvious idea to make another live action movie. Walter Mirisch had been told about the bad blood that occurred between Blake and Sellers on *A Shot in the Dark*, and that the two men, having earlier discussed the possibilities of doing a third film, had vowed never to work together again. He hoped that a bit of time apart might have healed this wound. 'The *Pink Panther* was a franchise that deserved to be continued, and they were both indispensable to it,' he said.[2] But Blake had no desire to return to the *Panther* series, instead, he wanted to pursue other projects. *The Great Race* (1965) was an epic homage to the silent movie comedies he adored and while fun and entertaining, with a great cast that included Jack Lemmon, Tony Curtis and Natalie Wood, it flopped at the box office. The project he had been working on with William Peter Blatty, when the two men took over on *A Shot in the Dark*, titled *What Did You Do in the War, Daddy?* finally saw daylight in 1966 and did not make much of a splash either. Then there was a movie version of Blake's TV show *Peter Gunn*, called simply *Gunn*, which came out in 1967 and ended up being something of a damp squib, too.

As for Sellers, he did not much fancy doing another *Panther* film either, or playing Clouseau again. According to friend Graham Stark, 'He didn't want to go on giving the same performance.'[3] Instead, Sellers starred in several international movie comedies that made decent money but did not necessarily stretch him as a performer or increase his reputation.

With Blake and Sellers unwilling to return, Walter Mirisch brought in the writers Tom and Frank Waldman to work on a potential third Clouseau/ *Panther* film. It was going to be called simply, *Inspector Clouseau*. The plot was to revolve around a series of organised bank heists across Europe. Suspecting a mole within Scotland Yard, Clouseau is brought to London to help solve the case. Walter Mirisch's hope was that by the time a script was ready, Blake and Sellers would have changed their minds. That plan stalled when the producer saw the Cold War comedy *The Russians Are Coming, the Russians Are Coming* (1966), about a Soviet submarine that accidentally runs aground off the American coast of New England. What caught his eye was the performance of a young actor called Alan Arkin, making his feature film debut in the role of the submarine's political officer. Arkin was to receive an Oscar nomination and win a Golden Globe. Walter felt that Arkin had the potential to be a big comedy star and might be a good choice to play Clouseau. His only reservation about offering him the role, was that Arkin might not want to run the risk of comparison with Sellers.

At the time Arkin was shooting the thriller *Wait Until Dark*, and perhaps as an antidote to playing a psychotic killer menacing Audrey Hepburn's blind woman, he agreed to take on the comedic challenges of Clouseau.

Arkin felt no pressure stepping into Sellers' shoes. As he told reporter Bobbie Wygant on the set of *Inspector Clouseau*. 'I'm playing the character. I am not playing him. I don't really feel like I'm competing with him. I am a great fan of his.'[4] The real pressure, he revealed, came from the fact that this was going to be his first starring role in a picture. Interestingly, Arkin also revealed that after saying yes to playing Clouseau he suddenly had misgivings and went back to re-watch *The Pink Panther* and *A Shot in the Dark*. 'And I felt I could do something different with the character than what he did. Not better, not worse, I just think different.'[5] Arkin also explained how it took him at least a month to get the French accent the way he wanted it.

With the casting of Arkin complete, Walter Mirisch returned to Blake to see if he wanted to direct the film. The answer was a firm no. Looking for another experienced comedy director, Walter offered the job to Bud Yorkin, who said yes. Yorkin began his career as an engineer at NBC in 1949 and later distinguished himself as one of the most sought-after directors of musical variety shows and specials on American television, working with such stars as Jack Benny, Dinah Shore and Fred Astaire. In 1959 he began a long creative partnership with producer and writer Norman Lear, churning out TV shows and films like *Come Blow Your Horn* (1963) and *Divorce American Style* (1967).

Just prior to *Inspector Clouseau* going into production Walter Mirisch received a telephone call late one evening. It was Sellers in London.

> He was furious at me and said, 'How could you do this without me.' I reminded him as gently as I could that I had on numerous occasions asked him to play the role. He brushed all this aside and said something to the effect that Clouseau was his role and I had to dismiss Alan Arkin and do the film with him. That is after he had seen the script.[6]

Walter was having none of it. He saw this for what it was, a delaying tactic, perhaps even a way for Sellers to sabotage the new film.

> I told him that we were close to starting production and that what he was asking was not possible. Replacing Arkin with Sellers

> would convert a go project into a new script development at a very high cost with no assurance of the mercurial Peter ever really doing the film.[7]

And so, *Inspector Clouseau* went ahead. Sellers never forgave Walter Mirisch and for the remainder of his life held a grudge against the producer and a feeling of real animosity. Blake Edwards told film journalist Alexander Walker:

> In all the years I knew Peter, and despite all the times when he swore that he was never going to do another *Panther*, he never stopped complaining about the fact that the Mirisch Company had chosen Arkin. Peter was a collector of grievances. But he seemed to bear more of a grudge concerning the Arkin thing than just about anything else.[8]

Walter Mirisch's relationship with Sellers had always been troublesome, or as he politely called it, 'exceedingly complicated'. Thanks to his gift for mimicry, Sellers would phone people up, impersonating Walter, once telling an actor to get off the Mirisch film he was on, that it was a load of crap, and to come and work on the new Peter Sellers movie. He even got Walter's wife on the phone once and engaged in a long conversation posing as her husband. Walter was asked once who was the most difficult actor he had ever worked with. Considering Walter worked with the likes of Robert Mitchum, Steve McQueen and Marilyn Monroe, he had no hesitation in saying Peter Sellers. 'He was a comedic genius. He was just always very, very difficult.'[9]

Inspector Clouseau was made at the MGM-British Studios, Borehamwood, and features a cast of predominantly British comedy and character actors including Frank Finlay, Patrick Cargill, Beryl Reid, and Barry Foster. Making his film debut was a young actor called Clive Francis, playing Clyde Hargreaves, the mastermind behind the bank robberies. Clive had just appeared in a prestigious BBC production of *David Copperfield*, alongside the equally young Ian McKellen. Indeed, it was McKellen who had been offered the role of Hargreaves and turned it down. He called Francis and told him to get in touch with his agent fast if he was interested in doing the film. 'Ian even lent me rather an elegant white suit in order to meet Bud Yorkin, and I got the part. So, I had a lot to thank Ian for.'[10]

Hargreaves is rather a sophisticated criminal, unlike the rest of his hoodlum gang, 'most of which were extras and at one time had been behind bars themselves,' reveals Clive. 'I behaved impeccably!'[11] One of them, playing his second in command, was a character by the name of John Bindon. Clive recalls:

> He was a good looking, fun loving, happy-go-lucky guy. Little did we know but he also had close links with the London underworld and was alleged to have had connections with both the Kray twins and the Richardson gang. He even boasted to me that he had once bitten off the lobe of someone's ear because he refused to buy him a drink and that he had sex with Princess Margaret while staying in her house in Mustique.[12]

Bindon was the son of a London cab driver and was spotted in a London pub by Ken Loach, who asked him to appear in his film *Poor Cow* (1967). *Inspector Clouseau* was Bindon's second screen appearance and he went on to carve out something of a niche for himself playing villains and hard men in numerous films like *Performance* (1970) and *Get Carter* (1971). In 1978 Bindon was tried for the murder of London gangster John Darke, but managed to plead self-defence and was acquitted. 'That's what I like about this business,' states Clive. 'You meet all sorts of colourful individuals along the way, a number you would rather never meet again!'[13]

Much of *Inspector Clouseau* was shot on location in and around a London experiencing the fag end of the swinging era, also in Switzerland, largely in Bern, Lucerne and Zurich. At Zurich's mainline railway station Clive, as Hargreaves, disguises himself as a chauffeur to pick up Clouseau. Clive was supposed to drive him off all in one long continuous take. This meant slipping away from the station compound and then circling the area through heavy early morning traffic and back to his original starting point for another take if required.

> No one asked if I had ever driven, or indeed had a licence, they just presumed I had. In actuality, I hadn't, apart from half a dozen lessons with an aunt around the back roads of Eastbourne. Something I confided to Alan Arkin as we drove round for the third time, narrowly missing an oncoming tram! I thought he would have been amused, instead the poor man went visibly white, refusing point blank to go around a fourth time. Fortunately, it was an automatic, so I managed to pull it off with a certain amount of panache.[14]

In a bid to reassure audiences that this film was still linked to the two previous Blake/Sellers entries, DePatie and Freleng came up with an animated title sequence featuring the Clouseau character. The animation itself was produced at TVC (TV Cartoons) studios in London, which was run by Canadian filmmaker and animator George Dunning. The studio had recently worked on The Beatles' animated feature *Yellow Submarine* (1968). However, their real claim to fame would be *The Snowman* (1982) based on the book by Raymond Briggs, which is now a perennial favourite on Christmas television.

Walter Mirisch must have hoped that his switch in who played Clouseau, 'with an actor that was more professional than Peter Sellers',[15] would ensure a future for the franchise. By and large, critics neither missed nor bemoaned the absence of Sellers, or particularly welcomed or disapproved of Arkin stepping into the role. If anything, it was the film itself that took most of the critical barrage. *Time* magazine wrote, 'Bud Yorkin's slovenly direction makes the film look as if every expense had been spared, trapping Arkin in a farce of habit that will probably retire Clouseau to oblivion — one picture too late.' Leo Sullivan of *The Washington Post* called the film, 'a mirthless failure', while *The Monthly Film Bulletin* said, 'This third film in the Clouseau series finally demonstrates that the joke has run out of steam. That it works at all is largely due to Alan Arkin's performance as Clouseau, which emerges as a hilarious blend of Keaton and Sellers.'

Life magazine went so far as to refer to the film as, 'historic' in its own way, proving that the character of Clouseau was now so well established that his name alone was enough to lure audiences into theatres. Well, not quite. *Inspector Clouseau* was a resounding flop at the box office when it opened in the UK in February 1968 and in the States that July, making it appear obvious that audiences only wanted to see Clouseau if Sellers was playing him. Arkin himself went on record describing his attempt to play Clouseau as 'a failure'[16]. For the most part he was to remain silent on the subject. In an interview for *The Times* in 1970 the *Inspector Clouseau* film was raised, causing Arkin to reply to the reporter, incredulously, 'You saw that!' before rapidly changing the subject. Arkin was to go on and enjoy a successful, if sporadic, career. *Catch-22*, the 1970 screen adaptation of the Joseph Heller novel, which Arkin was in talks about making with Mike Nichols during production of *Inspector Clouseau*, is perhaps his most famous film.

As for Bud Yorkin, things worked out rather well. During his time in London making *Inspector Clouseau*, he caught a few episodes of *Till Death*

Us Do Part, Johnny Speight's controversial BBC sitcom that centred on the working-class bigot Alf Garnett, played by Warren Mitchell. 'I couldn't believe anybody could put that on television,' Yorkin recalled.[17] He sent a tape back to Norman Lear, telling him, 'This will blow your mind.' Lear thought the show was great and suggested doing it on US TV. Yorkin said he was nuts, that they would never get it on the air. Taking a gamble, they bought the rights, changed the name of the main character from Alf Garnett to Archie Bunker and cast Carroll O'Connor. Two pilots were taped for ABC in 1968 but the network was reluctant to commit, calling it too controversial. Lear and Yorkin took the show to CBS, and the renamed *All in the Family* aired in January 1971, becoming one of the most successful shows on American television. In the 1970s, Yorkin and Lear also produced *Sanford and Son*, based on another BBC success *Steptoe and Son*. In 1982 Yorkin was executive producer on the sci-fi classic *Blade Runner*.

Over the years *Inspector Clouseau* was perceived to be something of a bastard offspring, illegitimate, purely because Blake Edwards and Sellers were not involved, even though it came from the same studio as its predecessors. In fact, it is a relatively entertaining '60s comedy caper, although the plot merely serves as a framework on which the filmmakers hang a series of physical comedy set pieces; in that way it very much foreshadows the way the '70s *Panther* films were to go. There is one amusing moment where Clouseau arrives at Heathrow airport only to step out of the plane a split second after the ramp has been pulled away. Scotland Yard also equips Clouseau with some 007-style gadgets, a cigarette-case-cum-tape-recorder and a cigarette lighter that is a laser. As for Arkin, he is highly watchable as Clouseau, but the spectre of Sellers looms large across the entire picture making it in the end quite an odd watch.

Ironically, Peter Sellers and Blake Edwards did make a film together in 1968, and even more ironically, it was for the Mirisch company and United Artists. Despite their vow never to work together again, there had been some recent conciliatory noises and friends like Herbert Lom were making efforts to bring them back together. 'I would tell Blake that Peter had been saying good things about him and vice-versa.'[18]

In the early part of 1967, Blake conceived a comedy about a bumbling Indian actor mistakenly invited to a showbiz bash at a Hollywood mansion where he proceeds to cause absolute mayhem. It was called *The Party*. The intention was for the picture to be largely improvised, and the more Blake thought about it the more he realised there was no one else but Sellers capable of doing it. For Blake, one of the joys doing the *Panthers* and what made them work so well, was the ad-libbing that went on, discovering things on the set. Blake and Sellers did so much ad-libbing on the *Panthers*, so why didn't they ad-lib a whole film?

By this time Sellers' health problems and unpredictable nature was scaring off studios. Sellers had behaved outrageously on the 1967 Bond spoof *Casino Royale*, causing numerous production hold ups, and eventually walking off the picture necessitating drastic rewrites and reshooting, which is why watching it today the thing makes no sense whatsoever. Blake's reputation had taken a whack recently, too. After the expensive flop *The Great Race* he was viewed as a profligate director who did not care about budgets or schedules. So, to sweeten the deal with United Artists, Walter Mirisch persuaded both Blake and Sellers to promise that if *The Party* overran its budget, they would pay the extra out of their own salary.

Blake and Sellers worked well together on *The Party* but their enjoyment did not translate into box office dollars. Overtime, though, the movie has acquired considerable cult status. At least it broke the ice a little between the two men, although audiences would have to wait another six years before they reacquainted themselves with the Pink Panther.

Chapter 4

RETURN OF THE PINK PANTHER

The financial failure of *The Party* did little to enhance the reputation of either Sellers or Blake and by the start of the 1970s both their careers were haemorrhaging fast. Blake had a string of major costly flops to his name, none quite so big as *Darling Lili* (1970), which starred his new wife, Julie Andrews. They had seen each other socially at a few parties over the years and enjoyed a couple of brief conversations, nothing more than that. One evening, Blake was at a party and there was a discussion going on about what made certain film people successful and Julie's name came up. Blake said something that cracked the room up. 'I can tell you exactly what it is. She has lilacs for pubic hair.' When the laughter subsided, Stan Kamen, an agent with William Morris, nudged Blake and said, 'With your luck, you'll wind up marrying her.'[1]

Blake had just moved into a new home after his marriage to former actress Patricia Walker had collapsed. Julie, too, was separated from costume designer Tony Walton. As a housewarming present Julie bought three lilac bushes and gave them to Blake. 'Aw, come on,' he said, when Julie arrived with them. 'Who put you up to this? How did you find out?'[2] Julie had no idea what he was talking about. Still disbelieving, Blake told her his joke at the party.

They started dating proper when Blake approached Julie to star in *Darling Lili* and married in 1969. *Darling Lili* was the most ambitious and expensive movie musical ever produced by Paramount Pictures. When it turned out to be a colossal dud, it almost bankrupted the studio. The vultures started circling. 'I was strung up, hanged, drawn and quartered and thrown to the wolves,' Blake complained.[3] The same people who were happy enough to hire him when he was making hits now didn't want to know. 'As soon as I made a bomb, they dropped me.'[4]

Like Blake, Sellers' career was flatlining. Several of his recent pictures had either received scant theatrical distribution or in the case of one, *Ghost in the Noonday Sun*, a pirate comedy, went unreleased. 'Financially he was not in a good state,' recalls his secretary Sue Evans, now Susan Wood. 'Film-wise he was having a dry spell. I would call up Peter's agent, Dennis Selinger, and say, 'Please send him something, even if you know he won't do it,' because he was in the depths of despair, not having any work. He was broke. It was as simple as that.'[5]

Susan came into Sellers' orbit in 1973 when the actor was looking for a new secretary. For most of the 1960s Sellers had been looked after by a woman called Hattie Stevenson. Hattie had quite remarkably suffered Sellers for seven years, despite on numerous occasions being sacked by him, usually for trivial matters or matters she had no control over, only for the star to beg her to return. Finally, she quit on her own accord and Sellers was left floundering. According to his son Michael, Sellers went through something like six secretaries and was now on the lookout for number seven.

Hattie came straight from secretarial school, happened to know Sellers' wife Anne, and turned up on the set of *The Millionairess*. Sellers took one look at her and said, 'When would you like to start?' For Susan, it was much the same. Her husband at the time knew Sellers and she was asked to come and see him at his home in Eaton Mews in Belgravia. Susan recalls:

> I cannot say it was an interview. We sat in the kitchen. I spoke to him for about eight minutes. Liza Minnelli was sitting there eating yoghurt with her feet up. And he just said, 'Can you start tomorrow.' I said, 'Sure. Ok.' And that is how it started.[6]

Susan was Sellers' secretary for the rest of his life.

What both Blake and Sellers were in desperate need of was a sure-fire hit. The obvious solution was to bring back Clouseau and the *Pink Panther*. In the summer of 1971, Sellers told a reporter:

> I think I had the most fun working with Blake on those two films. We are planning to do another, simply because of the terrific pressure from the public who saw them. Wherever I go in the world I get the impression that these two films are probably the most popular things I have done. I am always being asked to do another one.[7]

At least in their private lives Blake and Sellers had kept Clouseau alive. Sometimes Sellers would call Blake up as the Inspector at some strange time of the day or night, and they would spend hours on the phone thinking up crazy ideas for the character and laughing. However, given the erratic nature of Sellers, he was just as quick to turn against the idea of doing another *Panther*. Even so, Blake put pen to paper and came up with a twenty-page story outline of a thing called *The Return of the Pink Panther*. He gave it to Walter Mirisch who wasted no time in seeking backing from United Artists. Their response took him by surprise, a point-blank refusal to take another chance with Sellers or Blake. In any case, the Mirisch brothers' relationship with United Artists was fracturing and in the early 70s they sold their interest in the *Pink Panther* movies to the studio.

Meanwhile, in Britain, entertainment tycoon Lew Grade was trying to persuade Julie Andrews to star in a series of big variety television specials. To sweeten the deal, Grade promised to finance two movies developed and directed by her husband Blake. The first was a handsomely mounted espionage-romance called *The Tamarind Seed* (1974), starring Julie and Omar Sharif. While it did reasonably well in European territories, it made no impression in the all-important American market.

The second film proposed by Blake would again star Julie and was a remake of the 1948 RKO western *Rachel and the Stranger*, which starred Loretta Young, William Holden and Robert Mitchum. Under the new title of *Rachel*, the film would have given Julie a strong role to play, as a woman struggling for independence in the male-dominated world of American frontier society. Grade disliked the idea, seeing no commercial interest in it, and told Blake he would buy off the remainder of his contract. It was all agreed, then Blake had a change of heart and called Grade to say they had made a deal to do two films and he wanted to honour it. Besides, he was concerned that, such was his reputation in the industry, people might think there had been problems on *The Tamarind Seed* and Grade didn't want to work with him on another film.

Sympathetic to Blake's situation, Grade had another idea, what if he made a comedy instead, something that audiences knew and loved him for; even better, a *Pink Panther* film. Blake was interested but warned the British tycoon that getting Sellers on board would be tricky. Grade told Blake to leave that to him, the two were old friends. Picking up the phone, Grade asked Sellers to come to his office.

Had he been riding high on comedy successes it's doubtful that Sellers would have countenanced the prospect of playing Clouseau again for Blake. As it was, he was eager to see what Grade was selling. After a two-hour meeting, Sellers was agreeable. Grade called in his secretary to type out a short letter of agreement and Sellers signed it.

The original plan was for Blake's *Return of the Pink Panther* story treatment to form the basis of a pilot episode for a proposed twenty-six-part television series. This was to be produced by Lew Grade himself, no stranger to making international television deals, this was the man behind smash hit shows like *The Saint*, *Thunderbirds*, *Danger Man* and *The Persuaders*. Neither Blake nor Sellers thought a TV series was the right vehicle for the *Pink Panther*. Besides, the two men may very well have killed each other by the end of what would have been a long schedule, and so Blake tried talking Grade into doing it as a movie. 'At first, he absolutely and totally refused, but then he finally got around to saying. 'Well, how much is it going to cost me?' I've always been a gambler, so I said, 'Lew, I won't take a nickel, and I've talked to Peter and he won't take a nickel. All we each want is expenses and ten per cent of the gross from the first dollar on. Lew gave it to us.'[8]

When Grade brought the project to Eric Pleskow, the CEO of United Artists, he discovered, much as Walter Mirisch did before him, that the company was less than enthused about another *Panther* film. 'He said that he wouldn't touch it with a bargepole,' Grade was to recall. 'He thought it would be a total disaster.'[9] Pleskow was, however, prepared to sanction the licensing of the rights to the characters in exchange for world distribution and a share of the profits. The first *Pink Panther* film in ten years was a go.

At first, it was hoped to reunite as many of the original cast members as possible. David Niven was approached to reprise his role as debonair jewel thief Sir Charles Lytton, or as Clouseau calls him, 'Sir Charles Phantom, the notorious Lytton.' Sir Charles becomes the prime suspect when the famous Pink Panther diamond is once again stolen; the Phantom's trademark glove has been conveniently left at the scene of the crime. When Niven proved unavailable, Douglas Fairbanks Jr. was briefly considered before Christopher Plummer eventually signed on. Herbert Lom returned as Chief Inspector Dreyfus, now more unhinged than ever, attempting several times to kill Clouseau. And Burt Kwouk was back as Clouseau's man servant Cato. When Kwouk was approached about coming back his first response was, 'But I'm ten years older.' And the reply was, 'So is everybody else!'[10]

However, the story does introduce a new main character in Lady Claudine Lytton, Sir Charles' wife, whom Clouseau trails in a bungled bid to find out her husband's whereabouts. Austrian actress Catherine Schell had already established herself in film and television, appearing memorably as one of Blofeld's 'Angels of Death' opposite George Lazenby's James Bond in *On Her Majesty's Secret Service* (1969) and the Hammer science fiction thriller *Moon Zero Two* (1969). Recently she had appeared with Bette Davis in *Madame Sin* (1972), a thriller made by Lew Grade's production company ITC, which may have helped put her in contention for the *Panther* job.

Catherine was asked to go and see Blake, fully aware that she was one of many actresses up for the role, some of whom were very famous indeed. It came as a pleasant surprise when Blake revealed the part was hers. It was only later, when Catherine went in for a discussion about costumes and make up, that Blake revealed the reason why she had been cast: 'It's because you laughed during our interview, and I really like that.'[11] Laughter was important to Blake and Catherine remembers him as a very funny man:

> And I have got a good sense of humour, too. I laugh very easily. So, it must have worked in his mind that he liked the fact that this actress enjoyed a laugh. He told me that in the other *Panther* films the female lead was very straight and very serious.[12]

This tendency on Catherine's part to laugh is evident in the finished picture, when in certain scenes she is unable to control herself at some of Sellers' antics. 'Blake loved that I corpsed and that is why it was not cut out of the film. All of that was completely natural.'[13] For example, when Clouseau disguises himself as a telephone repairman and calls at Sir Charles Lytton's villa, Catherine can be seen hiding behind the door giggling. Then there is the nightclub scene where Clouseau arrives, masquerading as a suave playboy, and sits at her table. 'And he says something in his awful accent which made me laugh and instead of Blake going, cut, just the opposite, keep going, keep going.'[14] However, the film's denouement called for a little bit more decorum. Catherine is in bed with Plummer when it is revealed that she was in fact the thief all along. Another villain arrives with a gun, determined to have the Pink Panther jewel for himself. Catherine recalls:

> Then Peter barges into the room, and I really did laugh. I laughed so much that Blake had to cut. I said, 'I know, I can't be laughing because there's a bloody gun pointing at me, it's just not right.' But that was the only time when Blake said, 'Oh come on Cathy.'[15]

A couple of nights after winning the part, Catherine and a few friends went to Tramp nightclub in London's West End to celebrate:

> We were sat at this table and Peter Sellers walked in, on his own. He sat at another table and my friends said, 'We're going to tell him.' And I said, 'No, no, please don't.' But they did, they went over and said, 'By the way, your co-star in the next *Pink Panther* is sitting at that table.' He was very sweet. He did not come to our table but he sent a bottle of champagne. I think he was waiting for a lady. If my friends had not snuck up to him and told him he'd have never known.[16]

Another familiar face returning was Graham Stark, this time playing Pepi, a lowlife criminal type. After reading the script, Stark met Blake in London. 'I want him permanently in a sweat, filthy and dirty,' the director declared. 'Other than that, do what you like.'[17] All of stark's scenes were shot out in Morocco. Off he went to Casablanca with the wardrobe mistress and bought this terrible suit which he proceeded to dirty down, rubbing it on the ground and filing the edges until they were frayed. So filthy was the costume that during breaks in filming Stark was regularly refused entry to local cafes and bars. When Sellers invited him up to his hotel balcony for drinks one afternoon the waiter did his best to throw Stark out, thinking he was some tramp after free drinks.

To complete the image, Stark bought a pair of shoes and did the same thing, scuffing them until they were almost falling apart. 'I went back to the shop where I bought them and asked to see the assistant. "Listen, half an hour ago you sold me these shoes, look at them." She went mad. It was only a joke.'[18]

Oddly, no scene was written for Stark to share with his friend Sellers. Instead, all his moments in the film are played opposite Plummer. 'I did love working with Plummer though. He was a lovely man.'[19]

Among a crew of seasoned professionals and experienced technicians there was Peter Samuelson, a self-confessed, 'swot, a nerd',[20] not long out of Cambridge with a master's degree in medieval English history. That there wasn't a line of people at the door waiting to hire someone who knew a lot about medieval English literature hardly came as a surprise. What Samuelson did have going for him was a good command of French and he had already worked with Blake, doing some preparation for the proposed film *Rachel*, which was going to be shot on location in a French-speaking province of Canada. And so, with *Panther* going out to places like Morocco, Gstaad and Nice, Blake thought it made sense to have a production manager that was bi-lingual. 'And I guess that was me,' says Samuelson.[21] Still in his early 20s, Samuelson found himself in a position of huge responsibility and having to manage as best he could. He did have previous experience of being interpreter to the production manager on the Steve McQueen racing movie *Le Mans* (1971), which he had done prior to going to Cambridge, so at least he was used to life on a film set. Still, this was a huge gamble for Blake to take on someone with so little film experience. 'Blake was a joy,' notes Samuelson. 'He was kind, encouraging, very smart and funny man. Think of what he did, I was 23, it is a hell of a thing to make a 23-year-old your production manager. He took a big risk on me.'[22]

Even though Sellers was not to make an appearance in any of the scenes shot out in Morocco, the actor was on the location the whole time and Samuelson got to know and like him. 'Peter thought I was too serious, which I was, I had the weight of the world on my shoulders trying to keep this film on schedule and on budget.'[23] Samuelson also got to quickly know the star's various quirks.

> Peter was a very strange man. One of my jobs as production manager was, before Mr Sellers came on the set, I had to go around and look at all the crew and if anyone was wearing the colour green, I had to tell them to go to wardrobe and change their socks or whatever because he would not work. He had a superstition thing, which was also honestly a controlling thing, that he would not work if he could see green in his peripheral vision.[24]

Looking back, Samuelson identifies Sellers as a narcissist and incredibly insecure. As he explains:

> Inside every narcissist is a very insecure person. Narcissism is a manifestation of insecurity. There is this thing called classic narcissism. Here is an example, in a nursery school all the children transition well from being the sole apple of their mother's eye to being one of say twenty-five in a nursery school class, and where the teacher only gives them one 25th of attention. Almost all kids are fine with that. Except the one that goes on to become a narcissist who is estranged and feels terribly insecure because the teacher is not giving them the

> sole focus of attention. That leads to a life of misery, both the person's misery and inflicting it upon those around them because they are obnoxiously inflicting control on everyone around them.[25]

Alongside classic narcissism there is something called Acquired Situational Narcissism. Samuelson continues:

> This is where the kid in nursery school kind of adapted to being one of many but then something triggers their inner narcissist later in life, such as winning an Academy Award, becoming a star, and making a lot of money. I think Peter, who was one of the great comedic geniuses of the twentieth century, I think he had an inner narcissist. He was a sweetheart in many ways and I enjoyed dealing with him. But he was always testing. Why was it that he would not work if someone was wearing green? Was he really that superstitious? Or was it a ploy to see if he could make 150 people change their clothes if necessary? It is a control thing.[26]

Samuelson loved his stay in Morocco, loved the country, its people, the whole ambience of the place. Of course, the heat was tremendous and the work was arduous and slow. At one point a huge sandstorm hit Marrakesh and the production ground to a halt. It was a bit of a culture shock, though. One of the numerous problems he faced was the proliferation of hash, with so many people trying to sell the stuff to the cast and crew. 'You have never seen anything like it. All the hash in Morocco was in, on and around that film.'[27] Early on, Samuelson had to award a transport contract and someone came in for the interview with a block of hash that was the size of a gold ingot. The bribe did not work.

A few weeks into the filming, Samuelson was in his office when he received a petition from the local drivers who had been hired to ferry the cast and equipment to and from locations. They complained that the transportation captain had not been paying them their wages. They all had families to feed. Samuelson was outraged and called in the transportation captain to ask why, despite being given the money, the drivers had received nothing. The captain explained that the local custom was to wait and pay them all at the end of the film. Samuelson wasn't having any of it, they should be paid at the end of each week, and they should be paid tomorrow morning what they were already owed. The captain shook his head, 'Mr Samuelson, you are making a serious mistake.' Samuelson was adamant. 'I am not making a serious mistake. We are honest. We pay our people. You are going to pay them.'[28] The captain agreed, reluctantly, and walked out shaking his head and muttering dire warnings.

At 6am the following morning the drivers all arrived, looking deliriously happy to be finally getting their money.

> The next day not a single driver showed up,' recalls Samuelson. 'And when I went over to the transportation compound, they were all zonked out in their vehicles, completely stoned, incapable of working. I had to bring the crew over to drive the camera truck and the electrical truck and all the rest of it.[29]

And there was the transportation captain, a wry smile on his face.

In Morocco the cast and crew were based in Marrakesh and some of them stayed at the exclusive La Mamounia Hotel, with Blake and Julie Andrews occupying the royal suite. Sellers was installed in the Churchill suite, so called because it was Winston's favourite room, where he could indulge in his hobby of watercolour painting on the balcony, which had stunning views.

Graham Stark recalls that the pool became the centre of social life and that Sellers would stand on his head for half an hour at a time, doing his yoga, which was his latest fad. He had brought with him his new girlfriend, Christina 'Titi' Wachtmeister, a former model and socialite. Previously she had dated the future King of Sweden but broke it off to start a relationship with Sellers. Like many that had gone before, and would come afterwards, Sellers was convinced she was the right one for him. He even showed his son Michael some nude shots he had taken of her. 'Now can you see why I want to marry her?'[30]

The cast and crew had been filming for about a month when one morning Blake received a call from the hotel management. It was a polite reminder about one of the rules of staying in the royal suite, and that was a requirement to leave should any royalty turn up. It just so happened that the King of Cameroon was about to arrive with his entourage and some armed guards. Blake was not happy. 'I'm not moving out – that's flat.'

'I'm afraid you'll have to, sir,' came the reply. 'Or you will be ejected by force.'

'Well goddamn it,' fumed Blake. 'How the hell long do I have.'

'About half an hour, sir.'[31]

With the corridor outside quickly filling up with soldiers in battledress and machine guns, Blake and Julie herded up their children and moved to another suite. All this time Plummer was relaxing outside by the swimming pool and recalls hearing the commotion and looking up to see a row of snipers on the rooftops.

When it came time to leave Morocco for the next location, Switzerland, a plane had to be specially chartered. Back then there wasn't an airline that flew non-stop from Marrakesh to Geneva. Sellers was leaving a couple of days before everyone else on a small private jet. The morning of the flight Sellers came to see Samuelson in his office. He was carrying a small holdall. 'You know I'm going up this morning,' he said. 'I've got so much luggage. Would you mind bringing this with you when you come on the charter.' Samuelson was happy to oblige and Sellers put the bag on a table and left. Samuelson recalls:

> I looked at it, and I looked at it later the same day, and I looked at it the following morning, and I thought, something does not check out here. It is so small, why would he have me take it? And I thought, I know why he's bloody well let me take it. I know what is in it. That's why he's not taking it.[32]

Samuelson had forcefully laid the law down to the crew about taking any hash with them. 'I can only imagine how strict, how severe Swiss customs will be when bloody filmmakers arrive on a chartered 707 non-stop from Morocco,' he said to them. 'Don't take anything, do not, you'll spend your days in a prison cell and we'll have to replace you.'[33] And now here was Samuelson looking at the case Sellers had left in his office and thinking, that's it, it's got drugs in it for sure. But what to do? Samuelson went to have a look. It was locked, of course, and he did not have the key. He tried to pry it open, nothing doing. Defeated, he went back to his desk. Another few hours went by and he thought, what am I going to do? I am not going to prison for Peter Sellers.

The following day everyone was packing ready to leave and head off to the airport, this was the moment of truth. Samuelson took a large knife and cut the bag's leather strap.

> I opened the bag. It was full of dirty socks and underpants. That's all that was in it. And I realised what he had done. It was

> a prank. He wanted to see whether I would take it or whether I would cut it open or whether I would leave it behind. And when I gave it to him, clearly destroyed, cut, he thought that was the funniest thing. He said, 'So, we didn't trust me then.' And I said, 'Oh no, I think it was the customs that must have cut it, don't you think.'[34]

Gstaad is an upscale resort town in the Swiss Alps; Blake and Julie Andrews owned a holiday home there. It was off season so the place was just filled with movie stars and the rich playing tennis. During filming in the town Sellers, who stayed in a rented villa, fell in love with the place and bought his own chalet where he later enjoyed spending much of his spare time. Most of the crew and cast stayed at the prestigious Palace hotel, which also features heavily in the film. The nightclub sequence, where Clouseau arrives in a bungled bid to seduce Lady Lytton, was shot at the hotel's very own nightclub, The GreenGo, which still operates today.

Arriving in the town to start work on the picture were two very different actors at very different stages in their career. Victor Spinetti had been asked personally by Sellers to be in the film as the hotel concierge. Spinetti was a respected and experienced comedy actor who had worked in the West End, won a Tony award for his performance on Broadway as an obnoxious Drill Sergeant in Joan Littlewood's production of *Oh, What a Lovely War!* and appeared in the first three Beatles films: *A Hard Day's Night* (1964), *Help!* (1965), and *Magical Mystery Tour* (1967).

Mike Grady was in his twenties, had done a few bits and pieces on television, was at the Royal Court Theatre but still very much finding his way in the business. For him, this was Hollywood and the likes of Blake Edwards and Peter Sellers might well have been from another planet. 'But I had the best time on the film.'[35] Playing the hotel bell boy, Mike gets into a couple of comedy scrapes with Clouseau. 'And Sellers was so generous towards me. He was always cracking up and you didn't know when he was going to go. Both he and Blake were gigglers. They set each other off.'[36] As for Blake, Mike found him to be a very serious man – an anomaly perhaps, for someone who had made such great comedies. 'He was a processor.'[37]

Mike liked Spinetti a lot more. On that first morning Spinetti told him, 'Meet me for breakfast and I'll show you how films work.' He took Mike to the set, 'Let's make ourselves known,' said Spinetti. The crew were just setting up a shot. Blake spotted them:

> 'Hello Victor. How are you?' Then looking at Mike. 'What is the name of this other guy? Oh Mike. Hi Mike, how are you doing. Do you know Mr Sellers?' There was Peter, in the whole Clouseau get up. He looked over. 'I know Mike,' said Sellers. 'I was in London and saw you on a TV commercial. It's the funniest thing on television.' Those words went round the unit like wild fire. 'The crew were won over,' says Mike. 'After that, nothing was too much. I was accepted.'[38]

Spinetti was exploring the hotel one day when he came across a network of tunnels and small rooms carved into the rock down in the basement. An idea formed in his head. When Clouseau arrives at reception asking for a 'reum', the concierge tells him the place is full, except for one tiny room. He then produces a key, blowing a layer of dust off it, and sends him down into the bowels of the hotel. Spinetti took this idea to Blake who listened impassively. After he finished Blake said, quietly, 'That's funny.' The set of a ridiculously small hotel room was later built back at the studios in England. This work all added to the schedule and added to the budget, and in the end most of the scenes involving Clouseau in his tiny hotel room never made the final cut. But it demonstrates that Blake was always open to ideas; more than that, if he liked them, he did them.

One morning Mike Grady was on the set and there was a woman, dressed as a hotel chambermaid, her face riven with blotches and huge puss-filled boils. 'You know who that is, don't you,' said an assistant. 'No fucking clue,' said Mike. 'That's Julie Andrews.' Mike looked again, 'Fuck me, I'm doing a scene with Julie Andrews.'[39] Julie was around most of the time in Gstaad and either Blake convinced her to do a cameo or Julie insisted in being in the movie. The joke was that this chambermaid and her vacuum cleaner can hardly fit into Clouseau's cupboard of a room and the two of them are squeezed together. 'We thought it was hysterical,' says Peter Samuelson. 'But when we tested the scene with an audience, nobody laughed at it. The reason being that they did not realise it was Julie Andrews. We thought it was hysterical because we knew it was Julie Andrews being a chambermaid. However, if you did not know that, because of the make-up it didn't look anything like Julie, then it was just somebody banging around with a vacuum cleaner in a room. So that one came out. We thought it was gold dust.'[40]

More deleted footage involved the comedy actress Carol Cleveland, known for her work with the Monty Python team. She flew over to Gstaad to appear in a scene taking place in the hotel restaurant. Her outfit was an Indian sari, for reasons Carol never understood or were explained to her. The scene called for Carol, with an actor playing her husband, to arrive at the restaurant and wait in a small queue to be seated. Clouseau, in disguise, is standing behind her, spying on Lady Lytton who is already in the restaurant. 'Clouseau suddenly realises his zip is undone,' recalls Carol.

> So, he is trying to do up his zip but it gets caught in my sari and he's frantically tugging away. I look at him and he stops. Then the maître d' takes us over to the bar and because my sari has been caught in Clouseau's flies he has to go as well, walking right behind me.[41]

Sat at the bar, Clouseau tries once again to loosen the sari from his flies, frantically tugging and pulling at the material. 'But from my angle,' says Carol, 'I'm just seeing this strange man who appears to be wanking himself off.'[42] The maître d' rescues the situation by showing the couple to their table, but again Clouseau has no choice but to follow.

> And as we are walking, in this packed restaurant, my sari is gradually coming off. We had to time it just right, so that the moment we got to our table my sari completely came off and there I was in my underwear, with Peter holding the sari in his hand. My husband glares at him and chases him out of the restaurant.[43]

That was the scene and it took a full day to film, only for it to end up on the cutting room floor. Perhaps the humour was deemed to be a little too coarse.

Having done her job, Carol could now relax, with another few days before she was due to fly back to London. 'It was like a holiday. It was wonderful.'[44] That night she went down to the hotel disco with some of the other cast and stayed up very late, returning to her room at some ungodly hour.

> I had not been in bed very long when the phone goes and I'm asked, 'Carol, you swim, don't you.' I said, 'Yes, I do.' The voice said, 'Can you come straight down to the hotel's indoor pool please.' I got into my bathing suit and went downstairs and we rehearsed this little scene that Blake wanted us to do.[45]

The scene in question, a favourite with *Panther* fans, has Clouseau seated on the edge of the pool and as Carol dives in he follows her movement and ends up in the pool himself. For Carol, it turned out to be a strange experience going to see the film, upset that her big scene in the restaurant, the job for which she was paid, was cut, only for her diving bit to be included.

In any case, she enjoyed her last two days in Gstaad. Blake invited all the cast to his house for lunch. 'And that was a real treat. It had amazing views.'[46] And there was one memorable evening when Carol and some of the cast were relaxing in the restaurant and Sellers showed up, asking if he could join them. 'It was the most magical night. He regaled us with all these wonderful stories. We were all in fits of laughter. And at the end of the meal, we all went to pay and Peter said, 'No, this is on me.''[47] The very next evening Carol and the cast encountered a very different Peter Sellers:

> We were in the bar and we saw Peter, sitting by himself over in the corner, and wondered if he might like to join us. So, one of the actors went over to him and was told to fuck off, go away, leave me alone. He was obviously on one of his down days.[48]

One of the film's most famous gags is when Clouseau first arrives at the hotel and is approached by a man who asks for his coat, his hat, and his gloves. Thinking he is the hotel porter, Clouseau happily obliges only to watch as the man leaves, climbs into a car and drives off. He even has the temerity to wave, and Clouseau waves back. Peter Samuelson had arranged for the actor playing the role to fly in on the day the scene was due to be shot, rather than have him arrive the day before and incur extra salary and hotel costs. One thing Samuelson did not take into consideration was the English weather. That morning Luton airport was fogged in. Samuelson had to tell Blake the actor could not make it. 'Well bloody hell, you'll have to do it yourself,' said Blake. 'No, no, no,' said Samuelson. 'I haven't acted since I was a little boy in school plays.' 'That will do,' said Blake. 'You are an Italian clothing thief. Go to wardrobe and get yourself kitted up.'[49] So, Samuelson ended up in the role himself.

Something else, too, the hotel's entrance was a revolving glass door. That got Blake and Sellers' minds going and they concocted a neat bit of comic business where Clouseau loses his suitcase on the other side of the glass door and has the usual trouble trying to retrieve it. Directly to the right of the revolving door was a huge sheet of plate glass. It was on a hinge and had been open all morning while the crew came in and out with equipment. It was closed for the actual shot. Samuelson recalls:

> The gaffer called for an extra lamp, and an electrician who did not know that this window had been closed came belting up the hill, carrying a light over his shoulder, and went smashing into it. The window did not break, but he was knocked out. We had to get an ambulance and off he went to the local hospital.[50]

As the crew began packing up in Gstaad, Catherine Schell was in a car with Sellers going back to her hotel when he asked how she was getting down to the next location, Nice. 'I'm on a coach or something,' she said. 'What!' said Sellers, incredulously. 'You are going to be with the crew on the coach!'[51] He was livid. 'Peter thought, maybe they were going to fly me there in a private plane,' says Catherine. 'Because he was being flown in a private jet.'[52] Sellers then asked where she was going to be staying in Nice. It turned out to be the same hotel as the rest of the crew. 'No, you're not,' Sellers affirmed. 'How dare they. I am going to speak to the production. You are going to come and stay in the same hotel that I am staying at.'[53] And that's what happened.

This very much summed up the kind of relationship Catherine had with Sellers on the film, friendly and enjoyable.

> He was very delicate in a way. If you needed a study of a manic depressive, he was. Sometimes he would be in a wonderful mood and then suddenly down, it just depended what was happening in his life. And most of his moods did not come from work, they came from women. When he was up, he was lovely, he was fun, he was always funny. But when he was down, he was seriously down.[54]

Catherine recalls Sellers had his girlfriend, Christina 'Titi' Wachtmeister, with him for most of the shoot. 'She was Swedish and very lovely, but they weren't together terribly long.'[55]

Observing at close quarters how Blake and Sellers worked, Catherine calls their relationship, 'complicated'. She saw that both had a lot of respect for one another but at the same time each of them believed they brought the most value to the production.

> Blake wanted to be more important within the filming process and Peter wanted to be more important because he was the star. And so, there was this thing between them, who is more important, the director or the star. In Peter's mind it was a case of, you would not be working if I wasn't playing the part, and I'm sure in Blake's mind it was the same, you wouldn't be playing the part if I wasn't your director. I think it was a little bit like that.[56]

Filming in Nice went smoothly. Blake had assembled another crew of top-notch professionals, mostly British, including stuntman Joe Dunne, who started out in the business back in the early 1960s. In *A Shot in the Dark*, he had played one of the policemen that raid the nudist camp. Joe first started doubling for Peter Sellers on *Soft Beds and Hard Battles* and *Ghost in the Noonday Sun*, both 1974, and had been asked to stunt coordinate on *Return*. Joe does just about every stunt in the movie, he is the one driving the phone truck into the swimming pool and sliding down a zip wire between two buildings in the opening robbery sequence. With a very similar sense of humour, Blake and Joe hit it off. 'Blake was terrific to work with,' says Joe. 'He was great at listening and then he'd pitch in his own ideas that made the stunt even better.'[57] In all Joe worked on fifteen Blake Edwards movies. By the time they made *A Fine Mess* in 1985, Blake's screenplay would read something along the lines of: 'What happens next is what Joe Dunne comes up with.'

Joe liked to bring his family out on location whenever he could. During the shooting of *Ghost in the Noonday Sun* in Cyprus, Joe and his family were invited to have Sunday lunch with Sellers at a private villa he was renting in Kyrenia. 'We showed up to be met by Bert, Sellers' right-hand man,' recalls Mathew Dunne, Joe's son, who is today an assistant director and producer, and who was around 9 years old at the time. 'Bert told us that Peter had left the country that morning. He'd had an argument with his girlfriend, who had got on a plane back to London, so he followed her on the next plane to continue the argument. We stayed and had lunch by ourselves.'[58]

Joe's family was out on location in Nice for *Return*. One evening Joe introduced Mathew to the monkey they had used in the blind beggar scene. 'The animal promptly bit me,' says Mathew. 'I have the honour of being bitten by the infamous *Pink Panther* minkey. I'm probably not the only one.'[59]

The monkey scene is one of the most iconic in the entire *Panther* canon. Clouseau, on patrol, berates a blind accordion player on a street corner for not having a licence. The blind man has a monkey which proceeds to chew the end of Clouseau's baton. While all this is going on, a robbery is taking place inside a bank behind them, but Clouseau is too tied up in all this petty bureaucracy to notice, even when the masked robbers rush outside and get into their getaway car. The setting was supposed to be Paris, but with its similar architecture Nice was the perfect substitute and audiences did not spot the difference. It is also noticeable in this scene how much Sellers' French accent has become more twisted and outlandish than when we saw him in *A Shot in the Dark*, with words like monkey becoming 'minkey' and room is 'reum.'

Just to make things a little more relaxed, Blake rented a yacht in Antibes, just down the coastal road from Nice, where he and Julie stayed instead of a hotel. In subsequent *Panther* films, Blake usually made sure to film in places like the South of France, so he could live in the best hotels or relax on his yacht. 'Blake's thing was, he always wanted to go to a nice place,' confirms Mathew Dunne. 'He liked the good life.'[60] Often, he would time the shooting schedule to coincide with the Cannes Film Festival. It all made for a great atmosphere.

Sellers had some of his old mates come over to play a couple of roles, mainly to have them around; John Bluthal, most famous today as the fastidious minutes-taker Frank Pickle in BBC sitcom *The Vicar of Dibley*, played the blind beggar, and David Lodge appeared as Sir Charles Lytton's chauffeur. Sellers and Lodge had known each other from their days together in Ralph Reader's Gang Show, touring military bases during the war and playing seasons in theatres throughout the UK. Sellers had got Lodge a small role as the gardener at the Ballon estate in *A Shot in the Dark*. Theirs was a friendship that lasted until Sellers' death in 1980, with Lodge a constant support for Sellers, both emotional and professional.

Bluthal and Lodge's roles in *Return* were bit parts, really, and so they were very rarely required. Most days they hung out with Joe Dunne's wife around the hotel pool. 'John Bluthal used to do his Jack Benny impression and make her laugh,' recalls Mathew.[61]

Someone who kept themselves very much to themselves was Christopher Plummer. 'He was lovely, polite, a real gentleman,' recalls Catherine Schell. 'But he was also very reserved.'[62] Any relationship they had was purely on the set. And that seemed to be the same with everyone else. Plummer said his lines, then when work was done for the day, it was, 'Bye all, see you tomorrow,' and straight into his car and off. 'He had a convertible Rolls Royce that was given to him by the film company,' Catherine recalls. 'And my god did he love that car.'[63]

As Charles Lytton Plummer wore a wig, which is a bit of a puzzle since he had a perfectly fine head of hair. Perhaps the makers were after a certain look or style. Anyway, one day after shooting Plummer left as usual but must have been in a bit of a hurry on this occasion because he walked out still wearing his wig. The hair and make-up department went into a complete panic. According to Catherine:

> They knew that he had this convertible Rolls Royce and was taking the coast road back to the hotel, and they were terrified that a wind or a breeze or something would whip the wig off his head and blow it into the sea. They only had that one wig and it would take two weeks to get a replacement from the wig makers in London. So, it was panic, panic.[64]

Fortunately, the wig stayed firmly planted atop Mr Plummer's head.

Nice was the setting for many of the film's best comedy sequences. Disguised as a telephone repairman Clouseau arrives at Charles Lytton's chateau. He presses the doorbell, but this being Clouseau it does not stop ringing. He presses it repeatedly, but it does not stop. Drastic action is required and from his little tool kit Clouseau produces a screwdriver and wrenches open the casing and pulls out feet after feet of wire. Finally, he taps the bell with a hammer and it stops. The shot Blake was after seemed simple enough. When Clouseau bends down to put his equipment back in his bag he sees two shoes in the open doorway belonging to David Lodge. As Sellers rises, the camera follows his gaze from the shoes up the trousers and waistcoat to the face of Lodge who asks, 'May I help you?' To which Sellers replies, 'I have fixed your phone from the ringing, there is no charge.'

Blake wanted to do the whole thing in one take. Peter Samuelson recalls:

> We do it and we get all the way up to David Lodge at which point, before he speaks, Sellers burst out laughing and ruins the take. They go for take two. This time David Lodge burst out laughing. We got up to something like take fifteen, we are wasting time and Blake is going crazy because one or other of them, Sellers or Lodge, as soon as they lock eyes, would collapse laughing.[65]

Blake did a clever thing, which Samuelson has seen other directors do since. He lost his temper, or pretended to, and screamed at them. The point being to scare the crap out of them and break the moment of hilarity. It seemed to work. 'And we did it again,' says Samuelson. 'This time neither Sellers nor David Lodge collapsed in laughter. Instead, it was Blake Edwards who laughed so hard he fell off the camera dolly.'[66] The shot was abandoned and the scene was completed another way.

After leaving the Lytton's villa, Clouseau drives off in his little van, swerves to avoid another vehicle and ends up crashing into a private swimming pool. It was Samuelson's job to go all over the fashionable suburbs of Nice trying to find someone who wouldn't mind them performing the stunt. 'Easier said than done, because people who owned those houses up there in the hills, they're all very rich and shockingly they're not very interested in having people drive a truck into their swimming pool.'[67] In the end he found a large water container that was used for irrigation purposes and it was dressed to look like a pool.

For much of the filming Sellers and Blake had been on their best behaviour. Plummer observed that Sellers, not having had a hit for years, 'knuckled under and put his whole being into it'.[68] Blake said something similar, that Sellers on his uppers, when his career was in a bad shape, was, 'cooperative and wonderful to work with'.[69] This led, by and large, to a good atmosphere, just as the first *Panther* had been and how, by the end, *A Shot in the Dark* most assuredly was not. 'It was a happy film because Peter was in a very good place,' says Mike Grady.[70] He seemed to be off the drugs, temporarily, although suffered from back pain which he refused to allow to interfere with the work. 'He was praying a lot, too,' says Mike. 'He had a priest that came and prayed with him every morning.'[71] At Sellers' home in London he had a small altar where he put religious symbols, some Catholic things, items given to him by the Indian musician Ravi Shankar, in essence covering all the bases. He once brought a priest to a press conference for good luck.

Others, though, recognised the old Sellers not very far from the surface. 'He was fine when the camera was rolling,' recalls crew member John Allenby. 'But once the shot was over, he went back into his own little shell.'[72] It did appear that Blake got on much better with the crew than Sellers did.

One important scene scheduled for Nice was set inside Clouseau's apartment and the art department had found a suitable flat in a tenement block down by the docks. The whole interior needed to be dressed and because there were no lifts, and the flat was on the second floor, everything had to be carried up the stairs. On the morning of the shoot Blake arrived to okay the set. He took a wander round, studying and inspecting, then stood in the middle of the room. 'There is one thing wrong with this place, Sellers is not going to like walking up two flights of stairs every day. It's a wrap, we're going back to London.'[73] A call was put through to the production designer Peter Mullins at Shepperton studios. 'You're not meant to be back for another week,' he argued. 'The sets aren't ready.'[74] The order was: make them ready. Mullins and his team worked over the weekend to get everything prepared.

Peter Mullins was already a highly experienced and respected production designer and art director, with credits such as *Alfie* and *Where Eagles Dare* to his name. He had never done a *Panther* before and was working in his back garden one afternoon when the call came to go and see Blake at the Dorchester. Peter explained that he had not shaved for two days and was covered in muck. The assistant relayed all this to Blake and Mullins could hear the director in the background fire back, 'He's got forty-five minutes to get here or he hasn't got the job.'[75]

Peter did manage to get to the Dorchester in time. Blake was ensconced in the Oliver Messel suite. Peter knocked on the door and was pleasantly surprised to see it opened by Julie Andrews. Peter knew Julie from her early acting days and had not seen her for years. As for Julie, she was delighted to see that it was indeed that Peter Mullins and there were hugs and kisses in the open doorway, with Blake looking on wondering why this chap was so friendly with his wife. 'I thought I'd lost the job,' Peter jokes.[76] From that awkward first introduction with Blake, Peter went on to work on the next five *Panther* films.

At Shepperton work began on the interiors, with the emphasis always on improvisation. 'I used to turn up good as gold in my little bell boy's outfit never knowing what they were going to ask me to do,' recalls Mike.[77] Some of the funniest gags in the film were made up on the set, such as when Clouseau, disguised as a cleaner, searches a room while vacuuming and sucks a painting of some flowers out of its frame. Unable to replace the painting, he substitutes it with some real flowers from a nearby vase. Plummer saw how brilliantly Blake and Sellers improvised together, both having, 'a similar twisted sort of imagination'.[78]

Another gag saw Clouseau leave the bath tap running in his hotel room and when he and Cato later open the bathroom door they are engulfed by a huge tidal wave of soapy water. It was a big set up, with the crew pouring water from a huge vat down a chute suspended from the ceiling of the studio. On take one, the stunt men doubling Clouseau and Cato opened the door and there was scarcely a trickle of water. Blake was not happy. 'Come on guys. Give me more.'

Ok Blake, you want water, the crew was heard to mutter. Right, you will have water. The stunt was set up again and when Blake called 'Action' the force of the water literally ripped the set apart.

Mathew visited his dad Joe several times while the crew were filming at Shepperton. One day has stayed fixed in his mind ever since. They were shooting a scene on the set of a passenger plane and Blake was searching for a way for Clouseau to lose his passport before arriving at his destination.

> After getting my dad's attention I suggested to him that Clouseau goes to the bathroom, he bends over and his passport falls out of his top pocket into the toilet and he accidentally flushes it down as he tries to retrieve it during turbulence. The next thing I knew Joe was having a quiet word with Blake, and then pointing to me. All I heard was Blake say, 'keep that kid around!' Blake's wish to keep me around worked out, as years later I ended up working on six of his movies, eventually as an assistant director.[79]

A few days later they shot the idea Mathew had suggested and he proudly awaited the release of the film. 'I had told everyone, and a great showbiz lesson for me was that obviously that scene didn't make the final cut – you never even see Clouseau on a plane.'[80] A lot of ideas and footage that was meant to be in *Return* never saw daylight. For example, there was going to be an entire sequence at a tennis match featuring Ilie Nastase, although Mathew is unsure whether it was ever put on film.

The exciting robbery sequence that opens the film was also shot at Shepperton. Joe Dunne brought in stuntwoman Cyd Child to double for Catherine Schell as the thief, all in black and wearing a mask. Dunne had worked before with Cyd who made her reputation doubling for Diana Rigg on *The Avengers* TV show. The interesting thing here is that the audience is not supposed to know who this thief is, so Cyd had to be careful not to give the game away, by being too feminine in her movements. 'The cameraman wanted to do a close up of my eyes when I was lying on the ground firing the crossbow,' recalls Cyd. 'But Blake said no because my eyes were a different colour. So, Catherine had to come in to do that close-up.'[81]

At one moment the alarm goes off and the thief dives under a rapidly descending steel security door. According to Cyd:

> Even though it was fake, the door was still very heavy and I made sure I was well under it. Joe wanted it closer. I did it again. 'No,' said Joe. 'We need it a bit closer than that.' In the end he was practically holding me back when he gave me the cue to go so it looked really close. We did get it ok in the end.[82]

Cyd enjoyed her brief time working on the movie and the opportunity to sit and chat with Blake in a relaxed manner between set ups.

> He was a great fan of martial arts and had been a close friend of Bruce Lee. And so, we were talking about that because he found out that I did judo, that was my thing. Blake talked a lot about Bruce. But he had a wide range of topics that he could talk about. He was a very intelligent man.[83]

Cyd also makes a brief appearance at the end of the film as one of the geishas at the Japanese restaurant when Clouseau is attacked by Cato, who destroys his sukiyaki. 'I must have been a foot taller than the Japanese ladies. But I don't think anybody notices in all the mayhem.'[84]

Once filming was completed thoughts turned to post-production. Henry Mancini returned as composer and his score is a joy to listen to. However, DePatie and Freleng were too busy on the *Pink Panther* TV series and other projects to work on the by now trademark animated title sequence. Instead, Blake approached the respected Canadian/British animator Richard Williams, who had been responsible for movie title sequences like *What's New Pussycat*, the Bond spoof *Casino Royale* and *Charge of the Light Brigade*. As well as the hauntingly atmospheric kidnap prologue that opened *Murder on the Orient Express*.

The Williams studio, which was based at 13 Soho Square in Central London, did mostly work for commercials and was the best in the world. 'In that period of time,' says animator Tony White, 'from the '70s through to the early '80s, in terms of international awards for commercials, our studio won more than all the other studios put together. It was so dominant.'[85] Tony began there as Williams' assistant and apprenticed with him. 'He was my idol. I couldn't believe I got a job to work for him. And he was my idol till his dying day.'[86] Williams' great strengths were his love and passion for animation and a literal obsession for the craft. The downside of that was it shut him off from people. 'In the studio he was a tyrant,' admits Tony. 'If he didn't get what he wanted or if you didn't do something the way he wanted it he would really shout and scream at you. He was tough to work for.'[87] In the office some people dubbed him 'the Fuhrer'.

By the time the *Panther* commission came along Tony was no longer Williams' assistant. He had begun directing his own commercials, as well as assisting Ken Harris, the noted American cartoonist. Harris came from Warner Brothers, working with the legendary Chuck Jones and drawing, among others, Bugs Bunny, Daffy Duck and Porky Pig. He had also worked for the DePatie-Freleng studio in Hollywood. By the early '70s he was retired, although in the summer months always flew over to London from his home in California to work at the Williams studio. Williams never paid him very much, instead put him and his wife up in a nice hotel, and knowing Harris was a big tennis fan always got the couple the best seats at Wimbledon. The *Panther* job just happened to coincide with Harris being in London so Williams put him in charge. Williams worked out the concept, did the storyboards and the character poses, Harris did the actual animation, with Tony doing some assisting. 'We were working round the clock,' says Tony.[88] All except Harris, who by then was in his mid-70s and would tire easily, so by the afternoon always went back to his hotel.

Williams knew getting the *Panther* was a big break for the company and intended to pull out all the stops. He told Ken Harris:

> I don't care about profit on this. I want to out-Hollywood Hollywood on this. I want to out-Disney Disney. I want to out-Warner Brothers Warner Brothers. I want this to be the greatest thing. So, I'm not worried about money, we're just going to do the most amazing job.[89]

Williams enjoyed complete artistic freedom to come up with the new titles; Blake Edwards never interfered. 'We ran it half finished,' said Williams. 'And he just said, "Thank you."'[90] The scenario has Clouseau on the trail of the Pink Panther, following him to a glitzy Hollywood premiere. Here the Panther adopts the guises of various old time movie stars like Carmen Miranda, Gary Cooper, Chaplin, Groucho Mark and George Raft. The titles ran for something like four minutes and took twelve weeks to complete. The result was a smash, with every critic reviewing the film signalling out the titles as a highlight. 'And it won all kinds of awards and all kinds of accolades,' says Tony. 'But that project lost a huge amount of money for the studio.'[91]

The Return of the Pink Panther was launched in grand style with a special opening in Gstaad that lasted the whole weekend. Something like 250 journalists were jetted in from around the world. The streets were adorned with pink bunting, and pink paw prints led to the Palace hotel where guests were given *Pink Panther* goody bags and looked after by *Pink Panther* hostesses serving pink champagne.

Sellers put in a request to United Artists for round trip tickets for his children, for Bert his chauffeur, two tickets for George Harrison, and one for his date, although at the time Sellers had no idea who that was, since he and Christina 'Titi' Wachtmeister had broken up somewhat acrimoniously. It happened while they were on holiday in Cyprus. Eating at a local taverna a local man was giving 'Titi' the eye at her table and she responded. Sellers stormed off, grabbed her coat, and chucked it at her across the table, smashing glasses, bottles, and crockery. In the end Sellers took her sister Anna to the premiere.

Mike Grady flew in for the occasion with his wife on a pink aeroplane and they were put up in a suite at the Palace hotel. 'Every time you went back to your room there were piles of presents.'[92] This was hospitality on a grand scale. 'The bar in the hotel was open 24/7,' reveals Mike. 'You had hundreds of journalists and you had the cast and the production people. It was absolute fucking mayhem.'[93] Indeed, a showbiz reporter from one of the British tabloids fell ill at the airport on his way back to London from the premiere and died.

In the garishly pink decorated hotel ballroom Sellers and his co-stars were available for interviews. Sellers gave each journalist fifteen minutes. It was very tightly scheduled. Sellers went out of his way to be cooperative. When one reporter was too hung over to show up for his allotted slot, Sellers set aside another time for him to get his interview.

At the premiere itself, Mike and his wife sat next to Victor Spinetti. As the film played and neared its end, it was clear that most of Spinetti's part had been cut out. Mike recalls:

> He was very upset and hurt. He was crying at the end of the screening. He was crying with rage. He was very gracious

> towards me, saying I had done well. I asked if he was ok. He said, 'I'm just so angry.' If they would have rung him and said, Vic we have had to cut you, then he wouldn't have turned up, he said, or at least he would have known.[94]

Mike asked if Spinetti wanted to go to the post-premiere party with them. There was a big dinner taking place on the terrace of the Palace hotel. 'No,' he said. 'I can't face it.'[95]

Back in his room, Spinetti picked up the phone. He knew that his good friend and fellow Welshman Richard Burton was staying in his chalet in Gstaad with Elizabeth Taylor. He decided to give them a call. Burton picked up the phone. 'What are you bloody doing here, boy?' 'Well, there's this *Pink Panther* premiere and a big party tonight.' 'They haven't bloody asked us.'[96]

And for good reason, this most famous of couples would assuredly take the spotlight away from the film and its star. Which is exactly why Spinetti insisted they come along. When Spinetti announced to Sellers that he had invited the Burtons, Sellers slightly stiffened before saying, 'How kind of your friends to grace us with their presence.'[97]

Mike was in the ballroom when Burton and Taylor arrived. 'They turned up looking a million dollars.'[98] Burton was in a Nehru jacket and Liz loaded with jewels. 'When those big doors opened and they walked in everyone's heads turned. It was almost like that moment in a Western when the piano stops playing in the saloon bar.'[99] Of course, photographs of the couple dominated the front pages of the newspapers the following day. Blake and Sellers were not best pleased.

Burton and Liz sat at the top table. Henry Mancini always enjoyed telling the story that during dinner someone at the table said to Burton, 'Do you mind if I smoke?' And Burton answered, 'I don't care if you burn.'[100]

The dinner was arguably the highlight of the weekend. At each table there was *Pink Panther* champagne and *Pink Panther* gift wrist watches. Henry Mancini and his orchestra provided the musical entertainment. At one point Julie Andrews, who had arrived in suitable style wearing a glamorous pink evening dress, stepped onto the stage and her rendition of *Moon River* received the best ovation of the night.

The film's promotion did not stop there. Something like 450 *Pink Panther* products, including toys, games, sweets, umbrellas and toiletries, were already for sale in over forty countries. There was a *Pink Panther* toy car by Meccano, and shirts by Ben Sherman.

Sellers was gambling a lot on this picture to restore much of the star lustre he had lost over the last few years. Just before it opened, he wrote to his friend, actor John Le Mesurier: 'Had a marvellous time on *Pink Panther*. It looks as though it may be the best of the three, which would be good, as recent efforts have not contributed a great deal to my career.'[101] The two men first met on the set of *I'm Alright Jack* and Le Mesurier had appeared in the first *Panther* film as the prosecuting counsel in the final court scene. They shared many interests, not least listening to jazz as a form of relaxation. By 1974 Le Mesurier had become a household name in Britain as Sergeant Wilson in the sitcom *Dad's Army*.

Happily, Sellers did promotion for the film in the States, including an appearance on the popular Merv Griffith show, who devoted the entire ninety-minutes to Sellers and the new *Panther* movie. Sellers also appeared on the *Tonight Show*. While in New York he was named an honorary detective by the city police department, and dressed as Clouseau for the ceremony.

Return of the Pink Panther was everything Sellers and Blake hoped it might be, and more. Opening in America during the summer of 1975 it emerged as the fifth highest grossing film of the year, beaten only by *Jaws*, *One Flew Over the Cuckoo's Nest*, *Shampoo* and *Dog Day Afternoon*. Critically, it was mostly well received. *The New Yorker* called it 'One of the most delicately cataclysmic studies in accident proneness since the silents.' *Time* reckoned it was 'The most raucous of the lot, and possibly the best.'

British audiences had to wait until January 1976 to catch Clouseau's latest adventure. Again, the film proved a runaway success. Prince Charles jokingly wrote to Sellers that he had laughed so hard when he saw it that he had wet the dress of the woman in the next seat. Many view the film as the best of the '70s *Panthers*, although it does occasionally suffer from poor pacing. As the *Sunday Mirror* observed, 'The whole thing seems to sag whenever Sellers is off-camera.' That is the problem with a star vehicle, the film is so dependent on that one performer. This had become the case with the *Panther* films, they were now all about Sellers. 'It is that rare thing,' *The Spectator* said about *Return*, 'a film worth seeing again just to watch one comic performance'. As for the critic of the *Sunday Express*, he called Sellers, 'The funniest man in the world.'

It is also true to say that with this new *Panther* film the comedy had become almost as cartoonish as the opening credits, such as when Clouseau opens the door of his apartment and casually accepts a bomb with a burning fuse from an assassin. This is a gag that happens again in *Revenge*: 'A bomb, were you expecting one.' But overall, the comedy set pieces are brilliantly conceived and played. Comedy is never easy, especially on film. 'You haven't got an audience sitting there giving you feedback, was that actually funny,' says Peter Samuelson. 'You're sort of guessing. There is huge pressure. What if it flops? What if nobody laughs? We won't know for months.'[102]

Besides the financial rewards, out of the film came a lifelong friendship between Christopher Plummer and Blake and Julie. The actor had enjoyed working with Blake. 'He was easy and relaxed, at least on the surface. Plus, he had this quirky, zany side to him I found most appealing.'[103] As for Sellers, Plummer did not see much of him again. He considered him to have greatness as a comic, but Plummer saw Sellers as, 'A strange, tortured soul, just a stone's throw from schizophrenia. He could be delightful one moment and deeply sullen the next. The drugs, I am positive, were inviting him to self-destruct.'[104]

Catherine Schell did remain on friendly terms with Sellers after the film. He would ring her up sometimes in the middle of the night, 'Catherine please can you come over, I've got to talk to somebody.' She would get in her car and drive over to his apartment and sit up until six o'clock in the morning talking him up from his depression. 'Then he would go to sleep and I would be able to leave.'[105] Sellers hated to be alone. Susan Wood recalls being awoken at something like three in the morning with a frantic Sellers on the end of the phone threatening to jump off the balcony of his flat.

> I drove up there, thinking, oh my God, what am I going to find. I got there and the first words out of his mouth were, 'You know, I really feel like a salt beef sandwich. Do you think you could find somewhere round here.' He always needed someone to talk to. He was not a man who was comfortable alone. In so many ways he was like a little boy. Hence him being so much more comfortable in a character than in his own skin.[106]

Chapter 5

THE PINK PANTHER STRIKES AGAIN

The world-wide success of *The Return of the Pink Panther* totally rejuvenated Sellers' career, making him a box office draw once again. As a bonus, he and Blake also made a tidy fortune out of it, having both agreed to defer their salaries for a larger share of the profits. 'From where he had been to where he found himself so very quickly was just amazing,' recalls his secretary Susan Wood.[1] He moved from his mews house to a plush apartment in Roebuck House in Victoria, not far from Buckingham Palace. 'That was a big jump up for him,' says Susan. 'Laurence Olivier was on the next floor and Max Bygraves was on another floor. His whole life changed again.'[2]

And not just financially and professionally. Sellers' agent Dennis Selinger threw a dinner party for his major clients in a private room at the Ivy restaurant. The star-studded guest list included the likes of Sean Connery, Michael Caine, Roger Moore and Sellers. One of Selinger's lesser-known clients, a young actress by the name of Lynne Frederick, was there, too. Lynne had just finished work on the film *Voyage of The Damned*, appearing with Malcolm McDowell as a pair of star-crossed lovers. It was McDowell who invited Lynne to the party that evening as his guest.

During the meal a woman lost a diamond stud in an earring and became visibly upset and agitated. Sellers, who had been relaxing, almost dozing in a corner, sprang into life, and in the guise of Inspector Clouseau approached every person in the room mockingly accusing them of stealing the diamond stud. McDowell later recalled it as one of the funniest and most brilliant things he had ever seen. Later that same evening Sellers revealed to McDowell one of his character flaws, that he could walk into a room of say forty women, one of those women in that room would be poison for him, and he'd walk straight up to her and ask her to marry him. He didn't quite ask Lynne to marry him that night, but did become fascinated and infatuated enough to call Selinger up at 4.30 that morning for her phone number. Par for the course, during their first date Sellers asked Lynne to marry him. She refused but agreed they could continue to see each other.

Soon after meeting Lynne, Sellers began work on another *Pink Panther* film. The unexpected success of *Return* made United Artists think that perhaps they had another franchise to rival their other big studio cash cow, the James Bond series. *Return* must be the only comedy movie ever made that finishes with one of its main protagonists, in this case Dreyfus, strapped into a straight-jacket and put in a padded cell. Blake and screenwriter Frank Waldman decided in *The Pink Panther Strikes Again* to continue with the storyline of Dreyfus' obsession with killing Clouseau, essentially turning him into a mad super-villain. Kidnapping a renowned British scientist, Dreyfus forces him to build a giant laser weapon to threaten various capital cities unless the governments of the world combine their resources and kill Clouseau for him. In his attempts to locate the scientist, Clouseau arrives in the UK to work with Scotland Yard. Playing a police superintendent was Leonard Rossiter, then a big television star thanks to two popular TV sitcoms that were running at the time, *Rising Damp* and *The Fall and Rise of Reginald Perrin*.

Early in 1976, Blake and Julie Andrews flew into London, renting a house and setting up an office at Shepperton studios. Here Blake began to cast the movie. In a bid to appease the mad plan of Dreyfus, world governments have no choice but to send their best assassins out with orders to find and kill Clouseau. Russia sends their top spy, Olga, with orders to seduce and kill Clouseau. Blake cast Maud Adams in the role, an actress who had appeared in the most recent James Bond film *The Man with The Golden Gun* (1974). In one scene, Maud was required to wear a fur coat with nothing underneath and then to step out and slide into bed. From the outset Maud was having trouble. While no nudity would be seen on the screen (the camera was carefully placed behind her), the actress was still required to be naked, with pasties or patches placed over her nipples and pubic area for modesty's sake. During the long day of filming these kept falling off, causing Maud to feel uncomfortable. Her unease translated to Sellers and the crew and the atmosphere got worse and worse. In the end the decision was made by Blake to recast. Michael Sellers believed the real reason for Maud's departure was that she spurned his father's carnal overtures.

Blake, but especially Julie, were huge fans of the British period television drama *Upstairs, Downstairs*, which had been shown in America to great acclaim. Lesley-Anne Down had gained international popularity playing Georgina Worsley in the series and was at home one afternoon when her agent called saying Blake Edwards wanted to see her at his office at Shepperton. Excited, Lesley arrived, there was Blake, and Julie; it was not a screen test or an audition, they just chatted and asked a few questions and told Lesley how much they both loved her in *Upstairs, Downstairs*.

Then Blake asked Lesley to remain in the room while he and Julie left to talk privately in the next office. Lesley recalls that,

> The walls were very thin and I could hear everything that was said. I heard Blake saying, 'She does not look like she did in *Upstairs, Downstairs*. She looks completely different.' And Julie said, 'Oh, Blake it's just the costumes, the hair, the make-up, of course she looks different, but you know it's the same girl.' There was a brief pause. 'Ok, if you say so,' answered Blake. After that they both returned and I got the job.[3]

It was only later that Lesley discovered that Blake and Julie thought she was Nicola Pagett, her co-star in *Upstairs, Downstairs* who played the rebellious and thoroughly spoiled Elizabeth Bellamy. 'When they eventually found out I wasn't Nicola Pagett, it was fine,' says Lesley.[4]

Blake had found his new Olga but when filming began in February 1976, he had other things to worry about, not least an increasingly fractured relationship with his star. Things had been good on *Return*; Blake had even said that it was the most fun they'd had making a film together. But then both men were in desperate need of a hit. Coming into *Strikes Again* on the back of a big success, things began to unravel very quickly. For starters, Sellers was mentally and physically in bad shape. The medication he was being given for his continuing heart condition was not helping with his mood swings and appeared to sap his energy. 'As the days unfolded,' recalled Julie Andrews, 'he was chronically late for work in the mornings, asked for lunch breaks to begin early, and couldn't wait to be dismissed in the evenings.'[5] Sellers would phone in saying he was too sick to work, leaving Blake with no choice but to shoot around his star or pack in for the day. It was tough on company morale, especially so early in the production schedule. When Blake confronted Sellers with the problem the actor threatened to quit, or sue. 'Blake talked him down, but the détente would only last a day or two before problems flared up again,' revealed Julie. 'Blake confessed to me how difficult it was to do comedy with someone so depressed. He began to look for ways to build the comedy *around* Peter, rather than having it emanate *from* him.'[6]

With Blake and Sellers, it was a love/hate affair if ever there was one. When they were good, they were very good and when they were bad, they were horrid. According to Susan Wood:

> Peter seemed to delight in upsetting Blake, and yet he really owed him so much. And Blake put up with so much. If Peter did not want to do something, or he did not feel it was right, or he felt that Blake was interfering with the script, things became very difficult and strained. And then at other times you would think they were best buddies.[7]

The *Panther* regulars, Herbert Lom, Burt Kwouk and Graham Stark, had all seen this before, of course, and recognised that there was almost an inevitability about it. 'There was a lot of conflict,' admits Kwouk. 'And out of the Blake/Peter conflict came this wonderful stuff, which without the conflict might not have happened. They were both geniuses, really. And it is very difficult to get geniuses to work together.'[8]

Kwouk put some of this behaviour down to Sellers' poor health and the drugs he was taking for his heart. 'This had an impact on him. And sometimes when he would not turn up, people would say, oh he's being difficult. But I think it was his heart that said, don't go to work today.'[9] Kwouk's theory is that Blake and the production pushed this agenda of Sellers being difficult to hide his heart condition, otherwise they might not have got the insurance for him.

For the most part Stark kept himself away from the troubles:

> Once or twice, Blake would come up to me and say, 'Would you deal with it.' I was terribly torn because I used to think to myself, Peter maybe a shit in some ways, but he is the reason I'm here. He was always very good to me, very loyal. And I understood a lot about Peter. We were very close.[10]

Once again, Sellers had asked for Stark to be in the new *Panther*. He was to play a German hotel clerk on location at the Hotel Bayerischer Hof in Munich. However, it did not quite work out to plan.

> Blake said to me, 'I want you to look like Hitler.' And I got very nasty. 'Blake, I love you dearly, but you've got to understand, to someone like me who was in the war, he is the arsehole

> of the world.' I could see he was worried. Finally, he said, 'I'll tell you what, I'll be fair, we'll do it and if it's shit, out, I promise you.' I said, 'Okay, but you're going to get a nasty shock because I'm his fucking double.'[11]

Stark was led into make-up and the eventual result was eye opening to say the least.

> I'm with the make-up guy, and he stands back and goes, 'Jesus Christ.' And I said, 'I told you; I look like his fucking double.' I had the hair, the uniform, everything. I walk down this great big flight of stairs into the lobby and Peter and Blake are there at the bottom, and Blake goes, 'Oh my God.' He doesn't know what to do. 'I fucking told you,' I said. By now the public are coming in. And I had to stand behind this desk. We started the take and I put on this German voice, and Peter corpsed. And then this woman came up to ask for her key and looked at me in total disbelief. We could not go on, there were tears rolling down Peter's face, we couldn't shoot it.[12]

Instead, they got Stark to play a decrepit old Bavarian inn keeper. This is the scene that contains arguably the best joke in the entire *Panther* series. Clouseau sees a small dog and asks the inn keeper if his dog bites. The innkeeper says it does not. Clouseau turns back to the dog, gives it a reassuring smile, and bends down to pet it. Just then it becomes a mini Hound of the Baskervilles and viciously goes for Clouseau. The Inspector bolts upright and stares at the inn keeper saying, 'You told me your dog did not bite.' Cue a short pause and then, with masterful timing and deadpan delivery, Stark answers, 'That is not my dog.'

The delivery and timing of the punchline is even more admirable when one considers that by this stage Stark was stoned out of his tree. The prop man had given Stark an old pipe for his character to use, only the actor had recently quit smoking and did not want to puff away on tobacco. Sellers came up with the answer: herbal tobacco; he just happened to have a batch of it and gladly filled Starks's pipe with it. Only it was not herbal tobacco, it was marijuana. Stark revealed; 'I was stoned out of my fucking mind. I did all the words right, but I was out of my head, absolutely stoned for the whole take and all through lunch. Blake said to me, 'At lunch you talked absolute rubbish.' And I kept thinking, I have got this terrible headache.[13]

Not long after finishing that scene Stark was on the Pinewood set of Richard Fleischer's all-star cast movie of *The Prince and the Pauper*. He was playing the court jester to Charlton Heston's Henry VIII. Blake paid a visit to the set one day and went over to see Fleischer. Motioning at Stark, Blake told Fleischer, 'He's a well-known drug addict, you know.' The whole set went silent. Then Blake laughed and spilled the beans about the marijuana pipe story.

Stark was often the victim of Sellers' pranks. On another *Panther* film Sellers talked Stark into sending for some German virility pills in the post. The advertising copy, however, was a fake concocted and specially printed by Sellers and Blake.

It must be said that Blake was just as bad as Sellers when it came to pranks, and corpsing for that matter. 'Sometimes things were so funny that people started laughing,' said Herbert Lom. 'Unfortunately, it was very often Blake, who was such a grateful audience that very often he spoilt our takes by laughing right in the middle.'[14] Lom observed that whenever the actors broke up a scene to laugh, 'Blake was in seventh heaven.' Indeed, Lom claimed that this was one of the reasons why he didn't have such a good relationship with the director, since being quite serious by nature he would remain stony-faced, waiting to start the scene again.

> A normal director would have said, 'Listen, we are wasting a lot of time.' Blake loved us losing our characters and laughing and giggling. I was the only one among the actors that did not laugh or break character and Blake said to someone, 'That Lom, he hasn't got any sense of humour.'[15]

Often the schedules on the *Panthers* accommodated the fact that days, indeed weeks, would be lost to playacting or scenes taking too long because they were ruined by corpsing. Or simply because not very much work was done per day. Blake and Sellers would work on ideas and sometimes just get the one shot done. This, together with Sellers' behaviour, turning up late or not at all, pushed *Strikes Again* way over schedule and over budget.

The composer and lyricist Leslie Bricusse was a friend of both Blake and Sellers and recalled having dinner one evening with Sellers, who had found it most amusing that he and Blake had spent the entire day working and yet not achieved a single shot. The scene was Clouseau visiting his tailor in Rome. They needed a funny name for the tailor. Blake came up with, 'pederasti di roma.' But every time Sellers got to the point where he had to say the name he collapsed into giggles, or Blake went, or they set each other off. They switched instead to another scene, but that did not work either because they were still thinking of 'pederasti di roma' and burst out laughing. At the end of the day Sellers said that Blake had something like forty-five takes of just laughter, so they packed it in.

A lot of this was the responsibility of Blake, he was just as much to blame as Sellers, his style of directing was relaxed and far from disciplined. Inevitably this got him in trouble with the studio according to Peter Mullins. 'He used to start out alright with the management and then he would end up having problems with them because he'd go over budget and they'd all come over from America to curtail him and then he would disappear or tell them to fuck off.'[16]

Lesley-Anne Down is under no illusion that someone like Blake would not survive in today's film industry:

> With Blake it was like, 'Ok, it's 4 o'clock and we've laughed too much and we haven't got one single take, so let's all just go home and have dinner and come back tomorrow.' There simply wasn't anything to do with, you've got to keep on schedule. The films always went on much longer than the original schedule. He was much more into living life to the full and having as much fun. And having as much fun for everybody that was making the movie.[17]

Much later, in the 1980s, Lesley got to know Blake much better and became good friends with him when she married cameraman Don E. FauntLeRoy, who worked on several movies with Blake. They all lived near each other in Malibu. 'We used to see each other all the time,' says Lesley. 'Blake and Julie would have these wonderful parties.'[18]

In *Strikes Again* the slapstick element ratchets up several notches, leading to ever more bizarre comic situations. This is a criticism that can be levelled at the 1970s' *Panther* films. 'I think they became rather too broad,' admits Stark. 'They missed the subtleties of *Shot in the Dark*, which were wonderful.'[19]

By this time, the jokes had a familiar air about them, too, like a favourite pair of slippers. And yet they still worked, by and large. Like the Bond films, audiences came to see a *Panther* movie expecting certain elements to be in place: the animated opening, Clouseau's fight with Cato, his destroying of Dreyfus' office, his donning of increasingly ridiculous disguises, et al. These 'set pieces' remained funny precisely because they did not deviate from what most of the audience wanted to see. For instance, how many times can we laugh at Clouseau's mispronunciation of the word 'room' to a hotel receptionist, and yet we do, largely because it is Peter Sellers doing the delivery. It helps if your lead actor in a comedy is a genius on the level of Chaplin or Stan Laurel.

In *Strikes Again*, Sellers' assault of the French language took on new heights of absurdity, as if it had a life of its own. As Lynne Frederick was to say, 'Peter kept tinkering with his French accent till it very nearly became unintelligible.'[20] The Clouseau character was now barely recognisable from the one in the 60s films.

Filming on location in Munich, Sellers continued to play up. One night he stayed out until dawn with another member of the cast and did not show up on the set until the afternoon. 'Blake was furious,' recalled Julie Andrews, 'but didn't confront him, since he knew that it would only lead to sulking on Sellers' part and cost even more time.'[21]

Peter Mullins, returning as production designer, witnessed something eye-opening. Often, he would be hopping between the Munich location and the studios at Shepperton.

> I remember getting the last plane back to London and over in the corner I saw Sellers sitting there. I thought, he's on location tomorrow, what's he doing here? I did not acknowledge him but when I got to London, because I thought he was doing a runner, I put a call through to associate producer Tony Adams in Munich and told him because nobody knew he had left. Sellers returned the next day.[22]

Tony Adams was Blake's right-hand man and fixer, he sorted problems, dealt with issues Blake wanted done. He was invaluable and trusted. Born in Dublin to a large family, in his teens Adams managed local bands. 'Somehow he met the film director John Boorman and started babysitting his kids,' says Jeffrey Auerbach, one of Adam's closest friends. 'And when Boorman went over to London in 1969 to shoot the movie *Leo the Last*, Tony convinced Boorman to take him with him to watch the kids, hang out with them and make sure they didn't get into trouble.'[23] Boorman's next movie, *Deliverance*, was going to be shot in the US, 'and Tony begged Boorman to take him along,' says Jeffrey.[24] He went and, on the set, cultivated a good relationship with the film's star Burt Reynolds. 'Tony didn't want to go back to Ireland and convinced Burt to let him go work on his ranch in Jupiter, Florida.'[25]

While working there Adams was attending a local college, but feeling he was going nowhere and at the same time getting bored. Jeffrey reveals:

> Burt was dating Dinah Shore, Dinah gets a call from Julie Andrews, the two of them were buddies. Julie and Blake are moving houses in Beverly Hills and they lost the person who was working for them and she desperately needs somebody that she can trust, who is organised and can help facilitate the move. Dinah says, 'I know this really nice young gentleman that works for Burt here.' And Tony was keen. And so, it happened.[26]

Adams started to work for Blake and Julie, looking after stuff. 'Instantly Blake took a liking to him and Julie took a liking to him. They trusted him,' asserts Jeffrey.[27] According to Gregg Champion, a family friend of the Edwardses, Adams began as Blake's driver, mostly ferrying his children to and from school. Then, to the surprise of many, Blake fired his producer Ken Wales, with whom he had worked on five previous pictures, starting with *Gunn* in 1967. In his place Blake installed Adams, then still in his early 20s, making him associate producer on *Return of the Pink Panther*. 'Tony was very smart and very calculated about things,' says Gregg. 'He seemed very put together for a 22–23-year-old. He dressed well. He was like a clone of Blake. He was in an enviable position.'[28]

On *Strikes Again*, Adams was installed once more as associate producer; Blake, as always, was producer. 'He and Blake were on the same wavelength,' says Mathew Dunne. 'Blake relied on him a great deal to take care of the stuff he did not want to have to deal with. I also think Blake used Tony as a sounding board for a younger audience.'[29] Adams ended up producing all the subsequent *Panther* movies Blake directed, as well as producing all of Blake's other movie productions.

The Munich location saw the introduction of Olga, who infiltrates Clouseau's hotel room. On her first day on the set, Lesley-Anne Down admits to being 'completely terrified'.[30] She was just 21 at the time. 'But it didn't take me long not to be completely terrified.'[31] Her nerves were not helped when it was decided to send her down to have a perm done at the hairdressers that was based in the same hotel the cast and crew were staying at. The film's hair stylist informed Lesley that this would make it easier to blow dry and style her hair. Lesley recalls:

'Well, it didn't work at all. I got back to my room and called Tony Adams, 'I am going to kill everybody. I cannot go out. My hair is horrible.' And Tony came to my room and said, 'You're right,' and he helped me blow dry it back inch by inch. Seriously, it was an Afro![32]

The previous evening Lesley was informed by the film's publicists that Sellers was throwing a small dinner party and wanted her to come along so they could get to know each other. 'And then they just reeled into this litany of what Peter likes about people, what Peter doesn't like about people, how I should behave, what I shouldn't say, blah blah.'[33] Lesley was a bit bewildered by all this, and did not take any notice of it anyway. 'I was put next to Peter. It was a very quiet first half an hour and then we all had copious amounts of alcohol and everything kind of relaxed.'[34] By the end of the evening Lesley liked Sellers enormously. 'The entire time I spent with Peter on the movie, and then a week or two after the shoot, we were absolutely best buddies. Peter was attracted to me. I was 21, what wasn't there to like, quite frankly. We did get on, Peter and I, extremely well.'[35]

By and large Sellers got on well with most of his leading ladies. 'That's because they were in no shape or form any kind of threat to him,' believes Lesley. 'They were an adjunct. We were the pretty thing on the side to make him look good.'[36]

Added to this mixture, of course, was Lynne Frederick. 'Of whom we talked about A LOT,' admits Lesley. 'This was all in the throes of Peter going: Do I want to marry Lynne, don't I want to marry Lynne. He was in turmoil about it.'[37]

Something else Lesley noticed about Sellers was his drug use. 'Peter smoked a lot of dope. I smoked a bit but I certainly didn't smoke as much as he did because I would have been under the table.'[38] They socialised a lot together, going out to restaurants and nightclubs and hanging out in his hotel suite.

> We listened to music. He loved the band Manhattan Transfer; he would listen to them all the fricking time. One night we went to a discotheque and ended up back at his hotel and we talked all night through. And then the doorbell rang and his car arrived to take him to work. He had not been to bed.[39]

They certainly had fun in their seduction scene. At the point where Olga opens her fur coat, and it is very evident she is not wearing anything underneath, she takes Clouseau's head in her hands and he disappears inside her embrace. Shooting that day was one joke after another. If it wasn't Sellers, Blake, or Lesley corpsing, it was one of the crew. Lesley recalls:

> Blake came up to me, he said, 'Quick, quick, open your coat.' He'd got small bits of gaffer tape and made a face of Groucho Marx on my stomach. So, I'm doing the scene, keeping a straight face, and Peter gets on his knees to nuzzle into the fur coat, I open the coat and there's Groucho and everybody just fell about.[40]

In this sequence the audience are treated to a surprising cameo from Omar Sharif. The joke is that Olga seduces Sharif, playing an Egyptian killer, thinking he's Clouseau (for reasons too convoluted to waste time on here – watch the film). The joke is that when the real Clouseau turns up, Olga wonders where the great lover went. 'Omar was lovely and very sweet,' remembers Lesley. 'A tremendous flirt, of course.'[41] Omar agreed to do the cameo as a favour for Blake. Julie Andrews was to recall Blake telling her what a joy and a relief it was, 'To have a pro on the set.'[42]

One of the main reasons for shooting in Munich was Blake's desire to capture some footage of the famous Oktoberfest. In the end what they managed to get did not satisfy Blake and the decision was taken to shoot it later in London on the studio backlot. The film packed up and plans were put in place to return to Shepperton. Sellers upgraded Lesley's economy plane ticket to first class and they flew back together.

> We arrived at Heathrow. And a lady far away in the car park started waving her arms saying, 'Hello Peter.' And he turned to me and said, 'Fuck, it's Lynne's mother. Somebody in the office must have alerted her. Take this.' And he gave me a briefcase. 'I'll call you,' he said. 'I'll see you tonight.'[43]

At the time Lesley was in a long-term relationship with Bruce Robinson, then a struggling actor more out of work than in, and living on social security payments. After years of disenchantment Robinson was to leave the acting profession and turn to writing screenplays, making his directorial debut with the classic *Withnail and I* (1987). When Sellers called Lesley inviting her to his apartment she asked if she could invite Bruce. 'We go over to his place and he ordered curry. He said, "My favourite picture I've ever done, bar none, is *I'm All Right Jack*.'"[44] It turned out that Sellers had his own 16mm copy and set up a projector for a private showing. These were the days when you had to feed the film into the projector manually and Lesley recalls that:

> he couldn't thread this fricking projector to save his life. Bruce and I were sitting on the couch in front of a screen. We offered to help. 'No. no,' he said. 'I'm going to get it.' Time went on and Bruce and I fell asleep. We never saw *I'm All Right Jack*. We woke up in the middle of the night, oh shit, what's happening, what's going on. We look over the back of the couch and there is a vague movement under a giant pile of celluloid. And there's Peter. The whole film had completely unravelled from the reel, he never got it in, and there he was, sound asleep underneath the pile of *I'm All Right Jack* celluloid.[45]

According to production notes *Strikes Again* required seventy different sets, occupying four sound stages at Shepperton, including an exact replica of the Oval Office in the White House. Blake told Peter Mullins that he wanted the Oval Office set to look as real as possible and told him to go to Washington.

> I said, I've got all these photographs, but Blake insisted I check it out myself. So, I flew Concorde to Washington and somebody met me from the White House and took me to a hotel. And then next morning collected me and took me to the White House and I had the grand tour, including a look round the Oval Office. And I was given copies of the original plans of the Oval room. Then I was taken back to the airport and flew back home.[46]

The production design highlight of the film is Dreyfus' villainous lair, although it does look a bit like a cut-price Bond set. The 'Doomsday machine' was the result of a collaboration between the studio's art department and Sony Corporation researchers, which also supplied much of the electronic equipment used in its construction. Amusingly, Dreyfus is seen in his castle lair playing the organ à la Phantom of the Opera, a clever in-joke as Herbert Lom played the Phantom in a 1962 version of the famous horror tale made by Hammer pictures.

THE PINK PANTHER (1963)

Above: Cast as Inspector Clouseau in *The Pink Panther* at the last minute, Peter Sellers ended up stealing the film from its star David Niven.

Right: David Niven as the notorious jewel thief, 'The Phantom', entices Claudia Cardinale's princess.

The relationship between Peter Sellers and director Blake Edwards was often fraught, but their chemistry was undeniable.

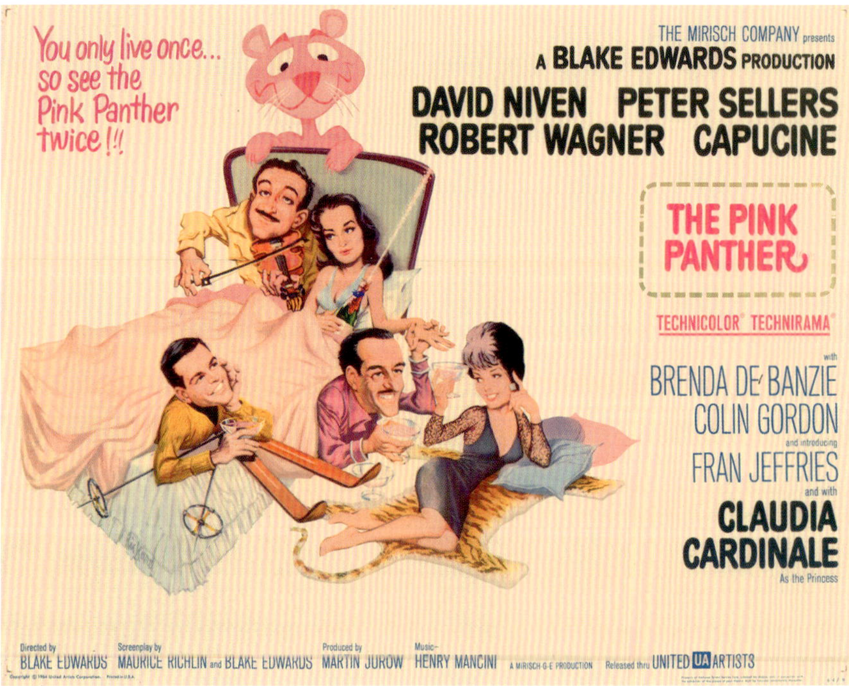

Released in 1963, *The Pink Panther* was a box office hit and began a franchise that spanned over four decades.

A SHOT IN THE DARK (1964)

Right: Sellers returned as Inspector Clouseau in 1964's *A Shot in the Dark*, considered the best of the series.

Below: In one of the film's most famous scenes, Sellers and Elke Sommer are trapped in a nudist colony.

Another comic highlight was Sellers' snooker game with George Sanders.

A Shot in the Dark was another hit, but Sellers and Blake Edwards vowed never to work together again.

INSPECTOR CLOUSEAU (1966)

When Sellers and Edwards refused to work together, the studio still wanted another Clouseau film and hired American comic actor Alan Arkin instead.

An example of some of the *Pink Panther* merchandise that was produced. This board game came out in 1974.

RETURN OF THE PINK PANTHER (1975)

After a ten-year gap Sellers was back as Clouseau in the appropriately titled *Return of the Pink Panther*.

The classic confrontation between Clouseau and the blind beggar and his chimpanzee 'minkey'.

Burt Kwouk as the iconic Cato; his fights with Clouseau were always a highlight of the *Panther* films.

In *Return*, Sellers co-starred with Christopher Plummer and Catherine Schell. The film was another hit.

THE PINK PANTHER STRIKES AGAIN (1976)

The plot of *The Pink Panther Strikes Again* sees police chief Dreyfus turning to villainy to rid the world of Clouseau.

Lesley-Anne Down stars as a Russian assassin with orders to seduce and kill Clouseau.

Of course, things turn out a little differently.

Released soon after *Return*, *Strikes Again* was another box office success.

REVENGE OF THE PINK PANTHER (1978)

Left: Sellers was so difficult to work with by *Revenge of the Pink Panther* that he and Blake Edwards never worked together again.

Below: Clouseau faces another perilous situation.

Revenge was another worldwide box-office success.

The end – Sellers makes his final bow as Inspector Clouseau.

On the press junket for *Revenge* Sellers had a risqué Clouseau doll made, which he delighted in showing people at parties. (Monica Mancini)

TRAIL OF THE PINK PANTHER (1982)

Back from the dead, *Trail of the Pink Panther* was comprised of deleted scenes from previous *Panther* movies.

Joanna Lumley plays a reporter on the trail of the missing Clouseau; here with the returning David Niven.

CURSE OF THE PINK PANTHER (1983)

Right: American TV star Ted Wass as Clouseau's 'replacement', the equally inept Sgt Clifton Sleigh, here with Lesley Ash.

Below: Herbert Lom's Dreyfus takes aim in *Curse of the Pink Panther*. Both this and *Trail* were box office duds.

SON OF THE PINK PANTHER (1993)

ROBERTO BENIGNI stars in MGM's comedy, Blake Edwards' **SON OF THE PINK PANTHER.**

P-T-3
Photo credit: David Appleby

Ten years after the last *Panther* film, Italian comedy star Roberto Benigni appeared as *The Son of the Pink Panther*. This was another box office flop.

THE PINK PANTHER (2006)

Above: Big shoes to fill, Steve Martin takes on the role of Clouseau in this 2006 reboot.

Right: Big hitters like Kevin Kline and Beyonce turned *The Pink Panther* into a financial success.

THE PINK PANTHER 2 (2009)

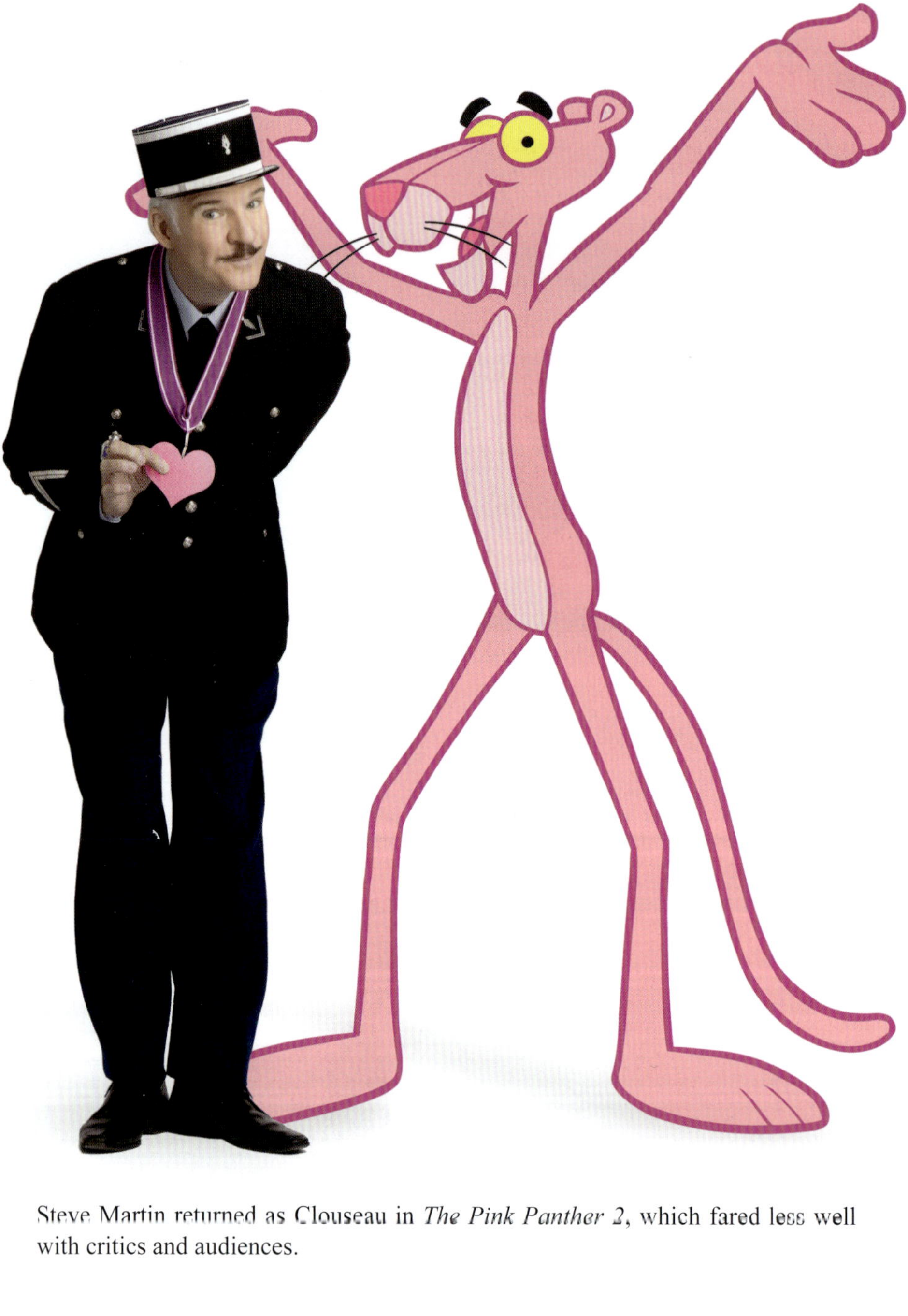

Steve Martin returned as Clouseau in *The Pink Panther 2*, which fared less well with critics and audiences.

Mullins work and preparation of the sets was hindered by Sellers' obsessive issues over the colour green and purple. Mullins recalls the time when he and his team had to get a set ready quickly because they were shooting on it after lunch. They were dressing the set, which included some green drapes. The wardrobe supervisor, Bridget Sellers, walked past, stood there, scanned the set, saw the drapes and said, 'You will never get him on here.' Mullins asked why. 'He doesn't like green,' she answered. 'He won't come on.'[47] By this time the crew were returning from lunch and ready to start work. Mullins had half an hour to sort things out, what should he do? He went round to Sellers' dressing room and knocked on the door. 'Peter, I have got a problem. I hear you don't like green.'

'Right.'

'Well, I didn't know that,' said Mullins. 'And I have hung up green curtains and other stuff.'

'Have you got any replacements,' asked Sellers.

'No.'

'Can you spray them or do something to them.'

'Yes, probably,' said Mullins.

'Well, do what you can,' asked Sellers.[48]

Mullins rushed downstairs and got a spray can of paint and darkened what he could and took other things down, basically just toning it all down a bit. 'And, of course, everyone was standing round waiting for Sellers to explode and say, I'm going home. But he walked onto the set and did not say a word. Everyone was in shock because they were expecting Sellers to have a fit and that I might get fired.'[49] Mullins had experienced this kind of behaviour before with some stars expressing an aversion to certain colours. With Sellers, he saw green as a harbinger of bad luck (interestingly, a lot of people working in horse racing have a superstition about the colour green), while he connected the colour purple with death. Gregg Champion, who worked as an assistant on *Revenge of the Pink Panther*, was told that when Sellers had his heart attack; he had seen the colour purple and that's why it terrified him.

Was this merely a power game by Sellers? A way of making people run around after one of his whims? Walter Mirisch claimed that on a film with Sellers he had to repaint a train, 'because the colour offended him'.[50] Or was this a very real superstition, one of his many quirks and oddities? Susan Wood recalls when Sellers' youngest daughter Victoria paid a visit to a *Pink Panther* location and she went to pick her up: 'I can't remember if it was green or purple, because those were the two colours that you weren't supposed to wear anywhere near him, and she had either green or purple on and he screamed at her, this poor little girl, on the set. He could be a pig.'[51] Tony Adams recalled the occasion when Julie Andrews' mother visited a *Panther* set and she was wearing a purple coat. 'Peter went ballistic, foaming at the mouth, pointing fingers and then ran off screaming like he had just seen the devil incarnate, literally not to be found for hours, or maybe days. And this poor old lady was left standing there wondering, what did I do?'[52]

The exterior of Dreyfus' castle, and the moat, was all built on the studio backlot. There is an amusing sequence of Clouseau trying various ways to infiltrate the castle, from pole vaulting over the moat, to approaching it in a canoe, all failing miserably. Much of this was again handled by stunt man Joe Dunne. Mathew's favourite stunt performed by his father in the film was shot in three parts. In the castle Joe swings across the laboratory on a rope and through a door, falls down a flight of stairs and hurtles out of a window to land in a pigsty, all while wearing a suit of armour.

Joe Dunne had been hired once again as Sellers' stunt double. He had a similar build to the actor and had learnt his mannerisms and the way he walked and moved. Although to play him on screen Joe wore a false nose and moustache and dyed his hair. On *Strikes Again* Joe also worked uncredited as the stunt coordinator when Blake fell out with John Sullivan, the man originally hired for the job.

For the most part Joe enjoyed working with Sellers and got on well with him, but they never met outside studio hours or socialised at all.

> He was an absolute genius. I used to watch him and he could make a little gesture and it would make that scene look even better. He had his good days, and he had his bad days. He was ok with me, because I never gave him the opportunity not to be ok with me. When we were on the set, I wouldn't chum up to him like a lot of people did. Sometimes one word out of place, and you were gone. So, I kept myself to myself. People took his wrath, but I never had to do that, and he knew I wouldn't stand for that.[53]

Joe reveals one act of kindness during the making of one of the *Panther* films. Sellers' chauffeur and assistant Bert Mortimer came to Joe saying he had a gift from Sellers. It was a top of the range all-in-one TV/radio/

tape player, at the time very new and no doubt very expensive. 'I was flabbergasted. It was totally out of the blue.'[54]

When it came to stunts and physical action, Sellers would not exert himself if he did not have to, happy to leave that kind of stuff to Joe. 'When it came to doing a stunt, it was great for me because Peter would not get out of a chair to do a stunt. He didn't want to know when it came to the stunts. Peter would get dizzy on a thick carpet.'[55] You also must add into that equation the danger of your star actor getting injured and fouling up the schedule if he ends up in hospital. Often, when Joe or another stuntman carried out a stunt, Sellers was not even there. 'A lot of actors stand by the side of the camera if you're doubling for them and watch exactly what you do,' says Joe. 'But Peter just said, he can do this, and walked away and that would be it.'[56]

There was another reason why Sellers did not tackle anything remotely physical. On *Strikes Again* there was a noticeable physical deterioration. Ironically, as the *Panther* films grew in popularity and size, so did the reliance on broad physical humour and stunts, something Sellers was not able to do, whether he was inclined to do so or not. A case in point were the Clouseau and Kato fight scenes which had now become marathons of destruction. 'They were great fun to do,' says Joe Dunne. 'Peter wouldn't be there when you were setting up the scene, he'd be in his dressing room, he'd take it for granted that when he came out, he would be able to do certain parts and I'd do the rest of it.'[57] In *Strikes Again*, Clouseau performs with Nunchucks, the martial arts weapon made famous by Bruce Lee. This was Blake's idea, who had been a friend and student of Lee back in the late '60s in California.

Dunne also doubled for Sellers when Clouseau leaps off some parallel bars and falls down a flight of stairs. Also, when he dons a Quasimodo disguise kit, with inflatable hump. Unfortunately, Clouseau overdoes it with the helium gas and the hump grows blimp-like on his back, carries him out of his apartment (Clouseau is oblivious to all this being on the telephone), and deposits him in the Seine, outside Notre-Dame, to the consternation of a couple of nuns. This was not a particularly dangerous job for Joe, but he did have concerns.

> I was told that nobody had been in the Seine for three years, on purpose, because it was so polluted. So, I had to have injections before I went in. They took me up by crane about 40 feet and dropped me. One of the French assistants working on

> the movie said they had a hard time getting the certificate to be allowed to go into the Seine. The guy who gave us permission warned us there might be bits of timber and other things just below the surface and I might possibly hit something, so the best way to go in was feet first.[58]

Joe performed the stunt just the once.

The Quasimodo kit is the latest in a long line of disguises that Clouseau employs in order to blend in with the criminal underworld. Part of the illusion that he is a great detective is that he is also a master of disguise. Of course, he isn't. Why he thinks dressing up as Quasimodo renders him inconspicuous is anyone's guess. In *Revenge of the Pink Panther* he disguises himself as a Swedish seafarer, with a rubber parrot on his shoulder in constant need of pumping up. All this to meet an informer on the docks who, upon encountering Clouseau, immediately says, 'good evening, Inspector'.

These disguises all come courtesy of one Auguste Balls, Clouseau's eccentric disguise maker whose shop the Inspector regularly frequents. This character was to make his first appearance in the series in *Strikes Again* and was played by the American comedy actor and Mel Brooks regular, Harvey Korman. Alas, the scene was cut from the finished film. It would appear later in Blake Edwards ill-fated *Trail of the Pink Panther*.

Part of the scene had Clouseau looking at a tray of false noses, each one as grotesque and ridiculous as the last. As the day wore on Blake told Peter Mullins that it was too late now to shoot the scene, they would do it first thing in the morning. He told Mullins:

> But what I want you to do is this. When Sellers pulls the tray out, we'll rehearse it with the noses, but when we come to shoot it, I want you to substitute them for a tray of dildo noses. I want you to find me all kinds of shapes of cocks and have them here in the morning.[59]

Mullins sent out one of his team into the sex district of Soho to buy all these dildos.

> We worked until midnight with the plasterer making up these things. We had about twenty in total and laid them all out. We did a rehearsal before Sellers came down. The continuity girl

> was so disgusted she walked off the set. Sellers comes on and we did a quick rehearsal with him. 'Ok, we go next time,' says Blake. We did a quick change over and put the tray in with the dildo noses. Sellers enters the store, ding ding, he comes in and looks down at the dildos, and he doesn't flinch. He picks one up, holds it up to his face, turns round to the camera and says, 'Fuck nose.' It was brilliant.[60]

Another scene that was shot but never made the final cut took place in a nightclub where an altercation, inevitably begun by Clouseau, ends in a massive custard-pie fight that harks back to those wonderful comedy silents Blake and Sellers adored (there is a huge custard pie fight at the end of Blake's *The Great Race*). 'We shot on that for days,' recalls Mullins. 'And at the end the set was a complete mess.'[61] Blake went over to Mullins to compliment him on a job well done and motioned towards a table set up with a magnum of champagne. Blake wanted Mullins to sit on a chair holding a glass of champagne, with the ruined set in the background, and for the stills guy to take a shot of it. 'I'm sitting there on my own and I hear this noise and I looked up and half the unit were above me with custard pies and they threw them at me and I got drenched.'[62]

In the film the scene plays out now minus the custard pie fight. Clouseau follows Jarvis, the butler of the missing scientist, to what turns out to be a gay nightclub. Jarvis is played by Michael Robbins, famous to British audiences for the ITV sitcom *On the Buses*. Jarvis is in fact the star attraction of the club's cabaret, in the guise of a drag singer called Ainsley Jarvis. In the scene Robbins' singing voice was eventually dubbed by Julie Andrews.

Playing the hefty bouncer of the club was Cyd Child, back again after her duties on *Return*. It was during a break in filming on the previous *Panther* that the subject of parrots came up. In *Return* Clouseau is menaced by a parrot when he is searching a room disguised as a cleaner. Cyd owned a parrot and so it was agreed she would bring him in for her role as the club bouncer, with it perched on her shoulder. She recalls:

> Michael Robbins started to rehearse his song, and that kind of singing used to appeal to my parrot, he loved Barbra Streisand, hymns, opera, that kind of singing, and he heard Michael singing and he just joined in. Fortunately, because it was only a rehearsal, everyone thought it was very funny.[63]

The parrot's name was Chrome and it had previously belonged to Diana Rigg. After working on *The Avengers*, the actress gave Cyd the pet. Chrome would not feature in any more *Panthers* but did appear in a couple of Bond movies. When Cyd worked on *For Your Eyes Only* (1981), Chrome is the talking parrot on Melina Havelock's boat. Chrome can also be seen in 1987's *The Living Daylights* as the parrot in the kitchen of the MI6 safe-house.

When Clouseau is in the nightclub the kidnappers arrive and there is an almighty brawl. At one-point Cyd had to pick up Sellers and swing him around. The pair never met on *Return* so here was a chance for Cyd to talk and interact with the star. 'And I found him extremely nice. I liked him.'[64] They chatted about judo mostly.

> In a scene, Peter had this thing where he would break up and start giggling. We would all look at Blake Edwards to see if he was laughing, and if he was laughing then we could all laugh. That would go on for a while. And then, eventually, you would look at Blake and he wasn't laughing anymore because he wanted to get on, so we wouldn't laugh. And then once Peter realised that his audience wasn't with him anymore, he would behave himself and get on with the scene.[65]

Cyd found the atmosphere on the set, 'extremely good'.[66] She recalls that the fight scene took a couple of days to complete, during which time the studio set aside a large room for all the stunt men to have lunch in. 'And they had painted a title over the entrance which said: The Pink Panther Reum.'[67]

For the fight Joe Dunne, as stunt coordinator, sent the word out for burly stunt men to show up. However, before the actual punch up, these stunt men had to be dressed up as gay/drag customers of the club. 'You've never seen anything so funny in all your life as dozens of butch stunt men dressed up as transvestites ballroom dancing,' recalls Vic Armstrong, a jobbing stunt man back in the '70s, today a renowned stunt coordinator and director. 'It was quite surprising the number of stunt men that wanted to wear dresses. Is my lipstick smudged? they were saying. Are my seams straight?'[68]

This was the first time Vic had worked for either Blake or Sellers.

> There was always an aura that surrounded the set when Sellers arrived, a negative aura for me. As for Blake Edwards,

> everybody had to leave the set while he walked round and decided what to shoot. It was like, God is here. Nobody was allowed in. Nobody was allowed to talk. With Sellers, if he got bad vibes off somebody or they were looking at him and he didn't like it, he would whisper to his minion, get rid of that guy, I don't like him. He was totally paranoid.[69]

According to Peter Mullins, Sellers was generally friendly with the people on the set, including the crew, except when he was in a bad mood. Even so, he was someone who needed to be treated with kid gloves at all times. 'Sometimes he would ignore you or not speak to you for days and you were left thinking, what have I done, when in fact you had done nothing, it was just Peter in a mood. Then he'd start talking to you again.'[70]

Off the set, Sellers mostly kept himself to himself, crew members hardly ever saw him after hours or got to socialise with him much. Mullins does recall one occasion when Sellers came into his office at Shepperton and asked what he was doing that evening. Not much, said Mullins. Sellers had found this wonderful Chinese restaurant and invited him along. His chauffeur would pick him up. When Mullins and his wife arrived, he noticed a few other members of the crew there. Everyone sat down. After a few minutes Sellers left the table.

> He came back as a Chinese waiter. He'd found a coolie hat somewhere and put make up on his eyes, and he had a note pad and took our order. It was very funny. But then the next day he wouldn't talk to you. He was very moody. You never knew where you were with him.[71]

It was this playfulness in Sellers that Mullins did find endearing. They were once shooting in Paris and Sellers was staying at the luxurious Le Bristol hotel, close to the Champs Élysées. Mullins showed up and there was Sellers, already in his Clouseau outfit, getting in a car about to be taken to the location. Mullins cadged a lift and sat in the back with Sellers. Driving through central Paris they approached a policeman stood in the middle of the road directing the heavy traffic. 'We got alongside this policeman and Sellers wound the window down, looked at him, and in his Clouseau voice said, "You are doing a very good job. Give me your badge number. I will commend you to the commissionaire." We fell about laughing in the car.'[72]

Lesley-Anne Down remembers everybody on the set being, 'tip-toey fearful of Peter'.[73] She never was, certainly not after that first dinner engagement in Munich. 'He was just a mate.'[74] In London they continued to see each other. Lesley and Bruce Robinson would go out to dinner with Sellers and sometimes they would be joined by Spike Milligan and Harry Secombe, Sellers' ex-comrades from *The Goon Show*.

> I remember many evenings with Peter and the Goon gang, and I knew I was in the presence of greatness and how lucky I was. But I was never overwhelmed by the awe-ness of the people I was with, so I could just truly enjoy all of it and be myself.[75]

As filming wound down on *Strikes Again*, it was almost like a repeat of what happened on *A Shot in The Dark*. The Blake/Sellers relationship reached a point where no one anticipated it could ever be repaired again. 'It always started off very friendly but halfway through the picture they weren't talking,' says Peter Mullins.[76] Once again, Sellers would send messages to Blake about a scene, and Blake used to send messages through his assistant back to Sellers. 'They could go for weeks without speaking to each other,' remembered Herbert Lom.[77] Blake showed Lom several telegrams that Sellers had sent him:

'You are a rotten human being.'

'You are a shit and I can afford to work without you.'

'I don't need you to get work. Love, Peter.'[78]

By the end it was not very pleasant, everything was tense and strained. 'You could feel it on the set,' says Mullins. 'You were standing around with nothing happening because Sellers wouldn't come out of his dressing room until a piece of script that he didn't like had been rewritten or something else.'[79]

Lesley says she never personally saw any animosity between Blake and Sellers, 'differences of opinion, for sure',[80] but not the animosity others encountered. 'They both wanted to be top dog, probably. I do think they had enormous respect for one another. They were both quite powerful and opinionated and that, in itself, is going to cause situations to arise.'[81] It got to a stage where Blake used the fact the film was credited as 'A Blake Edwards production' to needle Sellers, who thought the *Panthers* ought to be 'A Peter Sellers Film'. 'I always felt that Blake thought he was the puppet master and that Sellers rather resented that perception,' says Mullins. 'You've got two master egos there.'[82] Both Sellers and Mullins were Virgos. 'And Peter used to walk past me sometimes and say, in his Clouseau voice, we Virgos must stick together, you know.'[83]

Mike Grady, the bellboy in *Return*, had a friend who worked on *Strikes Again*, the character actor Dudley Sutton. When Sutton finished on the film, he told Mike that the atmosphere on the set was, 'hideous'. And that everyone was angry with each other.

At the after-premiere party for *Return*, animator Richard Williams was a guest. Williams was inclined to like his wine and was quite tipsy by the end of the evening. Blake Edwards came over and put his arm round his shoulders. 'I'm going to do another *Panther*,' said the director. 'So, promise me you'll do the titles again.' Williams nodded. 'Yeah, anything for you Blake.'[84]

Unfortunately, when it came time to do the titles for *Strikes Again*, Williams had been contracted to go to New York to work on an animated film. When Blake called him up, Williams had to say he couldn't do it. Blake wasn't going to take no for an answer. 'If you don't do it,' he bellowed down the line, 'I'm going to sue you because I've got witnesses to say that you promised to do it. We have based this all on you doing it.'[85]

In a quandary, Williams spoke with Carl Gover, his friend and manager of the animation studio, and it was decided to give Tony White the assignment. This was the chance Tony had been waiting for. He had been directing his own commercials for some time, but this was a big movie production and a great opportunity. Even so, he hesitated.

> Because Richard was very protective of something he had done and then someone else doing it. If he was in the studio, it would have been hell. So, I said to Carl, 'I'll do it on two conditions. One, that Dick has no say on it at all, it's between you and I Carl, we deal with Blake Edwards. And the other one is all that money Dick lost on *Return*, I will try and claw back as much as I can.' Carl and Dick agreed, because Dick was desperate. He didn't want to be sued. Hollywood works that way.[86]

The first thing Tony did was go and see Blake who was still working on the film at Shepperton. 'He had his own private office at the studio. I was very nervous. This was Blake Edwards.'[87] Tony asked what Blake wanted, if he had any ideas. 'I don't know,' said Blake. 'You guys are the guys. It was great last time. I want you to do something great this time.'[88]

The concept Tony came up with was to set the whole sequence inside an old time Hollywood movie theatre. Clouseau sits in the stalls watching clips of various movie characters, like King Kong, Batman, Dracula, all ending up being played by the Pink Panther. Best of all, Tony thought it would be a fun in-joke to include the Pink Panther in the Julie Andrews role from *The Sound of Music*.

A week later Tony went back to see Blake with a storyboard. Blake's office at Shepperton was more like a fancy apartment, there was a sofa and a coffee table and Blake made himself comfortable on a large pouffe as Tony went through his ideas. He was a little nervous about showing Blake the *Sound of Music* sequence; it was going to go one way or the other.

> So, I tried to rush through that bit and he went, 'Hang on, what was that?' He made me turn the page back and I'm going, 'It's an affectionate thing.' I was so nervous explaining this. And Blake had quite a severe face. He wasn't really like that in real life, but his appearance was quite terrifying. He was looking at the page and he didn't say a word. A minute went by and he said nothing and I thought, I've blown this. And he looked at it and looked at it, and then suddenly he burst out laughing and literally fell off the back of the pouffe and landed on the floor. 'I've seen enough,' he said. 'Go and do it. I don't want to see the rest, just go and do the whole thing. You're great.'[89]

The schedule was twelve weeks, just as it had been on *Return*, a bit of a rush since in those days it took something like twelve weeks to complete a thirty second television commercial, and this was essentially a two-and-a-half minute short. It made sense, then, for Tony to have an assistant, Richard Burdett, who worked on the end titles, which included an amusing pastiche of *Jaws*.

With the titles taking place inside one of those cavernous Hollywood picture houses, ideally Tony would have liked to have gone over to Los Angeles to take photographs of say the interior of Grauman's Chinese Theatre, but the budget wouldn't stretch to that. Instead, he asked Roy Nesbit, a wizard at special effects who worked at the Williams studio, to come up with a solution. Nesbit was a real moviegoer and went around several London cinemas taking photographs of various architectural features. After that he printed them up large, cut them out and joined them together before photographing it again. And that became the cinema. Tony also asked the film laboratory to mess with the negative at certain points, to make it look like a scratched and dirty piece of old celluloid.

For Tony working on those opening titles was an exciting and wonderful experience. Previously on *Return*, Williams had structured the Pink Panther character differently both to the television cartoon show and the '60s films. He had redefined it visually and Tony had all his drawings to work from. 'I didn't copy them, but I could see how he'd redrawn the character and then I worked out my own formula for drawing it. I knew it could never be as good as him because I was determined to make money for the studio, not lose money.'[90] The only downside was that when the job was finished, Tony was not allowed to present it to Blake. Williams was back from New York and he took charge of that. And when those titles won a design award, again Williams collected it. Tony didn't even get a credit on the film. 'I resented that in some ways. But then I knew that was the rules of the studio and that's the way it was. Saying that, I benefited in so many ways working there and learning there.'[91]

At least Tony and some of his fellow animators were invited to a preview of *Strikes Again* at United Artists' London office.

> We sat in this very plush screening room, and there were the suits of UA, producers, accountants, money men, marketing people. We shuffled in in our jeans and we sat through the movie and we were falling about laughing, our stomachs hurt it was so funny. The suits showed no emotion whatsoever. None. They just looked at it, bored. I think what they were doing in their heads, their little computer heads, they were ticking, oh that laugh is worth a few thousand dollars, and there's another one, this is going to be a hit. They were looking at the film like a balance sheet. It was a product, a brand. They don't care about sensibilities, artistry, humour, it didn't mean anything to them. They were just stone faced. It was such a contrast because we were falling out of our seats laughing.[92]

The Pink Panther Strikes Again opened in 600 theatres across the US during the 1976 Christmas holiday, preceded by an extensive promotional campaign. As for the critics, Roger Ebert of the *Chicago Sun-Times* was less than totally enthusiastic. 'Maybe because I have been over this ground with Clouseau many times before. That is not to say this film is not funny –

it has moments as good as anything Sellers and Edwards have ever done – but that it is time for them to move on.' Vincent Canby of *The New York Times* enjoyed the film better. 'Both Mr Sellers and Mr Edwards delight in old gags, and part of the joy of *The Pink Panther Strikes Again* is watching the way they spin out what is essentially a single routine.' While Richard Schickel of *The Times* said, 'Better an indifferent *Panther* than no *Panther* at all.'

However, it was a review written by Rex Reed in the *New York Daily News*, calling the film 'moronic' and audience members who enjoyed it, 'sub-mental', that prompted an angry written response from Gabe Sumner, United Artists' Vice President in charge of advertising. Sumner labelled Reed's review, 'An ugly self-indulgent piece of trash writing that diminishes all film criticism.'[93] Reed was banned from all future United Artists screenings. Reed countered by saying that he never attended United Artists screenings anyway, and compared Sumner's attitude to fascism, while sending the executive a supply of laxatives.

In Britain, the film enjoyed a royal premiere at the Odeon Leicester Square in London the week before Christmas. Sellers, however, threw a strop and did not attend. He had promised Lynne Frederick that she would be in the line-up that was presented to Prince Charles. Unfortunately, the committee organising the premiere had to limit the number of people being presented to His Royal Highness, and since Lynne was not married to Sellers, and was not in the film either, she was deemed ineligible. Sellers responded angrily, demanding Lynne be present, and tried to get United Artists to overturn the decision, otherwise he refused to play Clouseau ever again. But even Hollywood could not overturn Royal protocol. And so a furious Sellers stayed at home.

The rest of the cast turned up. Lesley-Anne Down had just come out of hospital following an operation and was still on medication. 'There's a photograph of me with Prince Charles and I look kind of weird because I was completely strung out on pain killers.'[94]

The British reviews were mixed. Derek Malcom in *The Guardian* called it, 'the fag end' of the series. Meanwhile, in France, the film courted some controversy when René Goscinny, famous as the co-creator of the comic series *Astérix*, slapped an injunction on the film. Goscinny had sent Sellers a comedy script called 'Le Maître du Monde' or 'The Master of The World', about an evil genius who threatens the planet with extinction from his castle lair. Sellers sent it back with a polite rejection letter. When Goscinny saw *Strikes Again* he noticed certain elements from his own script, contacted his lawyer and accused Sellers and Blake of plagiarising his ideas and intended to sue. Things, however, did not get very far due to Goscinny's death in 1977.

The international success of *The Pink Panther Strikes Again* proved there was a desire from the public for more *Pink Panther* movies. The problem was, and not for the first time, could Blake and Sellers be persuaded to work with each other again? Blake seemed to have made up his own mind that it was all over. *Strikes Again* had been much harder to make than *Return*. That had been, 'kind of a lark', he said, while *Strikes Again* was a chore. 'I thought, oh boy, we are getting into a sick area here. It's dangerous. It's too much grief.'[95] For Blake, it had become harder to communicate with Sellers, let alone try to get a performance out of him. His leading man's behaviour was now so decidedly bizarre and erratic that Blake confessed: 'If you went to an asylum and you described the first inmate you saw, that's what Peter had become. He was certifiable.'[96]

Chapter 6

REVENGE OF THE PINK PANTHER

After the difficulties experienced on *Strikes Again*, it was, 'sheer greed',[1] according to Blake, that brought him back to direct yet another *Panther* film. It was a decision that left him, 'feeling like a man condemned to an illness for a year with the promise of a cure at the end'.[2] The *Panthers* had made Blake and Sellers a small fortune, or what Stanley Kubrick once told Sellers was, 'Fuck you money'; in other words, security to do what you wanted to do. Blake knew that by agreeing to do another *Panther*, not only was he getting his biggest pay cheque yet, but the leverage to get more personal projects off the ground. One of those was a comedy he wanted to do with Julie called *10*. And it was the same with Sellers. 'The thing about the *Panthers*,' says Burt Kwouk, 'was the studio would say, "If you do this *Panther* for us, we'll back any project you want to do", which is how Peter got the money for *Being There*, something he'd been wanting to make for years.'[3]

Once Blake had finished the new *Panther* script, again co-writing it with Frank Waldman, the problems started. Sellers began to act up, making unreasonable contractual demands of United Artists. Soon the studio had enough and told Blake it was up to him to get Sellers on board. During the making of *Strikes Again*, Sellers more than once told the press that he had no intention of playing Clouseau again. 'God forbid that I should do a whole series,' he told the *Observer* in 1975[4]

Blake devised a plan. He and Julie would vacation in St Tropez, where Sellers had a holiday home. They would hire a yacht, paid for by United Artists, during which time Blake would meet up with Sellers and they would work on the film together. Herbert Lom recalled:

> So, they all decided to meet in the South of France. Peter suggested on his yacht. But Blake, being Blake, he hired a

> yacht and the two yachts were floating towards each other for this meeting and peace negotiation, as well staged as Napoleon's meeting with the czar of Russia when they made peace somewhere on a lake on the Russian border.[5]

It seemed to work, as Blake and Sellers took daily meetings. 'But the situation became even more crazy,' Julie Andrews recalled. 'Peter was hustling all sides, telling Blake one thing and the producers another.'[6] Lawyers and managers flew in to try and get things sorted out. And there was Blake in the middle, under enormous pressure to get the project moving and, according to Julie, 'growing more and more irritable'.[7] Once again, this was Sellers trying to seize control, to manipulate everyone like pawns on a chess board. And all the time perfectly aware that it was inevitable there was going to be another *Panther*, the money involved was just too much to ignore. 'Blake and Peter seemed destined to continue their merry dance,' said Julie. 'Part competitive, part love/hate, yet dependent upon one another for so many reasons.'[8] How much of this playacting revolved around what Sellers wanted to get paid is unclear. What is clear is that he came out of the deal with $750,000, plus 10 per cent of the gross.

With a working title of 'Curse of the Pink Panther', the plot of *Revenge* revolves around Philippe Douvier (played by Robert Webber), a crime magnet out to prove to his rivals that he is still strong and powerful by killing the world's most famous detective, Clouseau. When a petty thief steals Clouseau's car and clothes and is mistakenly killed by Douvier's men, the world believes that Clouseau is dead. Former Chief Inspector Dreyfus is released from a lunatic asylum to conduct the investigation into his murder, this despite trying to take over the world in the last film and literally disintegrating from his own laser weapon; bizarrely no mention of this is ever made. Meanwhile, Clouseau goes undercover with Cato to find out who tried to kill him.

Sellers new leading lady came in the shape of Hollywood star Dyan Cannon, who first came to prominence back in 1969's sex comedy drama *Bob & Carol & Ted & Alice*, which earned her an Academy Award nomination. After that she starred in such films as *The Anderson Tapes* (1971) with Sean Connery and *Shamus* (1973) opposite Burt Reynolds. By the time Dyan was cast in *Revenge of the Pink Panther* she had recently finished what would be an Oscar-nominated performance in the Warren Beatty comedy *Heaven Can Wait*.

Dyan was out in Las Vegas appearing on a late-night talk show when she got a call about playing the role of Douvier's girlfriend, Simone.

> The minute I came off stage they said there was an important call for me. It was my agent and he said, 'I've got Blake Edwards on the phone and he wants to talk to you. I've already negotiated so if you say yes, I've got the script and when you get back to LA you'll read it.' I said, 'Ok. Let me talk to Blake.' He came on. 'I don't want anybody but you,' he said, which was very generous, very kind. And I told Blake on the phone, 'I'm such a fan of Peter and such a fan of yours that there's no way that I'm gonna say no, I'm gonna tell you that right now.'[9]

Dyan already knew Sellers, when she was married to Cary Grant in the mid- to late '60s. On visits to New York Sellers would spend time with the couple, often shopping for kitchenware. 'He loved to buy things for the kitchen,' says Dyan. 'And he was always eyeing up the girls. We'd drive down the streets in New York, Peter, Cary and myself, 'Mmm,' he'd say, 'I'd like to add that to my cutlery.' Peter loved the women.'[10]

Principal photography on *Revenge of the Pink Panther* began in November 1977. The first two weeks was going to be a location shoot in Paris and the whole company moved out there. Among them was 19-year-old Gregg Champion, still in film school at the time. Gregg happened to run into Blake and Julie at a film screening; Blake was an old friend of Gregg's father.

> I had not seen them for years and I reintroduced myself and Julie said, 'Blake, don't we have a 16mm camera we can loan Gregg.' So, I started going over to their home and borrowing their camera to shoot my student films. Blake then offered me a job on *Revenge*. I got permission to go from my film school if I did a thesis on the making of the movie. I remember I called it: A Panther Too Far.[11]

Gregg was never to forget the first day of shooting. Some work was done in the morning but it was clear that Blake was agitated about the lack of preparation that had gone on. He decided to break for lunch early. 'I didn't know where to go,' recalls Gregg, 'so I just followed Blake into the trailer with Tony Adams and some other production people. And Blake was pissed off, "Why the fuck didn't they tell me they weren't ready."'[12] While the film was being prepped Blake was in Gstaad sending pages of the script to everybody in production. He never really showed up at the production office. Gregg recalls that Blake stood up and said:

> We're not ready. Let's go. And literally, after lunch, everybody was told they were going back to London. This was the first day of shooting. So, everybody moved back to Shepperton and sat around because none of the sets were ready. We had to wait. And the whole movie carried on like that.[13]

Like the other *Panther* films, *Revenge* was to go way over schedule and budget. The money being spent on the films was considerable, but Blake complained it wasn't enough. Peter Mullins recalls Blake used to complain on the phone to United Artists that the *Panthers* should have the same humongous budgets as the Bond films. The budget for *Revenge* was by far the biggest yet for a *Pink Panther* film. 'And the film started to go over budget very quickly,' Gregg confirms. 'And a couple of studio executives showed up to basically rein Blake in.'[14] These suits arranged a big showdown with Blake, and Gregg was in the room.

> Blake sat there and they said, 'We are over budget. What can we do to bring it down.' And Blake took out a script and yanked some pages out and started throwing them on the floor. The executives got sent packing and never reined Blake in. It was this kind of craziness going on.[15]

The studio was so desperate for another *Panther* that all the power was with Blake. 'Blake had a very up and down career,' says Gregg. 'And when he was in a power position, he really exercised it. I think he just wanted to say – fuck you – to everybody. He did as he pleased.'[16]

This attitude had much to do with the fact that Blake did not really want to be there in the first place. He had not worked since *Strikes Again*, instead, he had been busy writing and finishing the scripts for *10* and another comedy called *S.O.B*, along with trying to get another personal project off the ground, *Victor/Victoria*. These were the films he cared about making but nobody was buying. And going into *Revenge* Julie Andrews could see that her husband was not exactly looking forward to it. 'I have a hunch he'd love to get out of the madness of the next *Panther* film with Peter, but he's committed.'[17] And it did not take long for the madness to begin.

Sellers had come to depend more and more upon his own instincts and imagination to get through a scene. If the inspiration did not come to him immediately, he was in trouble. In a scene that eventually was left on the cutting room floor, Clouseau and Cato arrive at a hip Black nightclub dressed according to their own concept of what a couple of sharp Black dudes should look like, Afros and the most outrageous outfits. The scene was partly inspired by an idea of Blake's for a potential sequel to *Strikes Again*. Mathew Dunne recalls:

> Clouseau was up against a Black crime syndicate with Sammy Davis jr. mentioned as a possibility to star. Blake wanted to do a massive car chase in Paris and my father Joe was asked to come up with ideas. Eventually there was a whole sequence shot in a Black night club where Clouseau dons blackface.[18]

This is the club where in *Revenge* Dyan Cannon's Simone is abducted by the baddies.

As the day wore on, Sellers could not get a handle on things. He was supposed to come out with a lot of what Clouseau thought was very hip Black street lingo and, of course, screw it up. 'Peter absolutely couldn't get it,' recalled Blake. 'That made him very angry and resulted in a very unpleasant day on the set.'[19]

That night, Blake was asleep when the phone abruptly woke him. He struggled in the dark to answer it, noticing that the clock on his bedside table read two o'clock in the morning. It was Sellers. 'Don't worry about how we're going to do that scene tomorrow. I know how to do it.' Blake said that was terrific news and asked what he was going to do. 'I want to surprise you,' Sellers said, 'but don't worry, I've talked to God, and He told me how to do it.'[20]

When Sellers arrived on the set the following morning, he wanted to do the scene immediately. Blake said they still had some work to do with the cameras, but Sellers told him to leave things the way they were and just shoot it. Sellers made his entrance and it was quickly apparent that he had nothing planned at all, just a glimmer of hope that something intuitively brilliant might emerge. It was so awful that Edwards walked over to his star and said, 'Do me a favour Peter. In future, tell God to stay out of show business.'[21] It was meant as a joke but Sellers didn't laugh or take it the way Blake intended; he recalled:

> Instead, he drifted off into such a depressed, morose state that you could hardly hear him when he performed, and his whole physical being seemed to wither. We had to cut the entire sequence and replace it with a new one, which was a physical sequence in which we used a double. It was very sad.[22]

Julie Andrews was to write that Sellers, 'was becoming more and more eccentric – he was moody and paranoid. He was superstitious about the colour purple and holding regular conversations with his dead mother.'[23] The then head of United Artists, Eric Pleskow, recalls being invited once onto Sellers' yacht in the south of France. 'He had a cabin where he was in touch with his dead mother.'[24]

Pleskow also remembers a conversation with Sellers where the actor asked him if he still had his appendix; Pleskow did. Sellers said he ought to have it taken out and mentioned a doctor in Manila who put a sheet over you and pulled the thing out. When Pleskow died, not long after I interviewed him for this book, aged 95, he still had his appendix.

Pleskow often had to step in when Sellers was affecting the smooth running of the production and causing delays. 'Sometimes he didn't show up or he didn't know his lines, things like this used to happen. Quite often I went to London to try and help and get things moving.'[25] Blake, too, could be difficult to deal with sometimes, says Pleskow:

> He was a very tough character. One time I almost got into a fist fight with him. But he got things done. He was a very serious guy, and personality-wise you would never have thought that he had a great sense of humour, but it showed up in his films.[26]

Nine out of ten times, though, it was Sellers that Pleskow had to placate or deal with. 'I think his mind had gone. It was a shame because he was a genius in many ways.'[27]

For Blake, working with Sellers, accommodating his erratic behaviour, was having a profound impact on his mental and physical state. 'I developed pneumonia, which was entirely emotional from keeping my rage in check. I finally called my analyst here [LA] and told him, "I'm afraid I'm going to kill him or kill myself instead by holding back. I'm dealing with a madman."'[28] The analyst suggested Blake try a gentler approach and treat his star with kindness. This Blake did and it appeared to be working until Sellers caught on. 'Then he would throw a real tantrum.'[29]

One morning, Dyan Cannon arrived on set wearing purple and Sellers went crazy:

> I said, 'But Peter this is what they put me in.' He said, 'They should know. I told them. I'm not going to work. They must get you something else.' Now, in a film that is not easy because you spend hours in wardrobe fittings, going through what colours and the shoes and the nail polish, all of it.[30]

In the end wardrobe found Dyan something else to wear. It's interesting to note here how many times Sellers was reduced to an angry wreck when a bit of set dressing or the colour of a set was wrong, or when someone showed up from wardrobe wearing the wrong colour. It is inconceivable that these were mistakes. As Sellers told Dyan, he would instruct people about his colour phobias. Which begs the question, was this done deliberately by crew members, as a kind of revenge, just to piss the man off?

This was the one and only time Dyan saw Sellers lose his temper. 'I've never worked with such a kind, thoughtful, uplifting man.'[31] It shows on screen, the pair do share a great chemistry. 'There was just a nice warmth between us. The whole shoot was a total joy.'[32]

In the lead up to Christmas, Dyan's daughter flew to London and then the pair spent the holiday with Blake and Julie in Gstaad. Dyan enjoyed working with Blake on the film but found him tough going.

> I learned a big lesson with Blake. I was doing a scene in an office and I didn't like what I was doing and I said, 'Oops, I've got to stop.' And he said, 'Oh no, you never do that again. I say cut. You don't know what could have happened after that. And you don't know what happened in front of that that I might have loved.' And he was so right because later I directed and I remembered that and upfront I told my actors that. So, in that piece of direction was a great instruction and lesson and I was grateful for it.[33]

While her own working relationship with Sellers was good, Dyan was privy to the actor's love/hate relationship with Blake. 'Peter and Blake would get into it at times. They created sparks, they really did. Blake would come over to me and complain and then Peter would come over and complain. And then we would all just hug each other and get on with it.'[34]

Gregg Champion saw that it was very hit and miss with Sellers and Blake. 'It was a power struggle. And it was interesting to watch them work because a lot of it was improvisation.'[35] When Blake ditched the Paris location and moved the crew back to the studio, Gregg watched as he and Sellers rehearsed on the set.

> And Blake was already in a bad mood because he didn't like the way the set looked, and after rehearsal he was so pissed off that he wanted something changed and we had to wait through lunch before we even got the first shot. But I remember him rehearsing with Peter and Peter got very animated and at one point jumped up on the bed and was doing this comic stuff and Blake didn't like it. 'Why would you do that?' he said. And I could see that Peter was completely deflated. But I also remember a lot of laughter. The two of them would find that magical thing. And Blake would usually laugh at the end of every take and that would encourage Peter and then they would do another take. It was a love/hate thing, really.[36]

It was all about finding that bit of comedy gold, that little bit of business that made the scene dance. 'What Blake was so good at was creating a set piece,' says Gregg, 'something would build into something else. And they would find that in the moment. It came down, really, to Peter making Blake laugh.'[37] For example, Gregg remembers watching on set as they both came up with the sight gag of Clouseau walking too near a fan and getting his privates caught. 'They were always coming up with those little things.'[38]

The film's big location was Hong Kong. As everyone was gearing up to leave, Graham Stark popped into Shepperton. Sellers had once again asked him to be in the film, this time in the role of Auguste Balls, Clouseau's supplier of disguises. It was a Thursday afternoon and Stark was due to begin shooting the following Tuesday and was at the studios for a wig fitting. He walked into the restaurant and there was Blake; Stark joined him. 'What are you doing down here?' Blake asked. 'I've come for my fitting. I'm going to be shooting on Tuesday.' Blake said, 'You may be shooting Balls on Tuesday, we will all be in Hong Kong.' Obviously there had been a change in the schedule. Everyone was flying off on the Sunday. 'You fancy a trip to Hong Kong,' asked Blake. Graham looked stunned. 'You are kidding aren't you.' Blake called his assistant to arrange it. 'I was in Hong Kong for three weeks,' says Graham, 'never did a thing on the film out there. It was wonderful.'[39]

The cast and crew arrived in Hong Kong on a chartered flight, but what met them at the airport did not bode well. Graham recalls:

> There were sheets of water coming down. I'd never seen such rain. Blake looked out of the window of the plane and said, 'Oh God,' and then he delivered the coolest line ever quoted by any director ever. He turned round to his assistant and said, 'Check what the weather is like in Rio de Janeiro.'[40]

Peter Mullins, who had been in Hong Kong for two weeks setting things up, remembers things slightly differently, however. According to him, Blake was already in the city, staring gloomily out of his hotel window at the monsoon-like weather. With the charter plane on its way with the crew on board, Blake got Tony Adams to send a message to the pilot to make an overnight stop in Bangkok while Blake and his key people discussed what to do. That meeting went on till two in the morning, with Blake of a mind to turning the plane back to London. In the end the plane arrived in Hong Kong and the weather markedly improved.

Whatever the truth, it was a very long flight and Dyan remembers that when they finally arrived in Hong Kong the cast were given two days to sleep and rest to get over any jet lag. The main actors stayed in the luxurious Excelsior hotel and a lot of filming took place there. Gregg Champion was sent to Hong Kong ahead of the crew to help scout locations. This included finding the best hotels and checking out their room service and facilities. Blake had special requirements. Since his diving accident years before he suffered with back problems so there was always an exercise bike set up in his hotel room. Blake was also a hypochondriac, something he was fully aware of. 'One of the guys on the *Panther* crew was his doctor,' says Gregg. 'He travelled with us for the whole show and gave Blake his vitamin B shots.'[41]

Some of the rooms at the Excelsior were taken over and used as dressing rooms and make-up rooms for the actors. In one scene, Clouseau and Simone disguise themselves as an oriental couple; Simone rather more modestly than Clouseau who looks like Widow Twankey. Dyan is dressed in a sleek black dress, with sunglasses and a black wig. Finished in wardrobe, Dyan caught a lift down to the hotel lobby where the film crew were setting up. Dyan noticed that standing next to her was Blake's son Geoffrey, who was working on the movie uncredited as an assistant editor. He looked at her, then looked again. 'You're very pretty,' he said. Obviously, Geoffrey had failed to recognise Dyan, so the actress replied demurely in some quickly made-up mock Chinese gibberish. 'I mean *really* pretty,' Geoffrey stressed. Dyan replied the same way. Geoffrey asked where she was headed and Dyan pointed down and giggled.

> When we arrived at the lobby, Geoffrey had a look round thinking, what are you doing, because I walked straight up to Blake and I said, 'Blake, I'd like to introduce you to your son's new girlfriend.' I really fooled him and I thought, if I really fooled Blake's son, the audience will be fooled, too.[42]

Dyan also took to jogging up and down the corridors of the hotel. A keen jogger at the time, this was her daily routine and there was no other place to do it. 'You couldn't jog in the city or the parks, there were too many people. It was shoulder to shoulder. I couldn't believe it. So, Peter would stand guard and tell me when it was ok.'[43] The last thing Dyan wanted to do was sprint round a corner and crash headlong into a fellow guest.

Dyan enjoyed her sojourn in Hong Kong. The only thing that left a bad taste in the mouth was when some money was stolen from her room. 'Peter took us out to dinner so many times. And Blake did, as well. You can't replace those two men.'[44]

All the regular gang were on location: Herbert Lom, Graham Stark and Burt Kwouk. It was in Hong Kong that Stark realised the extent of his old friend's poor health. Of course, he knew of the health issues that had plagued Sellers for years, they went so far back that in truth Stark never really thought about them anymore. Then one afternoon the two of them were in a camera store, feeding their joint obsession for camera equipment, when Stark noticed, for the first time, that Sellers' fingers were trembling. Sellers had always hated any display of physical weakness. If he was ill, he would wave people's concerns away with the phrase, 'Just a touch of the lurgi.' But Stark sensed that this was different and more serious. 'I'd have liked not to have worried about the trembling fingers, but I was suddenly overwhelmed with a terrible feeling of sadness.'[45] Quickly Stark looked away, conscious of the fact that Sellers was trying to hide the shaking. What few people knew was that Sellers had been fitted with a pacemaker just prior to filming on *Revenge*.

In Hong Kong Stark made a point of staying with Kwouk most of the time, using the actor's inside knowledge of the best restaurants to go to. As Cato, Kwouk was heavily involved in a big car chase that forms the end of the picture. Joe Dunne was once again stunt coordinator and organised the car chase, along with doubling for Sellers, which he did far more of in *Revenge* due to the star's increased poor health. By this time, Sellers considered Joe his good luck charm.

The chase begins when the baddies leave the Excelsior hotel and speed off in a car. Cato sees them, grabs an ice cream seller's scooter and races after them. 'Blake calls action,' recalls Peter Mullins. 'Burt comes running out of the hotel doors and jumps on the ice cream cart, only this policeman sees him, runs after him, and pulls him off the cart. He didn't know it was a film.'[46]

A portion of Mullins time in Hong Kong was taken up appeasing local crime gangs. If the crew set up a camera anywhere in a street people would come up and say, 'My sign is in shot and if you want to use my shop, you need to pay me.' The counter argument to this was, 'Look, your shop is going to be seen by millions of people round the world.' That cut no ice, however, and it always ended the same way. 'You had to pay somebody off,' says Mullins.[47]

One of Mullins biggest jobs in Hong Kong was taking over one of the penthouse suites at the Excelsior to shoot an important scene. 'I remember we knocked down a wall to make one room bigger.'[48] His team also removed the windows to put in neutral density windows that would help with the light for filming. This was done with cranes on the roof that had suckers on them to remove the original windows and replace them with the new ones. 'We did all that which took days. We re-painted the suite and changed the look of it, and then the crew came to shoot.'[49] After about two days Mullins got a call to go and see Blake. In the office Blake was looking pensive. 'This isn't working,' he said.

'Why not?' asked Mullins. 'It's too hot here for Sellers. He doesn't like the heat. He's making noises about why are we here and we could have done this in the studio, all that kind of stuff. So, think about it in the next couple of hours and get back to me.'[50]

Mullins returned to his own office and put his thinking cap on:

> I rang the studios in Nice and spoke to the studio manager who I knew because I'd done several things there. He said the stages weren't busy. By the end of the day Blake called me

> back. I said, 'We can't go back to Shepperton because we're building other sets there, we don't have the stage space, and other studios are busy, but why don't we go to Nice.' I told him the stages were empty. He said, 'Let's do it.' So, we re-built the whole penthouse set in Nice. And that was all instigated by Sellers. We also had to put the whole penthouse suite in Hong Kong back to the way it was, including the windows.[51]

A second unit was left behind to pick up bits and pieces, mostly stunts for the car chase, while the rest of the cast and crew left and went to Nice. 'We literally sat around in the south of France for at least a week or two waiting for the sets to be built,' recalls Gregg Champion.[52]

Inevitably, Blake organised a yacht to arrive at Cap Ferret, where he and Julie planned to stay. The idea was for it to be used in the film, which it never was. On the morning the boat was due to arrive everyone was standing on the quay. It was late. 'And we are all waiting,' recalls Gregg. 'All of a sudden, we see the boat and it's getting closer and closer and Julie Andrews appears on the bow and breaks into "The Hills Are Alive with The Sound of Music." She broke everybody up.'[53]

Back in London Graham Stark finally got to do his scene as Auguste Balls. By this stage, audiences were waiting to see what ridiculous disguises Clouseau was going to use this time. Working with Blake and Frank Waldman on the film was television scriptwriter and playwright Ron Clark. During one meeting at Blake's office in Century City in Los Angeles, Sellers was there. The scene they were working on was Clouseau's visit to Auguste Balls' shop. Clark suddenly came up with the idea of Clouseau disguising himself as Toulouse-Lautrec. 'Sellers immediately got on his knees in the office,' Clark was to recall, 'and stayed on his knees for at least an hour, maybe longer, just walking around, playing the character, experimenting. He was hilarious.'[54] After the meeting, Clark drove home, arriving sometime after six. Later that night the phone rang. It was Sellers. 'He called to say that he enjoyed the session so much he wanted to call me to thank me.'[55]

In the scene Blake had given Stark as Balls a little poem to say:

> I went to Blake on the day we were going to do it and I said, 'You know what you've done, don't you.' He said, 'What, what.' I said, 'This poem I have to say as Balls: Through wind and mud, snow and hail, whether long or short, dark or pale,

> remember that when duty calls, you've got balls. Well, we're never going to get through this.'[56]

Sure enough, as soon as Stark began Sellers collapsed into giggles. 'We did eight takes, no good. In the end I had to send Peter out.'[57]

Again, much of the schedule was eaten up with corpsing and general larking about. Dyan Cannon recalls that each time she and Sellers got to one particular word in this scene they were playing, both would absolutely crack up.

> We could not control it. And that's not me. I'm pretty disciplined. So, finally after six or seven takes Blake said, 'Alright, the two of you, ok, that's enough, go take a break. Get in your car. Go for a half hour's ride. Go get some ice cream. Do whatever you have to do for half an hour and come back and we will continue.'
>
> So, he broke the entire cast and crew. When we came back, what do you think happened, the same thing. Ultimately Blake had to change the word.[58]

There was so much giggling going on, ruining takes and costing money, that in the end Blake warned Sellers and Dyan, 'No more. No more laughter. If you guys laugh, you're going to have to pay for it, because I'm not.'[59]

Of course, it wasn't just the corpsing that added to the schedule. 'With each film, Sellers cooperated less and got stranger and madder,' said Blake. 'And the sicker he got, and his illness had a lot to do with it, the less he was able to function.'[60] The heart condition, while obviously affecting Sellers physically, also appeared to hamper his memory. If Blake gave him any kind of intricate physical moves in scenes in which he also had lines, Sellers became literally incapable of doing both. There was a scene in *Revenge* that Blake incorporated all kinds of funny moves. These were directions and actions that would have been par for the course in the early *Pink Panther* movies, and yet during rehearsals it became apparent that there was absolutely no way Sellers was able to do it. Blake had no choice but to keep his moves to a minimum. 'Under normal conditions, that scene would have taken no more than the morning and possibly part of the afternoon to shoot. It ended up taking about two-and-a-half days.'[61]

Revenge does feature one of the most renowned bloopers of the entire *Panther* series. In a bid to expose the baddies, Clouseau dons yet another disguise, this time as a mafia godfather. At one point, Clouseau gets into a lift with a bunch of heavies. In ominous silence the men eye each other suspiciously. Then one of them breaks wind. This 'sound effect' was to have been added in post- production, but the actors needed a cue, so this was provided by Blake off camera. However, each time he blew a raspberry Sellers and the other actors broke up. Take after take was ruined. Blake then dispensed with the raspberry and instead just said the word, 'Now,' which for some reason had an even worse effect. 'All this sniggering made it difficult to shoot the scene as planned at the Excelsior hotel in Hong Kong,' recalls Terry Ackland-Snow, who was with the art department. 'So, we built the lift back in the UK to re-shoot, but the same thing happened. After some time and many laughs, we finally got the take.'[62] The take that Blake finally used was in fact the very last take, and even that was only barely usable, as Sellers couldn't contain himself any longer and literally turned round to face the back of the lift.

Other scenes shot at Shepperton included the presumed-dead Clouseau returning to his flat in Paris, only to discover that Cato has turned it into a brothel. One of the working girls had to be this Amazonian beauty, clad in leather and wielding a whip. Cast in the role was Valerie Leon, a familiar face to audiences thanks to appearances in Carry On and Hammer films, the recent Bond film *The Spy Who Loved Me*, and a series of TV commercials for Hai Karate aftershave. It was explained to Valerie that in order to play the role she was required to be proficient with a whip.

> This guy arrived at my house one day with a selection of whips that we took into the garden so he could teach me how to hold it, how to wield it, how to use it basically. I ended up having a lot of fun, and I remember looking up and I could see all the neighbours peering out of their windows wondering what on earth I was getting up to.[63]

Next to come was the outfit. 'It was leather and skin tight,' recalls Valerie. 'It was literally welded onto my body. I doubt it would have fitted anybody else, and that's why I was allowed to keep it after the film. I did have to be helped into it.'[64]

As for Sellers, Valerie had no chance to get to know him. 'He was ill on that picture.' Indeed, Valerie's participation was held up for a few weeks because of Sellers' health. 'It was a difficult scene to shoot because when I was on the set Peter wasn't well and he wasn't around that much. He would do what he had to do and then disappear very quickly. I think it was lucky they finished the film frankly.'[65]

The final shot of the movie sees Clouseau taking Simone out to dinner in a souped-up Citroën 2CV, dubbed The Silver Hornet. Only it predictably falls to pieces. 'The effects guys had it rigged,' recalls Gregg Champion.

> There were all kinds of springs to make the car fall apart. One of the springs shot up into the air and hit a pigeon and the bird came down right in the frame. Blake walked over and picked up this poor bird that was dying and gasping for breath. I remember seeing that over and over in dailies, they kept running it and everyone was in hysterics. It was a weird thing.[66]

The shot remains in the film and the plummeting pigeon is clearly visible, while Sellers and Dyan carry on with the scene.

Principal photography on *Revenge* was completed in mid-April, much to the relief of Blake Edwards who afterwards claimed he almost had a nervous breakdown during the shoot. 'I had so much pent-up rage and frustration within me.'[67] Somehow, he got through the picture. For Blake, Sellers was now almost impossible to work with. 'He would sulk, he would get into black moods, he would withdraw, and he would punish himself by not being able to do something.'[68] It reached a point where if Sellers could not get a handle on what was required, it would frustrate him to the point where the situation just got worse and worse. According to Blake:

> And he would blame it on somebody else. Blame it on conditions, blame it on God – blame it on anybody except Peter Sellers. And he was very cruel to people during those periods. He would threaten, even pretend physical violence. If it wasn't so sad, it was laughable.[69]

A lot of the problems caused by Sellers Blake would pass over to Tony Adams who had to contend with them almost daily. One time even Adams was stumped and put a call through to United Artist executive Dan Rissner, who oversaw European Production and was based in England. Rissner had already had a few run-ins with Sellers. On *Strikes Again* he was awoken from a deep sleep in the middle of the night by Sellers calling him to say that his mother had told him to quit the picture and go to Hawaii. Now,

Sellers had locked himself in his dressing room and was refusing to come out. Rissner arrived at the studio sporting an expression that said, why call me, you sort it out. Rissner knocked on Sellers' dressing room door and walked in. He was out ten minutes later. 'He's crazy,' said Rissner. On entering the room Rissner had sat down. Sellers did not say a word for a full five minutes. He just looked at Rissner. Another thing unsettled Rissner, he noticed candles and an altar in the room dedicated to the actor's dead mother. When Sellers finally spoke, he said, 'People love me, you know. People really love me. The guard on the gate loves me. He waves to me every day.' Sellers did not speak again and Rissner left. Adams listened to Rissner explain all this, but what he wanted to know was when Sellers was going to be on the set. 'I have no idea,' said Rissner. Adams sighed, 'Now you see what I go through every day.'[70]

Dyan prefers to remember the happy moments, and when Sellers was on form, he was a joy to watch. On the day they were shooting Sellers in disguise as an old Swedish sailor, with the plastic parrot on his shoulder, Dyan was not required but turned up to watch anyway. 'I had a pillow around my face and fell on the floor. That's how deeply and endlessly this man had the gift of making people laugh. He was a genius.'[71]

Gregg Champion has fond memories of Sellers, too. 'I loved him. He was really kind to me. He was very quiet. You couldn't really tell where his head was at a lot of the time.'[72] Gregg met Sellers again only once more, this was in LA when Sellers was making *Being There*.

> We ran into each other one evening and he took me to a restaurant and we had drinks and then we went across to a disco across the street. And Peter really looked at the top of his game. He was like a different person. He was outgoing, he was friendly. He immediately recognised me and remembered me. He was by himself. He wasn't with Lynne.[73]

Like others, Gregg sensed that it was not a happy union. 'They fought and argued. Lynne was on the set of *Revenge* in London. Peter was very withdrawn around her. She'd show up for lunch. She wouldn't watch on the set much.'[74]

United Artists intended to pull out all the stops when it came time to launch the latest in the *Panther* series, holding a press junket in the paradise setting of Hawaii. Then, with just weeks to go, Blake suddenly decided that the climax of the picture, a shoot-out in a fireworks factory, was not working. Quickly he rustled up some money, got most of the crew back, rented a soundstage at MGM, had the set rebuilt and shot new footage in record time. Then it was a race to edit it, and according to Julie Andrews, Blake did not see the completed result until the screening in Hawaii. 'I was so nervous for him. To be so down to the wire and to take such a gamble, but everything worked, brilliantly.'[75]

The launch itself was a triumph. Chartered jets were laid on to ferry seventy-five journalists in from London, Los Angeles and Paris for the weekend bash. In total 300 guests arrived, including comedian Steve Martin. Sellers and Lynne took the presidential suite at the Kuilima Hyatt hotel, which was decorated with all things *Pink Panther* related. Guests also received *Pink Panther* goodie bags upon arrival and every room was decked out with flowers, fruit baskets and gifts. Sellers' children Sarah and Michael had been invited, given first class air tickets and a beach cabana each and told they could order anything they wanted from room service. Dyan recalls taking her mum and dad to the launch and everything was paid for. United Artists ended up with a bill in excess of $300,000.

Sellers seemed to enjoy himself according to Monica Mancini who was there with her father. She had met Sellers before at her home when he came round to dinner, but at the Hawaiian junket he was being especially, 'goofy'. He had brought a doll with him, a Clouseau doll that he must have got some prop guy to build for him. It had on a hat and trench coat, but was naked underneath and Sellers would flash people with it at dinner. 'It was the silliest thing,' says Monica. 'I was captivated by Sellers really because I didn't see him as Peter Sellers, I saw him as Inspector Clouseau. So, when he was out of character, I didn't know who it was. It was like, who is this guy?'[76]

In London there was another Royal premiere, which Sellers turned up for this time. Prince Charles was absent, however, so Prince Philip attended. As usual, the cast were introduced to the Royal guest before the film was screened. An actress happened to be wearing a dress with four rows of pearls along the bottom. Unfortunately, she caught it on something and the pearls started rolling across the floor. Dyan recalls it being:

> Like a scene in a movie. Prince Philip and I were on our hands and knees crawling on the floor, not looking where we were going, picking up these pearls. And I looked up and we were

> right next to each other. If we hadn't lifted our heads up, we would have bumped into each other. I said, 'What a lovely way to meet you.' He said, 'Same here.'[77]

The publicity drive for the film went global. In the States, *Revenge* opened at the Los Angeles Cinerama Dome, where a giant inflatable Pink Panther was erected outside the theatre. This inflatable was later sent to Tokyo, where it was suspended from a skyscraper to promote the Japanese opening.

As had become a pattern with the last few *Panthers*, critical reaction was decidedly mixed. Philip French in the *Observer* called it, 'A sad affair, destructive, uninventive, very expensive and only occasionally funny. Rarely has so much expensive film wrapped so many cheap jokes.' However, Vincent Canby wrote in *The New York Times*, 'If you have the Clouseau habit, as I have, there's very little that Mr Edwards and Mr Sellers could do that would make you find the movie disappointing.' The film went on to win the Evening Standard British Film Award for best comedy. Sellers himself expressed his own disappointment in the film, that he and Blake had been rushed into making it by United Artists. 'Neither Blake nor I was ready to make it, but UA put such pressure on us that we said: "OK, we'll do our best."'[78] Again, we see Sellers hating on a film once it's finished. His PA, Susan Wood, recalls that Sellers was not above threatening to take his name off a film, despite being the star.

As for the public, they flocked once again to the latest Panther in droves that summer of 1978 and *Revenge* was another box office smash. 'The *Pink Panther* films were very important films to United Artists,' reports company head Eric Pleskow. 'They were very successful. They made money for us.'[79] It was the reliable revenue from the *Pink Panther* and Bond franchises that allowed UA to take chances on more auteur filmmaking and challenging material.

It was reported at the time that the *Pink Panther* films were United Artists' top sellers in terms of merchandising, with roughly forty companies licensed to manufacture Pink Panther products. A July 1978 UA press release named several of the items in production, they included: Pink Panther greeting cards and party supplies from Hallmark Cards, Pink Panther toys from Mattel, along with comic books, puzzles, colouring books, themed soap and toothbrush holders. Prior to the release of *Revenge*, Safeco, a Seattle-based insurance company, began using the Pink Panther cartoon character as its advertising mascot. There was even a seventy-five-acre Pink Panther-themed skate park and campsite erected in Slidell, Louisiana.

For some members of the cast there was a feeling that perhaps the films were growing stale and becoming guilty of repeating themselves. 'You can't really milk a subject forever,' said Herbert Lom. 'And as the films progressed, they suffered.'[80] All United Artists could see were dollar signs and the sound of busy box offices around the world. They wanted more *Panther* films. But would Blake and Sellers play ball? 'I've honestly had enough of Clouseau myself,' the actor was telling reporters. 'I've got nothing more to give.' He'd finally had it with Blake, too, and one suspects Blake with him. Sue Wood recalls Sellers saying to her after completing *Revenge* that he and Blake were finished. It was the end, no more. Sue had heard this all before. 'So many times, at the end of a working day, never mind the end of the film, it was, "I'm not going in tomorrow. I can't work with him. It's impossible." And, of course, it was never Peter's fault.'[81] The difference was, this time he meant it.

Chapter 7

THE PANTHER THAT NEVER WAS

When Peter Sellers flew into London on Monday 21 July, 1980, taking his usual suite at the Dorchester, he had a draft script with him entitled *Romance of the Pink Panther*. Three days later he was dead.

Had *Romance of the Pink Panther* been made it would have looked very different to the previous films in the series. Sellers was set to return as Inspector Clouseau, but Blake Edwards would not be behind the camera. This time their relationship was beyond repair. Senior executives at United Artists had tried and failed to effect a reconciliation. As senior vice-president at UA Steven Bach put it: 'What with seemingly endless volleys of recriminations and hostilities shooting back and forth between Blake Edwards and Peter Sellers, each of whom claimed full credit for the popularity of the series with such vehement animosity that it was clearly a situation irresolvable with mere diplomacy.'[1] Some referred to it as a hatred of each other. Ironically, they lived for some of the year in the same town, Gstaad, and took to ignoring each other should their Rolls-Royces pass in the street. Adam Fields worked as an assistant to Sellers' US agent, Martin Baum. 'Apparently there were only two good restaurants in Gstaad at the time. So, I used to have to get up at something like four in the morning to call and make reservations for each of them at the other place so they didn't run into each other.'[2]

Martin Baum worked for the recently formed Creative Artists Agency (CAA) and Sellers was one of its top clients. The deal for the new *Panther* film was not only going to be the biggest in the agency's short history, but one of the biggest Hollywood had ever seen. Baum was getting \$3m for Sellers to return as Clouseau, which would make him the world's highest paid star. As for Blake, another of Baum's clients, he was going to receive \$3m NOT to direct the picture, as he held some rights in the property. Baum also represented Jim Maloney, the man Sellers had chosen to write the script with, along with the director, Clive Donner, and the film's two producers, Dan Rissner and, at Sellers' insistence, Lynne Frederick. In all, it was something like a $9m package. This was a game changer for the agency. United Artists in their desperation for another Sellers/*Panther* film were going to have no option other than to pay up.

Sellers was understandably delighted with the money on offer, but according to his son Michael something was eating away at him:

> Privately he felt that the *Panther* movies had come to the end of their natural life span and that every feasible comedy situation involving Clouseau had been exploited. He worried about artistic prostitution, but even he had a price, for as he remarked to me: 'I would have been crazy to turn down that kind of deal. It's going to set me up for the rest of my days.'[3]

Never mind artistic prostitution, Sellers was now in such poor health that he was finding it hard to walk and breath at the same time. Would he be able to handle the physical rigors of doing another *Panther*, he was going to need an army of stand ins and stunt doubles this time. His PA, Susan Wood, certainly had her doubts. 'He was so ill at that point in time that it was very hard for me to visualise him even getting on the set to do it.'[4]

Following *Revenge of the Pink Panther*, Sellers made *The Prisoner of Zenda*, a lamentable comedy remake of the classic drama that was produced by Walter Mirisch. On the set his physical deterioration was clearly in evidence. The film had starred Lynne Frederick, along with two former *Panther* co-stars in Elke Sommer and Catherine Schell. Sellers had been happy to see them both again. Catherine recalls:

> And it was so sweet, because when I arrived at the hotel there was a box of chocolates for me and some flowers and it was – with love from – and Peter signed it with the name of the telephone repairman he had played in *Return of the Pink Panther*. It was so sweet.[5]

It did not take long for Catherine to see how truly ill Sellers was.

> He was a lot slower. He could not work in the afternoon, so a lot of the scenes that I was supposed to do with him I ended up doing with his stand in reading the lines. There was one

> evening when we did have dinner together, with Lynne, and after a certain time he would get extremely tired so he had to leave the table and she took him back to the room.[6]

Zenda was another troubled production, dominated by Sellers' erratic behaviour. Elke Sommer recalls that Sellers had a poor relationship with the director Richard Quine and was irritable on the set:

> I found him to be more depressed and more aggressive, to other people, but never, never with me. He was very friendly with me and very sweet. I am very sensitive and had he been aggressive with me, even once, I would have burst into tears because he was the actor that I admired the most in my whole career.[7]

Sellers' mood was not helped by personal issues with Lynne. Their marriage was in trouble. Their therapist had advised them not to work together, but Lynne had insisted on a role in the film. Soon the newspapers were awash with stories that the couple were looking at a divorce. According to Catherine, Sellers was desperate and wanted her back. Lynne agreed to return on condition that he alter his will, leaving everything to her. Sellers capitulated and his children were virtually locked out of his fortune. With Lynne back in his life, Sellers seemed to perk up. He must have benefited, too, when a project he had wanted to make for years was finally green lit.

Sellers first read the novel *Being There*, by Jerzy Kosiński, back in 1971. He recognised the central character as a perfect role for him, Chance the Gardener, a child-like man whose horticultural sayings are misconstrued as searing pronouncements on American politics. It is no mystery why Sellers wanted so desperately to play Chance, here was a character that had no real personality of his own. Sellers always recognised in himself that he was pretty much an empty vessel in which he poured the people he played into. Chance was the perfect embodiment of this. As Herbert Lom once said, 'Peter never knew who he was.'[8]

There was another reason for playing the role. Sellers felt that people now only saw him as Clouseau, and just wanted more *Pink Panther* films. He was sort of stuck with them in a way, although his feelings about them were ambivalent, since they made money and if he continued to do them the studio would sanction other projects. Susan Wood, however, is in no doubt that had Sellers lived, the success of *Being There* would have completely changed his career and that after doing *Romance* he would have favoured playing more mature character roles. 'That was how he had grown to see himself, as a serious actor. He felt that he wasn't being taken seriously enough.'[9]

Directed by Hal Ashby, *Being There* was completed by the spring of 1979. That summer, Sellers commenced work on another comedy, *The Fiendish Plot of Dr. Fu Manchu*, which ultimately would prove to be his final film. Now thoughts turned to *Romance of the Pink Panther*. Sellers was out to prove that he could make a *Panther* film without Blake Edwards, and perhaps also demonstrate that their success owed more to him than anything Blake may have contributed. As it was, Blake was soon to be riding high on the phenomenal box office success of *10* and so for now at least did not need the *Panthers* any more.

Sellers undertook the scriptwriting chores himself, along with Jim Moloney, a former actor turned writer who also worked on *The Fiendish Plot of Dr. Fu Manchu*, and whom Sellers liked and admired, according to Susan Wood. The plot of *Romance* saw Clouseau falling in love with a beautiful French countess, who unbeknownst to him is really a master criminal that he has been trying to track down. This entry in the series, Sellers hoped, would offer a 'different slant' on the character. 'And having him in love should be interesting. If this is to be the last *Pink Panther* film, I'm determined that it's got to be a good one.'[10] Susan Wood was one of the few people who read it. 'It was ok. It was very much like the other *Panthers*. It was funny.'[11]

With Blake persona non grata, numerous names were mentioned to replace him. In January 1979 the *Los Angeles Times* reported that Sidney Poitier was in the frame. Best known as an actor, Poitier had successfully directed several pictures since the early '70s. In the end a deal was not able to be done and so Sellers turned to an old friend, Clive Donner, with whom he had made the '60s sex comedy smash hit *What's New Pussycat*. Since then, Donner's career had been erratic to say the least, and he had not made a cinema feature since 1974's dismal Dracula send-up, *Vampira*, with David Niven.

As for the cast, United Artists drafted a list of possible candidates to play the criminal countess but Sellers, who had right of approval over any of the actors, had already chosen who he wanted, a young comedienne then making a name for herself on a BBC comedy series called *Not the Nine O' Clock News*, Pamela Stephenson. Sellers considered her to be exceptionally talented and asked Susan Wood to personally send the script to her.

Of course, it would not have been a *Pink Panther* movie without the participation of Graham Stark and Sellers phoned his old friend up from his home in Gstaad and spent the whole call talking about his role in the film. Stark was to reprise the role of Auguste Balls, and in one scene sells Clouseau a Louis XIV chair disguise kit. This turned out to be the last time the two friends ever spoke.

Sellers also personally reached out to Burt Kwouk about the film. The pair had only recently worked together on *The Fiendish Plot of Dr. Fu Manchu.* Sellers had invited him over to Paris for a week to play a role in the film. 'What do you want me to do?' Burt had enquired. 'We'll work something out when you get here,' said Sellers.

Burt flew to Paris and on arriving discovered that his role included him being set on fire. 'Peter, you must have known about this when you phoned me!' Kwouk protested. 'Yes Burt, but if I'd told you, you wouldn't have come.'[12]

When Sellers called about the new *Panther*, Kwouk was a little surprised that Blake Edwards was not involved. Despite that he was interested and Sellers promised to send over the script. That script never came. Burt heard nothing more about the new *Pink Panther* film until the news broke of Sellers death.

Sellers also hoped to reunite as many of the old *Panther* crew as possible. Peter Mullins was going to return as production designer and was sent the script. All he can recall about it was that at one point an orangutan falls in love with Clouseau and follows him everywhere. Whenever Clouseau gets into a scrape, the ape comes to his rescue. This was obviously a parody of the recent Cint Eastwood movie *Every Which Way but Loose* (1978) that featured an orangutan. Sellers also reached out to Joe Dunne as he wanted him to handle all the stunt work. Joe was currently working with Blake in Hollywood as his second unit director on *S.O.B* and was not so keen because Blake was not going to be involved. In the end Joe did agree to do *Romance* and was negotiating with the producers when Sellers died.

Inevitably, the scriptwriting process of *Romance* was fraught with near constant drama and problems. Sellers would incessantly call CAA and want to talk to Martin Baum and they would be on the phone for an hour, sometimes ninety minutes. It was always Baum's assistant Adam Fields that took the calls. He was the gatekeeper to his boss. 'Sellers called every day, almost. And they never seemed to be about anything.'[13] At the time, Lynne was staying in LA, and so Sellers was alone in Gstaad. 'Maybe he was phoning because he was lonely,' says Fields, 'and needed someone to talk to.'[14]

Other times the calls were more serious, with Sellers threatening to quit the film or quit the movies altogether and Baum would have to persuade him not to. The *Panther* project was just too big, both for the agency and UA, to let it go. Sellers took to calling Baum at all hours of the night. It got so bad that Baum moved out of the main bedroom in his home to a guest room so his wife could get a proper night's sleep. Baum told Fields of a recent trip he made to London to see Sellers. He and his wife Bernice, having had dinner with Sellers, were standing in the rain on the street waiting endlessly for a cab. Sellers came by in his chauffeur driven car, wound down the window and said, 'What are you doing?' Marty said, 'We're waiting for a cab, it takes forever.' Peter said, 'Yeah, it can take a long time,' and then drove off.[15]

Adam Fields was in his early 20s when he came to work as Baum's assistant. Graduating from the University of California at Berkeley, working at CAA was his first job in Hollywood. Fields would later move to Universal Pictures where he oversaw the development and production of the classic John Hughes film *The Breakfast Club* (1985) as well as produce his own films, including *Donnie Darko* (2001). Fields knew it was a crazy town but nothing could have prepared him for someone like Sellers.

> He made my life so miserable. He would call me in the middle of the night when he was in Europe and ask me to drive by Lynne Frederick's house up in the Hollywood Hills and see what cars were in the driveway and write down the licence plates. People would say, 'Why didn't you just say there were none.' But you never knew, he could be testing you and he would call Marty Baum and I'd get fired. So, I had to do it.[16]

This kind of stuff was not what Fields signed up for when he came to work at the agency. 'Every day was like a search and destroy mission in Vietnam where you just wanted to get home safely every day.'[17]

Sellers had a habit, too, of calling the office pretending to be somebody else, a producer like Dan Rissner or Walter Mirisch, and Fields, so new to Los Angeles and unfamiliar with these names, would innocently put him through.

> I'd go to Marty, 'Walter Mirisch is on line two,' and it would be Peter doing a perfect imitation of Walter Mirisch baiting Marty into a conversation about himself and Marty would fall for it. Peter was trying to see what Marty really thought, so he'd say, 'Do you find Peter sometimes a little odd.' Marty would go, 'Odd! He's fucking driving me fucking crazy.'[18]

Then half an hour later Sellers would call again and say to Baum, 'I hear you've been saying nasty things about me.' After that Fields would get yelled at for not telling Baum that it was Sellers all along. 'I'd say, "But you didn't recognise him either."'[19]

While Sellers worked on the script for *Romance,* he had been nominated for an Oscar for Best Actor for *Being There*. It was his first Academy Award nomination since *Dr Strangelove*. The ceremony was due to take place at the Dorothy Chandler Pavilion in Los Angeles on April 14, 1980. 'I dreaded Peter coming,' admits Fields, 'because I just knew there would be a tremendous number of arrangements and changing of arrangements, and completely unrealistic expectations that I would be responsible for and surely accountable for if it wasn't perfect.'[20] In the end Sellers decided to stay in London. 'Which for me was a big sigh of relief,' says Fields.[21]

The day of the Oscars came. Fields was hoping to get out of the office early so he could get home and switch the TV on to watch the stars arriving for the ceremony on the red carpet. At 5.30pm, the phone rang. Of course, it was Sellers. 'I thought, this is going to be a goddamn hour; there were no short calls with Peter.'[22] Fields put him through to Baum. As an assistant, Fields could always listen in to the calls. 'Peter was going on and on about all these people that had been calling him all day saying, don't worry if you don't win, it's being nominated that counts. He goes, "What is wrong with everyone in Hollywood. They're so shallow. They think I'm not going to win!"'[23] Finally, Baum ended the call and put the phone back on its hook. Fields remembers:

> And I hear my favourite sound of the day, which was the jingle jangle of Marty's keys, which meant he was packing up to leave, which means I could follow him out of the door in five minutes. And just then a telex came in. And, of course, it was from Peter. It went: Dear Martin (and when he said Martin you knew he was mad), in our entire conversation tonight you couldn't find time to wish me good luck. And that tells me everything about our relationship.[24]

Baum got straight on the phone to call Sellers, who was in a Paris hotel suite, but he had put a do not disturb on his phone. He could not be reached. Baum turned to Fields and told him to send a telex right away. It read:

> Dear Pete, in case you've forgotten, I want to remind you of the fact that I'm Jewish and there's a superstition among European shtetl Jews that if you want something badly you don't mention it because if you do a Cossack will come and take it before you got it. And that is my superstition about something I want so badly for you. All my love Martin.[25]

Fields sent the telex. Baum then dictated a note to send out if Sellers won, and a note to send out if he lost. Baum also had Fields organise with the hotel to send up two bottles of champagne to Sellers' room along with his breakfast with either the winning or the losing note.

Hollywood can be a sentimental town and many Oscars have been bestowed upon actors, not necessarily for the best performance, but for a body of work, it's their time. Think John Wayne for *True Grit* for example. One would have thought, given his age and health, that Hollywood would have given Sellers the nod for *Being There*. Maybe he had pissed off so many of his fellow actors, directors, producers, agents et al over twenty-plus years this was never going to happen. Nor did it help that the nominees for Best Actor that year was one of the strongest fields in recent memory. Sellers was up against Dustin Hoffman for *Kramer vs Kramer*. Jack Lemmon for *The China Syndrome*. Roy Scheider for *All That Jazz*. And Al Pacino for *And Justice for All*. Hoffman won.

Fields came into the office the next day thinking, this is going to be interesting for sure.

> Eventually Peter called Marty, and he didn't mention the awards, he just said, 'You know Martin, as long as you're my friend I don't really care if I ever work again.' And I thought, it was a brilliant piece of agenting on Marty's part, what a genius telex to send back, and it did the trick.[26]

It wasn't just Baum and Fields that Sellers was driving nuts. Steven Bach was an executive at United Artists and had been put in overall charge of bringing *Romance of the Pink Panther* to the screen. A problem had arisen with the script and Bach flew into Gstaad for an emergency meeting with

Sellers. What he saw made a deep impression. Physically Sellers looked like death. He had a 'wraithlike' appearance, Bach later wrote. 'The smile he wore seemed paralyzed in place, and I thought I had never seen so delicate a man. His skull, his fingers, the tightly drawn, almost transparent skin, all seemed frail, infinitely fragile.'[27] Bach compared him to a, 'spectral presence, a man made of egg shells.'[28]

Producer Dan Rissner had sent his notes on the script to Sellers, who at the time was relaxing on his yacht in the Aegean. Sellers' reaction to them had been, in Bach's words, 'hysterical', and the star vowed never again to speak to Rissner. It was only the intervention of Lynne, Sellers said, that prevented him jumping overboard. Bach arrived at Sellers' home in Gstaad. The two men chatted for quite a time, seemingly about everything except the script for the *Panther* film. Sellers happily showed Bach around the house. Bach knew about Sellers' love of photography and noticed that in several of the rooms hung enlarged photographs that he had taken. One in particular impressed Bach, it was of a bird in flight, backlit by a bright sun. He told Sellers who seemed delighted that Bach liked it. Dinner was then served after which Sellers insisted that they all go to the local nightclub. As the evening wore on, Bach saw that Sellers seemed to come alive in the company of strangers, in among the crowd. He also observed that Lynne was ever alert to any slight change in her husband's mood. Despite her age it appeared to Bach that Lynne was the calming influence in the household, keeping everything together.

Still, Sellers would not talk about the reason Bach had flown all the way over from the States – the *Panther* script. When Bach raised the subject Sellers told him, 'Leave it to Lynne.' The next day Bach arrived at the house for lunch. The atmosphere was relaxed, Sellers appeared calm. Lynne came into the room. 'Now,' she said, looking first at Bach, then her husband. 'What about this movie, darling.'[29] Sellers began to talk, hesitatingly at first, then with more confidence, going over the ideas and gags that he and Jim Moloney had been bouncing off each other. Bach found what Sellers had to say, 'institutive and intelligent'.[30] All the time, he noticed, Sellers never once let go of Lynne's hand. It was his life support system, giving him calm and energy. It was decided that Sellers and Moloney just get on paper what they wanted the film to be. Sellers seemed surprised by the resolution, asking Bach, 'May we?'

Bach returned to Los Angeles. When Martin Baum received a cable from Sellers he read it out to Bach on the phone: 'Script on way to you by courier. No joking, I think it's bloody terrific, and I hope you will.' The cable was signed, 'All the best, Peter Shakespeare and Jim Bacon.'[31] Adam Fields recalls the script coming into the office and Baum telling him to make a copy and then to send it to Sellers in Gstaad. This was late on a Friday, pre-FedEx and DHL days. A lawyer by the name of Michael Wolfe, who represented both Sellers and Blake, just happened to be going to Gstaad that evening to see Blake, so Fields got him a copy of the script to take and give to Sellers. Fields recalls:

> Sunday morning Marty started calling me three or four in the morning screaming and yelling at me. Apparently what happened, the script had got to Peter but it wasn't in a sealed envelope and he was convinced that Blake had intercepted it and read it. And he was quitting the *Panther*. And it was all my fault. And I had to call the homes of all the top execs at United Artists to tell them the *Panther* was off – and it was my fault.[32]

The only reason Fields did not get fired was that the blame fell on the mail room guy who was the son of one of the senior partners.

Sellers was now staying more and more in his chalet at Gstaad which he bought in the summer of 1979. It was isolated, on a hill and Sellers took great joy and comfort in staying there with Lynne. Susan Wood remembers staying there on Christmas Eve.

> It was the most relaxed I think I ever saw Peter. And then also a couple of weeks before his death, I went over there with his son Michael and we spent a weekend with Peter. He wasn't terribly well, but again he was the most relaxed I'd ever seen him. Because relaxed and Peter are not the words you would choose to use in the same sentence.[33]

As usual with Sellers the storm clouds were never very far away. Susan was at the house in Gstaad when several ravens or crows descended on the garden. After Susan left, she learned that Sellers had burned many of his old home movies and photographs and stills. 'He had seen that as a kind of omen. It was most bizarre.'[34]

When Sellers flew into London on Monday 21 July 1980, he was already a dying man. What few people knew was that he had recently suffered quite a serious heart attack while on holiday in the South of France. He ended up in a private hospital. 'And he behaved like an absolute pig, throwing things at the nuns,' says Susan. 'After that heart attack you could see the physical deterioration.' Making *The Fiendish Plot of Dr Fu Manchu* he was very frail. 'There were times when, literally, me or Lynne would help him get on the set,' says Susan. 'He really was not well by that point.'

Once in London Sellers took a suite at the Dorchester. He only expected to stay a couple of days. With him was the script for *Romance of the Pink Panther*. He had spoken to Spike Milligan to organise a meet up with fellow Goon Harry Secombe for the 22nd. He even wanted them to all get back together and write some more Goon shows. In a telegram to Milligan several weeks earlier, Sellers had broached the idea, saying how he didn't want any money and wanted to work just for the sheer joy of being with them both again, 'as we were'. Milligan had not taken this at all seriously, passing it off as a Sellers whim that would pass just as quickly as it arrived. Sellers and Spike did have a complicated relationship, says Susan. 'They were very close in many ways, but they were also pretty competitive with each other.'[35] Still, it is interesting to note that in the weeks leading up to his death, and Sellers must have known how gravely ill he was, his thoughts returned to that period in his life that he always said was his most happy, his time on The Goon Show. Ironically, Milligan had contacted Secombe telling him that they ought to meet up with Sellers for dinner, 'before one of us is walking behind the coffin'.[36]

On the 22nd both Susan and Michael Jeffery, Sellers' new assistant (Bert Mortimer had been unceremoniously fired) were in Sellers' suite. They shared a light lunch together. Susan recalls:

> When we finished lunch, Michael went to get Peter's clothes out. Peter suddenly said to me, 'Oh, gosh, I feel a bit hot. Could you get me some water, darling.' I got up, turned, and went over to the table to pour some water for him and I heard this thud and he had fallen off the chair and he was immediately going this terrible dark purple colour. It was frightening. I screamed at Michael. He called downstairs. I called downstairs. The ambulance came within minutes.[37]

Susan and Michael followed the ambulance in a car, but by the time they reached the hospital news had broken about Sellers. 'When I tried to get out of the car,' says Susan, 'I got knocked down to the ground by all these people.'[38]

As Sellers lay unconscious in a hospital bed it was not long before Lynne arrived and his children Michael and Sarah. Britt Ekland was there too, and had brought their daughter Victoria. 'We were all there,' says Susan. 'We were all keeping watch.'[39] After a while the doctors told everyone to go home and get some rest. He would be fine. He would get through the night, nothing to worry about. Susan drove back home only to be called straight back to the hospital. 'By the time we all got back he had gone. I think that is the saddest thing. This was a man who didn't ever, ever, want to be alone, and he died alone and it breaks my heart.'[40]

Peter Sellers died on 24th July, 1980. He was just 54 years old. He never did regain consciousness during those days in hospital. The hope was that, somehow, he did feel the presence of those closest people in his life when they were around his bedside.

In LA Adam Fields took the call that Sellers had died and told Baum. CAA was a small office then and the news spread quickly. Steven Bach heard about it, too, and got a surprise just a few days later when he received a parcel in the post from Susan. She wrote in a covering letter that Sellers had wanted him to have this. Rolled in a tube was the photograph that had so impressed Bach in Sellers' home of that bird in flight.

When Burt Kwouk heard the news of Sellers' death it deeply upset him, although he wasn't entirely surprised. 'His heart problems had been in the background and he had told me, "I'm living on borrowed time."'[41]

The first thing Julie Andrews did when she heard the news was phone Blake. The couple had known for a long time Sellers had a weak heart but never imagined it would take him so soon. 'Despite their differences in recent years, their friendship had been long,' Julie said. 'And they had shared so much laughter together. His loss came as a real shock.'[42] By this time Blake had somewhat mellowed regarding his attitude to Sellers. His view was that the way you make peace is to forgive and forget. And the way you forgive and forget is to try to understand why people are the way they are. Very possibly today, Sellers would be diagnosed with bipolar disorder. 'He could be so lovely and so charming,' says Susan, 'and then he'd turn on a sixpence to be an absolute so and so.'[43]

The last time Blake saw Sellers alive was in Gstaad at Christmas. Blake and Julie, along with their children, were enjoying an evening together at a local disco. Geoffrey had brought his girlfriend, a young budding actress by the name of Denise Crosby. Sellers and Lynne came in. Sellers did not acknowledge Blake's presence. Blake watched them from where he was sitting, saw them have an argument and leave. A little later someone caught sight of Sellers through the window. He was standing alone outside in the snow across the street. Blake thought this was strange, even for Sellers. Although not on speaking terms, remembering all the good times, Blake told Julie that he was going to go and talk to him. According to Denise Crosby,

> Blake went out and had a conversation with Peter, and this light snow was falling on them. It was almost like fairy dust was falling. Blake was out there for something like fifteen minutes. And I'll never forget, Blake put his hand on Peter's shoulder and this beautiful moment happened between them.[44]

Blake returned to the table but wouldn't divulge what they had talked about except to say that Sellers was in a depressed state. They never saw each other again.

Following the death of Sellers, *Romance of the Pink Panther* was scrapped and the cast and crew, who had scheduled their working calendar, now had no job. Peter Mullins heard that Blake was shooting his latest picture in London, *Victor/Victoria*, and even though he had heard Blake was not too happy with him for accepting the Sellers *Panther* film, gave him a call. 'Hello Blake, it's Peter Mullins.'

'What can I do for you,' Blake answered blankly.

'I hear you're doing a picture in London,' said Mullins, hopefully.

'I've got somebody,' and with that Blake put the phone down.[45]

Who knows what may have happened if Sellers had gone on to make *Romance of the Pink Panther*. Surely it would have been another hit and prompted calls for more *Panther* films. 'If Peter had lived, I think we would have made another two or three,' claims Burt Kwouk. 'I think there was scope for more.'[46]

For Susan Wood, the passing of Peter Sellers left her with many years of memories, some good, some not so good. 'I really feel so privileged to have had that period of time with such an extraordinary talent.'[47] There were splendid meals in the best restaurants, staying in top hotels, and travelling the world, meeting extraordinary people. Sellers treated Susan well, although he did fire her several times, as he had done with his previous secretary Hattie Stevenson. She recalls:

> We were in Cyprus, Peter knew I was getting married. I flew back to England. Peter came, too, he was a witness at the

> wedding. He then went back to Cyprus and sent me a telegram firing me saying my loyalties would now be divided and he didn't feel that I would be able to do my job as well. And then a couple of weeks later he called me. I said, 'But you fired me.' And he said, 'You know I don't mean what I say.'[48]

This happened a few times, Sellers would fire Susan only to later change his mind. Susan walked out, too, a couple of times, but always came back.

Overall, Susan prefers to remember the good times. Like when she was in restaurants with Sellers and people would come up for autographs. 'He was very good with fans. And what he did like was, if we were walking down the street and say there were some builders on scaffolding and they'd shout down, hello Pete, he loved all that.'[49] If Sellers was in a good mood, and he was with a group of friends or in a social situation, he always enjoyed making everyone laugh. According to Susan:

> He really enjoyed making people happy. Which is so strange when you think what a depressed person he was. He couldn't make himself happy. His chauffeur and assistant, Bert Mortimer, used to say Peter was great until he remembered he'd brought himself with him. Peter couldn't be really Peter. He was much better as a character than he was as a person.[50]

Chapter 8

FLOGGING A DEAD PANTHER

Blake was in trouble. Pre-production had already started on his new film, *Victor/Victoria*, a musical comedy with Julie. But the company backing it, Lorimar, who had financed Blake's previous film *S.O.B*, was having serious financial problems and pulled out. Cue several days of frantic phone calls and meetings between Blake and various lawyers and producers. Finally MGM, who had recently purchased United Artists, agreed to take over the movie – but at a price. They wanted Blake to sign a two-picture deal and the second film after *Victor/Victoria* had to be a *Pink Panther*. Blake scratched his head, how was he going to make a *Pink Panther* film with no Peter Sellers as Clouseau, and so at first, he resisted the suggestion. In the end, with *Victor/Victoria* on the line, he had no choice but to accept.

Blake faced many late nights thinking about how to approach a *Panther* film without the man that was the most recognisable component of the franchise. The only choice left open to him was to recast the role, and he approached Dudley Moore. Blake and Dudley Moore had an interesting relationship. They first met in group therapy. Blake went to therapy over many years. At the time Blake was setting up the film *10* starring his wife Julie, and George Segal as a middle-aged man who becomes infatuated with a young woman that he has never met but keeps on seeing. Then, with mere weeks before shooting was due to start, Segal pulled out following an argument with the producers. According to Denise Crosby, then dating Blake's son Geoffrey, Blake bumped into Dudley in the hallway after therapy one day and a bell went off in his head. Blake had always liked Dudley as a performer and asked him to take over from Segal. The film was a huge hit and made Dudley's name in Hollywood.

So well did they work together on *10* that Blake wanted Dudley for his next project. This was to be called The Ferret, which Blake hoped would become a film series to rival the *Pink Panther*. The character Dudley was set to play was the long-lost son of a master spy, codenamed 'the ferret'. When this great spy dies, 'the ferret' moniker reverts to his son, who unfortunately turns out to be something of a bumbling idiot. Blake knew comparisons with Clouseau would be inevitable, but stressed that this film would be more of a suspense comedy than slapstick. Moore liked the concept and signed on to do a potential five 'ferret' pictures. Blake was positive that in Dudley he had found another comedy actor capable of improvising and bringing ideas to the table, in much the same way Sellers did. Perhaps this was a way for Blake to recapture those happy early days with Sellers. Unfortunately, the film was cancelled due to issues with the script and budget problems.

The opportunity to work again with Blake on the *Panther* film certainly appealed to Moore, the two had stayed friendly. The idea of stepping into Sellers' shoes and the comparisons that would be drawn, were rather less appealing; although no doubt the role of Clouseau would have been re-shaped by Blake to suit Moore's screen personality. MGM also wanted Moore to sign up to a potential series of five new *Panther* films. In no mood to be tied down in such a way Moore politely declined.

With no star, Blake decided that Peter Sellers would have to play the role of Clouseau after all. Or at least his ghost would. The idea was to concoct a new story around deleted footage from previous *Panther* films, along with some classic clips. The result is *The Trail of the Pink Panther*, a mongrel of a film if ever there was one. The early part of the film comprises of never-before-seen footage of Sellers as Clouseau, predominately from *Strikes Again*, a film that Blake cut twenty minutes out of prior to release. This footage consists mostly of Clouseau's trip to England, including being taken to the airport by François, Dreyfus' assistant, played by André Maranne in six *Panther* films. Predictably, Clouseau sets François' car on fire thanks to the vehicle's faulty cigarette lighter. In disguise as a mustard salesman from Dijon, for some reason with his leg in a cast, there is an amusing scene where Clouseau tries and fails to use the plane's small onboard toilet. This deleted footage of Sellers is a joy to see. It is when Clouseau disappears from the film that the whole enterprise flounders. It is almost as if Sellers himself perished midway through the shoot and the writers had to scramble a way of making the story make sense. The thin scenario baked up is that Clouseau has disappeared after once more being asked to investigate the disappearance of the famous Pink Panther diamond. An investigative reporter, played by Joanna Lumley, sets out to track him down and encounters both friends and foes from Clouseau's past, including a local crime boss, played by Robert Loggia, who had appeared as one of the heavies in *Revenge of the Pink Panther*.

Joanna's reporter arrives to interview Clouseau's former colleague, Hercule, played by Graham Stark, living out his retirement on a charming canal barge. It was a simple scene, but one that presented certain problems, as Stark explains.

> We were in Paris and I was on a barge by the river Seine. We rehearsed the scene. Suddenly three big Cadillacs arrived and out stepped Blake. He looked through the camera finder, and there was complete silence among the crew, and suddenly he said, 'How long has that been there?' And he's looking at the Eiffel Tower. And someone said, 'Quite some considerable time, guv'nor.' Blake said, 'Well in the script this is supposed to be a fucking backwater. How do I shoot with that thing in the frame? Pack up.' And the whole day was cancelled. We ended up parking the barge in Teddington, near London, and filming there.[1]

It is a director's prerogative to do this kind of thing, of course. Art director Alan Tomkins had found a perfect vineyard for one important scene set at the Clouseau ancestral home. It was located just outside Nice and looked down over a scenic valley. Because it was winter when they were shooting, and the vines were all bare, Tomkin's crew spent five days dressing the set with fake leaves and hanging fruit to make the field look like the height of summer. Blake arrived on the Saturday, looked around and his eyes fell on the opposite field and suggested this is where the shot should be. 'Of course, you never argue with a director of his standing and experience,' recalled Tomkins, 'but it doesn't mean you can't scream silently in your head!'[2] With work due to start on the Monday, the crew had to work all day Sunday to strike the original field, move it all in boxes to the other field, and dress the vines all over again.

The thing with Blake, he worked a lot on instinct. He didn't like to prep too much. One of the biggest elements of doing a movie is planning. Less so with Blake. He rarely went on a location scout for example. He would rely on other people and then he'd show up. Blake's production manager, Derek Kavanagh, was often driven crazy because he would scout these locations, get them ready, and then Blake would show up and say, 'I don't wanna be here.' Or he'd throw a fit and go back to the office. Someone would make him a cup of tea, he'd sit down, mull things over, discuss it, and then announce, 'I know how to make this work,' and everyone would follow him back to the set.

Blake relied a great deal on his talent and his creative spark. As Peter Mullins recalls. 'He would let you do what you wanted to do. You would show him a few photographs and say, we can do this, or we can do that, and he'd look at you and say, "Surprise me." And you'd leave the meeting thinking, which way do I go.'[3] One of the reasons why Blake never liked to see anything beforehand was because it pre-empted his thinking. 'I often wondered why I could never get him on a set to look at something,' ponders Mullins.

> I remember one time he was leaving the studio and on the next stage we had the next day's work, which was a nightclub, quite a large and important set. I said to him, 'Have you got a moment to spare?' And he said, 'Yeah, what do you want?' And I said, 'Well, the next set is right here. It's what we're shooting on tomorrow. Can you pop over and run through it with me?' He said, 'When are we shooting it?' I said, 'Tomorrow.' He said, 'Right, I'll look at it tomorrow.'[4]

Crews who worked with Blake had no choice but to put up with this erratic behaviour. Mullins again: 'We've been to countries and shot for two days and he'd say, "We're going." And I'd say, "We've got two week's work in this country. We've got all the hotels booked. We've paid the local crew." And Blake would say, "We're going."'[5]

Blake was keen for as many *Panther* regulars to appear in the film as possible; Stark, Burt Kwouk and Herbert Lom all return. David Niven also reprised his role of Sir Charles Lytton from the very first *Panther* film, along with Capucine. The scene was shot at Niven's villa in the south of France. Alan Tomkins recalled that Niven entertained the crew royally with a choice of different tea blends and continental pastries. Joanna Lumley easily fell for the veteran star's 'charm and humour'. But it was obvious that he was not well. In fact, the actor was gravely ill and putting on a brave show. Joanna recalls the on-set doctor prescribing him a cocktail of, 'very strong drugs', to get him through.[6]

Weeks before shooting Niven had written to Blake saying he might not be fit enough. He got a cable back: 'Learn your lines. Much love, Blake.'[7] The problem was, Niven's voice had gone. Henry Mancini had scored Niven's previous film, *Better Late Than Never* (1983), and saw that he was having trouble articulating and that his words were sometimes garbled and slurred. The composer could see in many scenes Niven was struggling. By the time Mancini came to work on *Trail* things had markedly deteriorated. Watching the film, it is sadly obvious that here was a dying man. Blake watched the scene in post-production and realised that Niven's voice was just too weak and that it was going to be impossible for the actor to come in and post sync his lines. Blake made the decision to bring in Canadian-American impressionist and voice artist Rich Little to dub him.

Trail is very much an origin story. We hear and see stories of Clouseau's youth, learn of his lifelong desire to be a policeman and his efforts in the French resistance during the Second World War. The young Clouseau is played by British actor Daniel Peacock and the offer came quite out of the blue. 'My agent phoned up and said they want you to play the young Clouseau. I went, "fuck, ok, brilliant." I can't believe it.'[8] Peacock had done a few bits on TV and film, including a role in the British film drama *Quadrophenia* (1979). Obviously, Blake or the casting director had seen him in something and thought he had the right look for the juvenile Clouseau because Peacock was not required to do a screen test or an interview. The next thing that happened was he found himself on a plane to Nice, staying in a plush hotel on the Riviera and working with Blake Edwards. 'It was kind of surreal.'[9]

Peacock was on the film for a week and found Blake, 'the kind of guy that lets the actor get on with what the actor does. I can't remember any direction from him at all apart from, Dan you sit there, look out of the window and look dramatic.'[10] His biggest scene was the blowing up of a bridge as a convoy of German troops cross over. Of course, Clouseau fouls up and the dynamite plunger does not work. Cursing, he wanders down to the bridge just as the plunger falls on its own accord and the bridge goes up. This was a big stunt and was shot back in the UK. The effects guys had built a safety box, camouflaged by a strategically placed bush, for Peacock to get in. The whole stunt was going to be shot in one take. Peacock recalls:

> The box was quite small, and I remember saying to the effects guy, 'Do you really want me to go in the box?' And he said, 'Yes, I really do want you to go into the box. Because if you don't go in the box bad things will happen.' But being a young man thinking you're immortal, what bad things could happen? This is a film. It's all effects and stunts. Anyway, as I was

> walking down towards the bridge I thought, I'd better do what I'm told and got in the box, shut the door and a couple of seconds later I heard – BANG! Then a year or so later when I saw it on the screen, I realised why he insisted I get in the box. It was a huge explosion.[11]

Peacock had a great time on the film and didn't even mind the fact that his voice was later dubbed. And while it may have been a small part, it was still playing Clouseau and Peacock ranks among a very small group of people to have played that character on screen. 'I was just amazed to be given the honour to be the young Clouseau and step momentarily into Mr Sellers' shoes.'[12]

Not only do we get to see the young Clouseau, we are also introduced to Clouseau senior, played by Richard Mulligan, who had come to prominence in the hit US TV comedy *Soap*. Mulligan had also starred in Blake's *S.O.B.* Denise Crosby recalls:

> During the making of that film, Richard was on Blake constantly about, 'Can I have my wardrobe. I love these suits. I love what I'm wearing. You'll let me have them, right.' Blake said, 'Absolutely, but Richard you'll have to wait until the end of the picture.' But Richard kept on and it was driving Blake nuts. So, at the end of the film Blake took all of Richard's suits and shortened them a few inches, the pant legs and the sleeves, and didn't say a word and gave them all to him.[13]

One of the challenges making *Trail* was matching up the old footage with the new. Peter Mullins sometimes found himself having to replicate an old set for the new linking material. 'It was quite tricky.'[14] Inevitably Joe Dunne was used a lot, such as linking shots of Clouseau walking down a street. Joe enjoyed working on the film, especially being in the company of David Niven. The veteran star asked for Joe to come to the set after he'd finished his last shot to specifically say goodbye.

Along with Joe and Peter Mullins, Blake had his usual crew with him. He always surrounded himself with his trusted lieutenants: Tony Adams as producer, Harry Frampton on makeup, sound guy Roy Charman and his trusted and long-time assistant Francine Taylor. It was a very tight knit group. 'Blake liked to work with people that he knew and trusted,' says Denise Crosby. 'And he liked having his family around.'[15] Because a lot of the same people working on the film had done the previous *Panthers*, making this one without Sellers produced a strange atmosphere on the set. And whenever something weird happened or there was an odd little incident Blake would go, 'That's Peter.' Cameraman Don E. FauntLeRoy worked on several movies with Blake in the '80s and remembers Blake kept cursing out Sellers when things went wrong on the set, blaming it on Sellers looking down on him.

Trail of the Pink Panther opened in December 1982 and met with a disastrous critical reception. The *Los Angeles Times* called it, 'A melancholy affair that makes us feel the loss of Sellers all over again.' *The New York Times* was more forgiving: '*The Trail of the Pink Panther* is less a conventional comedy than an uproarious retrospective devoted to the particular achievements of the Edwards-Sellers collaboration. Not all the material is terrific, but all the memories are fond.' The film stiffed at the box office.

Further ignominy was to fall on Blake. While Sellers' children had no objection to the deleted scenes and outtakes being used in *Trail*, Lynne Frederick had never been happy and in March 1985 took Blake and United Artists to the High Court in London claiming damages. It was her argument that Sellers, being the perfectionist that he was, never found those cut scenes funny or worthy of his talent and had always refused his consent for them to be used or seen by the public. 'I could never, ever let pieces of film of that quality go into a film meant to be a tribute to Peter,' Lynne told the press. 'He would have hated it.'[16] The actress revealed that she had seen *Trail* and far from regarding it as funny, regarded it as an insult to her late husband.

Blake and United Artists denied any wrongdoing, arguing against the fact that Sellers' contract for each *Panther* film implied that extracts could not be used from them without his permission. Indeed, their claim was that such a contract ended anyway upon the actor's death, and since they had copyright of the *Panther* movies were therefore not prohibited from using any material from them. In the end though the judge did not agree with them, ruling that the use of clips and discarded footage was unlawful and that Miss Frederick's permission was required. The actress attended almost every day of the nineteen-day hearing but was not in London to hear the verdict, that the Sellers estate would be awarded $1m in damages, along with a percentage of the film's profits. Blake would appeal the court's decision but in vain.

By then, of course, the next film in the *Panther* franchise had already come and gone and been swiftly forgotten. To cut costs, *Curse of the Pink*

Panther was filmed at the same time as *Trail*, using the same crew and many of the same actors. Joanna Lumley pops up in a completely different role, that of Countess Chandra, a rather dubious owner of a health clinic who in fact masterminded the theft of the Pink Panther diamond. In her interview for the role of Chandra, Blake was so impressed with Lumley that he wanted her to play the journalist in *Trail* as well.

Curse continues where *Trail* pretty much ended, with Clouseau still missing. What essentially Blake was attempting here was a *Panther* film without Clouseau/Sellers. What was the point? Since Clouseau/Sellers was surely the raison d'etre for the whole enterprise, it was like making a James Bond movie without 007. *Curse* was Blake's mission to breathe new life into the series with the introduction of a new main character. Blake had no intention of directing any future instalments, rather he would oversee them in an executive capacity and pass on the directorial chores to others.

In *Curse* the President of France himself steps into the case with a plan to hire the world's greatest detective to find Clouseau. This is bad news for Dreyfus, of course, who rather fancies the idea of Clouseau remaining on the missing list. The President's scheme is to feed a computer with files from Interpol on every police agency in the world. Dreyfus rigs the computer so instead of coming up with the best detective, it chooses the worst – a certain New York police officer, Sergeant Clifton Sleigh, who is just as much of a buffoon as Clouseau.

A very long list of candidates to play Clifton Sleigh was put together. One of Blake's choices was Richard Mulligan from *S O.B*. However, Mulligan had been contracted to open in a Broadway play and so had to back out. Unfortunately, the play in question soon closed, and so Mulligan could have been available for the lead, instead of the small part he ended up with in *Trail*.

On that list was American actor Ted Wass, who had made his television debut on the US comedy show *Soap*, gone on to make a few TV movies, starred in two Broadway musicals and was now keen to make the move into features. Blake and Julie were big fans of *Soap*, which had just been cancelled. One afternoon Ted got a call from his manager. 'Don't ask how we did this, ok, but we got you a meeting with Blake Edwards. He's doing a new *Pink Panther* movie and everybody in town is trying to get this part. Go in there and listen to him, make a good impression, and see what happens.'[17]

Ted arrived at Blake's office, and someone was already inside having a meeting and making Blake laugh every time he opened his mouth. Ted thought he had no chance. 'I'm pretty much shaking outside, thinking about going into that room. The door opens and Martin Mull walks out. He looks over at me like, no chance kid.'[18] Ted is ushered inside. There's no one else in the room except Blake. He's all smiles and makes the young actor feel relaxed and comfortable. He then pitches what the movie is about, going through the whole story.

> After about seven or eight minutes I'm thinking, I wonder if there is anything in this movie for me, I don't get the drift at all. He finishes and turns to me and says, 'I think this will be a great role for you. Will you do it?' And my instant reaction was, of course I will do it. Sure.'[19] Blake shifts awkwardly in his chair. 'You know,' he says. 'I'll be honest with you. I wish I could get Dudley. But I made Dudley a big star and now I can't get him on the phone. He's booked for the next ten years. But they're going to give me who I want. We'll be in touch.[20]

Ted left and went home. His manager called to see how it went. 'Blake offered me the part.' There is a pause. 'He did not. It's Chevy Chase, Richard Pryor. Everybody wants this part. He did not offer you the part.' Ted said, 'Ok.'[21]

The next day Ted received another call to go and see Blake.

> I run over to his office in Century City. I go in. He says, 'Heh Ted, thanks so much for coming back. You see those glasses on that table over there.' I go, 'Yeah.' He says, 'Put 'em on.' I put the glasses on and he starts laughing. 'They look so funny.' He calls for Tony Adams, 'Come in here, come in here.' Tony comes running in. Blake says, 'Look at Ted.' Tony starts laughing. Everybody's laughing. Then Blake goes, 'Ok, great, thanks for coming back. Leave the glasses on the table. You'll be hearing from us.'[22]

Ted left none the wiser. 'Eight days later I got a call from my agent who said, "MGM/UA called and offered you a six-picture deal to star in the next six *Pink Panther* movies." Amazing.'[23]

When Ted signed on to do *Curse of the Pink Panther* he didn't know very much about the part he was going to be playing. There was no script yet. Blake had gone to Gstaad and from time-to-time Ted's fax machine would ring and he would get two or three pages of script.

> I read some of it and I'd think, oh, this is good, then I'd read some more and go, Peter already did this. That's already been in a *Pink Panther* movie. Blake gave me his number in Gstaad and I was trying to call him and Julie's mother always seemed to answer the phone. She didn't know who I was, she just thought I was some horrible American kid. She'd go, 'Leave Blake alone for God's sake, don't call,' and hang up the phone. I'd go, 'No, I need to talk to him about the pages, I'm sorry…' Click.[24]

Blake came back to LA to attend William Holden's funeral and Ted saw a chance to voice his concerns. All Blake said was, 'It's going to be great! All you need to do is pick out what colour Rolls Royce you want.'[25]

Ted never really got a complete script. Harold Lloyd's name came up a lot, that was the glasses thing, and obviously the silent comedy star was a model for the kind of character Blake and his son Geoffrey, who co-wrote the script, had in mind. Ted loved Clifton Sleigh's backstory, that he came from a long line of highly decorated police officers. 'And he was the next heir in the family and they would have been much more appreciative if he had not gone into law enforcement.'[26] For Ted not enough was made of that in the film. On the page he felt that the character was something of, 'a cipher,'[27] and in some of his scenes didn't have much to do. Ted kept wanting Blake to help him out, furnish a bit of information. 'And that wasn't always forthcoming.'[28]

On one of Ted's first days at Pinewood he went to see Harry Frampton who had done all those silly Clouseau disguises and makeup. He sat down in the makeup chair and lining the shelves in Frampton's makeup room were life-size wax heads of Sellers, thirty of them. Most of them were intended for the scene where Clifton Sleigh goes to Clouseau's apartment to look for clues, only Cato has turned it into the Clouseau memoriam museum. Sleigh breaks in and comes face to face with life-size replicas of Clouseau's greatest disguises.

> And I remember saying to Blake, 'We sure we want to do this. You want me standing eye to eye with him. I have such respect for Peter's genius in the part. These are colossal comedic

> treasures, his disguises, I'm just starting and I'm feeling a little like, maybe film three something like this when I've got more of the character underneath me.' It was daunting.[29]

When Ted first agreed to make *Curse* he knew what an amazing opportunity it was, but also how much of a big deal it was. 'I'm not just playing my first lead role in a feature film, I'm playing a lead role for Blake Edwards in the most successful comedy film series ever made.'[30] Ted's first work on the picture was in the South of France. Robert Wagner, returning as the nephew character he played in the original movie, drives him up to a splendid yacht in the harbour to meet with Niven's Sir Charles Lytton. Sitting in a Ferrari convertible with Bob Wagner, about to act his first scene with David Niven, Ted was tense and nervous. By comparison Wagner was charm and kindness personified, talking about sports and families, everything but the job in hand, all of which had the effect of totally relaxing Ted.

Playing those scenes with Niven were one of Ted's truly cherished memories, having been a fan of the veteran star for years. 'And he was charming. He was almost like what an American might imagine royalty would be like. He was exquisite.'[31] They would be working and then Niven would start to struggle with the words.

> And he was so self-conscious about it, and he would privately say to me, 'Why did Blake make me do this. I told him I wasn't well. I wish I wasn't doing this.' And then he would apologise to me, profusely. And I said, 'David, please, it's an honour to be on a set with you. I adore you. You have nothing to apologise to me about.[32]

Despite only appearing in a couple of scenes Blake gave Niven top billing in *Curse*, in what turned out to be the last film he ever made. There are several other returns, such as Herbert Lom and Burt Kwouk, a cameo from Graham Stark as a waiter, and Harvey Korman as Auguste Balls.

Also back is Robert Loggia's crime boss. Understandably concerned that if Clouseau is found his criminal empire will suffer, he arranges to have Clifton Sleigh assassinated before he finds the truth. Playing Loggia's moll girlfriend was Denise Crosby who already had a very special relationship with Blake. Denise had appeared in *10* in alternate versions of scenes that Blake shot to accommodate eventual network television screenings. Denise was just getting started in the business and Geoffrey introduced her to his father. The two had a connection; back in 1960 Blake had directed Denise's grandfather, Bing Crosby, in the film *High Time*. Blake had lots of stories about Bing and he and Denise hit it off. Denise ended up marrying Geoffrey in 1983 and Blake became her father-in-law.

> And he became very much a father figure. I never knew my father and so he really stepped into that place for me. Blake was so well versed in so many things, a consummate artist, he would paint and sculpt, he had exquisite taste. I welcomed his opinion. I would cherish his opinion.[33]

Denise became part of the Edwards clan, spending a lot of time at Blake and Julie's Malibu home.

> Blake would have these Sunday get togethers, screen a movie and have a dinner. And all the family would come. And you never knew who was coming through the door on a Sunday, people like Sean Connery, Jack Lemmon was a regular, Carrie Fisher, Stephanie Powers, Bob Wagner was there often. Blake and Julie were great hosts.[34]

On location in Nice, Denise was given carte blanche with the costume designer to come up with the look of her character. 'We were shopping at these fabulous little boutiques. We just tried on some stuff, the campier and more outrageous the better.'[35] Blake, as we know, was that kind of director, happy for the actor to give his input and come up with ideas. According to Denise:

> He was fantastic. He always was willing to try anything. He was spontaneous. He could change his mind in a heartbeat if he suddenly came up with an idea, some inspiration. Blake had been an actor for many years before directing so he understood the personality and what actors respond to and how they need to be spoken with.[36]

All Denise's scenes were played opposite Robert Loggia, a highly experienced actor, and although Denise was to have a successful career, notably playing the recurring role of Tasha Yar in television's *Star Trek: The Next Generation*, here she was something of a novice. 'Robert was so generous and kind to me. He was patient and made me feel at ease and comfortable. I mean, you're in this lingerie and you hop into bed with this guy, it could be awkward, but he made it very, very safe and fun.'[37]

Not so much fun was the intense security that surrounded one of the members of the cast. For some reason Blake had cast in the role of a Paris TV reporter Patti Davis, the actress daughter of Ronald Reagan, then the incumbent president. 'There were all kinds of secret service detailed in and around the hotel we were staying in,' Denise recalls.[38] It did not help that just days before the *Panther* company arrived in Paris to do some location shooting, there had been a car bombing close to the hotel the cast were staying at.

> It was really a heightened urgency going on, and Geoff and I were on the same floor of the hotel as Patti was and we asked to be switched to a different floor because whenever we walked out of our room it was just wall to wall guys in black suits. We thought, if something's going to happen, it's going to happen on this floor.[39]

Even going out for a meal turned into a James Bond-like affair recalls actress Leslie Ash:

> You'd get a message saying: can you be down in the hotel foyer at half past seven. Blake would like you to join him for dinner. So, you'd be down there all dressed up to the nines and suddenly all these secret service men would come buzzing around. Then we all went into cars and I was in the same car as Patti and there were about six cars around our car. We went into the restaurant and it looked quite busy but, on each table, there was a guy talking up his sleeve. Patti said to me that she wanted to go for a run the next morning and was going to try and give the slip to these secret service men. She told me that her life was just like being in a cage.[40]

Leslie was just 22 years old at the time, an up-and-coming actress who came to prominence in *Quadrophenia*. It was her agent who put her name up for *Curse*. 'I grew up on the *Pink Panther* films,' says Leslie. 'And I was a massive fan of Peter Sellers. I just loved all his films, that was my type of humour. One of my ambitions was to be in a *Pink Panther* film.'[41]

She went to see Blake at Pinewood. 'I had short blonde hair at the time. And because I was a model for so many years, I had a wacky dress sense and I think that's what he really liked.'[42] For Leslie, working on *Curse* was her first taste of big budget movie making.

> In *Quadrophenia* we were all huddled together trying to keep warm in doorways, not a Winnebago in sight, not a stand-in in sight. And then a few years later here I am sitting on the set in the South of France, a chair with my name on it, and sharing a Winnebago, but nevertheless I got a Winnebago. On my first day, going into makeup in this studio just outside Nice, walking in and seeing David Niven sitting there, I almost passed out.[43]

Not Just Niven, there was Bob Wagner, too.

> I could sit and listen to his stories all day. He was a bit of a sex symbol, so when I got a call, what are you doing tonight, I thought, oh my God, he's going to ask me out. Instead, he said, 'I need someone to watch my daughter while I go out to dinner with Blake.'[44]

Leslie was amused to find out that one of her co-stars from *Quadrophenia* was in the film, Michael Elphick, in the unlikely role of a chief of police in some scenes that were set in Spain. At his interview Blake thought Elphick looked Spanish and cast him in the part. 'There I was,' Elphick recalled, 'flying down to Spain in this pink jet called Panther 1 with Blake's wife Julie Andrews. Me and Mary Poppins. I thought, this isn't real.'[45] Leslie recalled Elphick spent most of his spare time on the film in local bars.

Julie Andrews was often around. She was on location over Easter and put large chocolate eggs in everyone's hotel room. 'Blake told me,' Leslie recalls, 'that when he got to the hotel, he'd be taking all his clothes out of the suitcase and she'd put little notes and messages in, I love you and all that. The relationship between the two of them was so lovely.'[46]

As for Blake, Leslie enjoyed his sense of humour. 'He could make you laugh so much.'[47] And while it did feel a little superficial at times, that the crew would all laugh at Blake's jokes, nevertheless for Leslie it was lovely to be a part of. 'Blake was adorable.'[48] This is what Denise liked best about working on *Curse*, the fun atmosphere that Blake created on the set.

> You're not going to get this screaming yelling maniac director. You're not going to get this moody director where you don't know how to approach him, what mood is he going to be in today. Blake didn't tolerate that. It was, I come to have as much fun as anyone.[49]

For Leslie, her most complicated scene involved a street brawl with some baddies. The actress undertook several months of martial arts coaching in preparedness, although much of what she had been taught ended up not being used, to Leslie's disappointment. Still, the fight is decent enough and well-choregraphed. 'This one stunt guy, in the scene I had to punch him in the jaw, and he said, 'Go on then, just do it. Just hit me, go on, do it.' So, I really hit him and he went, 'Oh Christ, not that bloody hard.'[50] The scene includes an appearance by Ed Parker, a renowned American martial artist who had appeared as an assassin in *Revenge of the Pink Panther*. Given Blake's interest in martial arts, Parker was someone he knew and learnt from. Parker's most famous pupil was Elvis Presley, and he also served as one of the singer's bodyguards towards the end of his life.

The atmosphere on set was good for the most part. The crew were happy, and there was a positive vibe going round among them that maybe this was the start of another ten years or so of making *Panther* films. Ted Wass heard horror stories from the crew about Sellers and his various antics. 'They would say to me, it's so nice that you're always here, and I was like, yeah, that's kind of my job.'[51]

The crew were deferential to Blake. 'You didn't hurry Blake. You worked at Blake's pace,' says property master John Allenby.[52] When everything was ready to shoot Blake invariably made his way down. Beforehand there would be calls of, 'Where's Blake.' Then, 'Blake's coming. Blake's here,' and everyone would congregate. Ted, whose memories of his time on the set appear to contradict those of Leslie and Denise, remembers that:

> On more than one occasion I saw Blake walk to a set and he'd look around, and he'd turn around and he'd walk out. I'd go, 'Where's Blake going? Are we going to shoot?' They'd go, 'We don't know what's happening.' Blake would get in his Rolls Royce and he'd drive to where his private plane was and he'd fly to Gstaad for four or five days and we'd all be sitting there. And they'd send me out with the second unit and we'd do some crazy shit like hanging me from a parachute or

> something. And everyone would be going, 'Where's Blake? Is Blake coming back?' What happened was he saw things he was unhappy with and stormed out.[53]

For Ted, filming in the South of France was a great adventure, and working at Pinewood, too. But inside him remained nagging doubts: is this working? And from Blake it was always, 'Don't worry kid. Just pick out your Rolls Royce colour. It's going to be great.' Going into dailies, the crew seemed to be enjoying it, but for Ted his character wasn't making an impression in any of the scenes he was in, just recreating the physical comedy antics of the Sellers' *Panthers*. 'And I just felt like I didn't have the opportunity in some way to really truly establish the character that I wanted to play.'[54]

Leslie Ash picked up on this creative conflict going on between Ted and Blake. 'Ted would complain continuously about, I don't want to do that scene like that. He didn't really want to do it like Peter Sellers, and I think Blake might have been trying to make him fill Sellers' shoes.'[55]

It was a shame, because Ted came into the movie with the highest respect for Blake. This was a man capable of making films as diverse as *Days of Wine and Roses* and *The Great Race*. 'Who has that cinematic range. Only the greats had that.'[56] Ted saw glimpses of that creative spirit sometimes on the set, when Blake would be energised, enthused, excited, and Ted would have happily done anything for him. Sadly, it wasn't there enough and Ted wondered why. What Ted ended up being told was that Blake still harboured deep bitterness over the way he was treated over the *Romance of the Pink Panther*, that the studio decided to side with Sellers and leave him out of the project.

> And when Sellers died, they went back to Blake and said, heh, would you like to make one for us now, and he went, sure, I'll fucking make you a *Pink Panther* movie, you bastards. That was the climate of that movie. I felt like there was a conflict in Blake where he was wanting to be there because he created it, he was genius at it, and he wanted to do it all again and basically give the finger to MGM/UA and say, you might want to rethink the way you do things in the future because I was the one that made this great – not him. And he wanted to make it for those reasons, but I don't know if creatively his heart and spirit were in it.[57]

While not nearly as bad as its reputation may suggest, *Curse of the Pink Panther* is still a pale imitation of its illustrious predecessors. Even a cameo from the then incumbent James Bond, Roger Moore, cannot save it. The film ends with Clouseau undergoing plastic surgery to give him a new identity and a new life. This turns out to be Roger Moore, doing a not terribly convincing Clouseau impersonation. Moore had a house in Gstaad and knew Blake well. He had also been a good friend of Sellers. Over dinner one evening, Moore did a Clouseau impression and Blake suggested he be in the movie. 'Roger was like Niven, a gentleman,' says Ted. 'And he was nothing but kind and generous to me. And so funny. And then he put a fucking ice bucket on his head and was doing a bad Sellers. These are glorious memories for me.'[58] Ted thinks Moore worked on the picture for two days. 'I made an off-colour joke. At one point he said, "Aren't we finished with this yet?" and I said, "They're still loading your fee into the trucks, Roger." I remember he looked at me a little funny. I had a great time with him. I adored him.'[59]

Curse features some amusing comedy set pieces, Herbert Lom, as always, is pitch perfect as Dreyfus, and there is some good physical action, including a decent comedy car chase where Sleigh takes a cab and is set upon by gun-wielding baddies. Playing the taxi driver was American actor William Hootkins, one of those familiar faces that turn up all the time in movies; he's in *Raiders of the Lost Ark*, Tim Burton's *Batman*, *Star Wars* et al. Leslie Ash was having breakfast with him on the day they shot the car chase. 'Bill told me, "I'm so nervous," and I said why, and he said, "I can't drive." He had to get somebody to give him a crash course quickly before he walked on set.'[60]

For Ted, some of the aspects of the film work, his scenes with Leslie Ash, he recalls fondly. 'But there are unfortunately long stretches of it that feel like an ode to a different time.'[61] Maybe too much of the thinking was stuck in the past, placing Clifton Sleigh into all the same predicaments that were successful before, like annoying Dreyfus, having silly disguises, fighting Cato etc. According to Ted:

> The concept was, 'let's get this guy, we'll put him in this film and then the sheer fact of the weight of the *Pink Panther* world that's around him will make this work. And I believe that maybe that was not the best idea. I think the best idea would have been to have had just a flavour of the *Pink Panther* movies.[62]

The fact that both *Trail* and *Curse* were shot concurrently didn't help much either. There would be times when Ted sat around for maybe three days while the cast went off to work on scenes in *Trail*. 'It was a split focus.'[63]

Curse of the Pink Panther was another box office flop when it opened in the States in the summer of 1983. The critics were not overly fond of it. Philip French in the *Observer* called the film, 'A further act of tomb-robbing.' Janet Maslin in *The New York Times* wrote that the film itself was, 'not unfunny, and not really an offence to the memory of inspector Clouseau, it's merely a movie with very little reason to exist.'

According to Julie Andrews, Blake regretted having agreed to do *Trail* and *Curse*, feeling that at that point in his career, approaching his sixties, he ought to be focusing on other more personal and challenging projects. 'Blake was not in a good mood on those films,' is the personal recollection production designer Peter Mullins, 'it was a real mess.'[64] The whole thing was made worse by the media backlash, with some accusing the director of exploitation and disrespect, making the two films on the back of a corpse.

In any case, the failure of *Curse* put paid to any further instalments of New York police sergeant Clifton Sleigh, and perhaps even signalled the end of the *Pink Panther* movie franchise.

Blake blamed the film's commercial failure squarely on MGM/UA, saying they violated a verbal agreement to spend $3.5m on publicity. Blake took his umbrage to court, suing the studio for a staggering $180m. MGM/UA thought, well two can play at that game, and promptly countersued Blake for $340m, alleging that he had overspent and squandered large sums of money on unnecessary expensive items while making *Victor/Victoria* and the two recent *Panthers*. During filming on *Trail/Curse* there had been financial issues. Ted recalls that work in the South of France was shut down for several days. 'These studio executives flew over from the States and there was a serious pow wow going on where they were thinking about shutting down the film. That was the story going round the set.'[65]

Angry that his name and reputation was being dragged through the mud, Blake countersued on the grounds that MGM/UA had libelled him. This was getting ridiculous and very expensive. 'It was hugely stressful,' said Julie, 'and we spent a good deal of time that year meeting with our lawyers.'[66] Everything was eventually settled out of court. 'But the experience took its toll on Blake emotionally,' confirmed Julie.[67]

Even before the picture came out and wasn't successful, Ted knew it hadn't worked and that an opportunity had not been realised. Even so, he was looking for contact with Blake. 'I would call and he wouldn't return my calls. It just makes me sad to think back on it.'[68] Ted never spoke to or saw Blake again. 'But my esteem for him is still at an all-time high.'[69]

Chapter 9

THE ITALIAN CLOUSEAU

It was another ten years before Blake Edwards brought the *Pink Panther* series back to the screen. He had tried to move on, making other films, quite a few in fact; Blake was nothing if not prolific, making almost forty features during his career, along with various TV series. All his new films were comedy-based, such as *The Man Who Loved Women* (1983), starring Burt Reynolds as a womanising sculptor going through a mid-life crisis, *Micki & Maude* (1984) with Dudley Moore, the apparently autobiographical *That's Life* (1986) with Jack Lemmon and Julie Andrews, shot at Blake and Julie's Malibu home, *Blind Date* (1987), which paired Bruce Willis with the wild Kim Basinger, and *Sunset* (1988), a portrait of silent movies and a lost Hollywood starring Bruce Willis and James Garner.

It is no surprise that Blake tended to make films of a comedic nature, he was so inherently funny himself. 'Nobody loved a joke more than Blake did,' says Denise Crosby. 'The family were constantly trying to crack each other up, the kids and Blake, outdoing each other with jokes and pranks.'[1]

Denise once asked him, because he did such an extraordinary job with the searing drama *Days of Wine and Roses* back in 1962, why he didn't make dramas like that anymore. And he said, 'It's just too heavy. I would rather enjoy the spirt of comedies and the fun of making comedies.'[2]

On his sets Blake still liked to retain an atmosphere of fun and good nature. He liked to live well and didn't see why he couldn't live well making movies, too; going to nice locations and staying in the best hotels. Cameraman Don E. FauntLeRoy worked on some of Blake's later films and thoroughly enjoyed the experience. 'Blake liked to have a good time. He'd do exactly what he wanted.'[3] Don worked on *The Man Who Loved Women* and recalls doing a week of night work in Los Angeles. 'And Blake and Burt Reynolds didn't like night work. We had 6.30pm calls. Blake would wrap about 9.30pm and we'd go home.'[4] Don recalls that Blake bought four new cars that week. 'We were shooting on Rodeo Drive and there was a luxury car dealership nearby and Blake would disappear. He'd give us a set up and we'd start lighting and he'd disappear and then he'd pull up in a brand-new Porsche or a Bentley. It was crazy.'[5]

Blake loved his gadgets, too. He was one of the first people to get a phone in his car. One afternoon he was driving in his Rolls-Royce Corniche and pulled up alongside a friend, scriptwriter Tom Waldman, at some lights. They both happened to be on their phone. Waldman motioned to Blake, heh, we've both got car phones. Blake picked up a second phone.

Blake's fondness for pulling practical jokes and pranks on his sets never faded either, according to Mathew Dunne. 'In *Micki & Maude*, there's a scene where Dudley Moore is packing a suitcase and goes into his closet to get some clothes and Blake had the prop guy dress up in a white gorilla suit standing in the closet.'[6]

One of the all-time great Blake pranks happened when he had an office at Culver Studios, over in Culver City, Los Angeles. The studios had a set of four bungalows, dating back to the 1920s and '30s, that used to be occupied by writers and actors; one was occupied by Clark Gable and Vivien Leigh during the making of *Gone with The Wind*. In more recent years they were used as production offices. Blake had been there for years, while other bungalows were rented out from time to time to the likes of Michael Jackson and Francis Ford Coppola. Producer Jeffrey Auerbach worked there for Blake, alongside Tony Adams, and in 1990 the bungalow next to theirs was rented out by the production team for the film *City Slickers*. And soon an incredibly realistic model of a cow appeared, tied to the front of the building, so that Billy Crystal and the other actors could practice cowboy lassoing. Jeffrey recalls:

> One morning there were twenty people standing around this cow, scratching their heads, trying to figure out, what the fuck, because there's a mound of cow shit under this cow. Funny joke. Funny joke. Next day, the cow shit is back. They were going, come on, what's going on. Five days go by and I'm having lunch with Blake and Tony Adams and Blake says, 'So, you like the cow shit thing.' He hired somebody to come in at two in the morning and put the cow shit under the cow on the lot. That's total Blake.[7]

Jeffrey worked for Blake from around 1989 to 1993 and loved every minute of it. Today he realises what a privilege it was. To Jeffrey, Blake was, 'a legend' of the industry. Somebody who was real Hollywood, who had literally grown up in the film business but operated outside the system and wasn't afraid to ruffle a few feathers. He was a maverick. At first, Jeffrey was a little in awe of Blake, but the director quickly put him at ease. A lot of people were intimidated by Blake. 'There was something about Blake that scared them,' says Jeffrey. 'He'd always wear these tinted or dark glasses with the executives. It was hysterical. Whenever executives were around, he'd wear the glasses.'[8]

Working for Blake, Jeffrey never really knew what to expect next, who was going to walk into the office or who was going to be there at lunch.

> I remember I was in my office and Blake called and said, 'What are you doing?' I said, 'Working, what do you think I'm doing.' He said, 'Come on in, I'm having a meeting with Raquel Welch, I want you to be in on it.' This kind of thing was a daily occurrence with him. Or he'd get crazy ideas. I was sitting in my office and he walked in and threw a copy of *Playboy* on my desk with these two blonde twins on the cover. And he says, 'I'm thinking of doing "20."' Four days later he says, 'Come over to the office.' I walk in and the two Playboy twins are sitting there. That's how Blake rolled.[9]

Jeffrey got to know Blake so well that he figured out which Blake was going to show up at the office, personality-wise, based on the car he chose to drive in that morning.

> If he took the black turbo Bentley he was in a really good mood. If he took the black Porsche – watch out. If he took Julie's car, which he did sometimes, which was a black four-seat Mercedes-Coupe, it was undecided, he didn't know; see how the day goes.[10]

Jeffrey spent a lot of his working day with Tony Adams and the two became instant friends. 'We had an unspoken trust and loyalty.'[11] Jeffrey saw how important Adams was to Julie and Blake, 'Tony was part of the family. He and Blake were like father and son. Tony was Blake's fixer, he was Blake's henchman, in a good way, and he was Blake's protector.'[12]

Proof of the esteem with which Blake held Adams, and his importance within his company, Blake made him the producer on the film *10*, after his role as associate and executive producer on the 1970s *Panther* films. After *10*, Adams produced all of Blake's movies, a position he was to undertake on the new *Panther* film, which had been bubbling away for several years, despite a less than enthusiastic response from the studio.

In truth, most of Blake's post *Curse* films had not been successful, only *Blind Date* was a commercial hit, despite lousy reviews. Maybe Blake saw in *Panther* one last shot at the big time before he packed it in. Blake was now approaching his 70s, getting tired of the business and feeling his age.

The plan was to introduce another new character that hopefully the public would accept and respond to in a vastly more positive way than they had Ted Wass' unrealised Clifton Sleigh. The plot has something to do with the kidnaping of a Middle Eastern princess by terrorists, but really the film is centred around Jacques Gambrelli, the illegitimate son of inspector Clouseau and a lowly gendarme.

As co-owner of the *Panther* franchise rights with MGM, Blake did eventually receive positive encouragement about the project; the artist and the studio's propensity to sue each other obviously forgotten and forgiven, this was business. That was until the studio was bought in 1990 by Italian financier Giancarlo Parretti. The new regime not only stymied production on any new *Panther* film but prohibited Blake from looking elsewhere for funding. Blake filed a $25 million lawsuit for breach of contract. Meanwhile Parretti was in trouble, financial storm clouds were gathering over MGM and cheques started bouncing. When the Italian was ousted after just two years in charge, a new financial structure was put in place and Blake's *Panther* was back on.

Blake's original choice to play Jacques Gambrelli was Gérard Depardieu. The French star was approached and according to producer Tony Adams, 'was very interested, but the project wasn't ready, and his schedule changed.'[13]. Instead, Blake drew up a list of numerous British and American comedy actors. According to press reports Kevin Kline was attached for a while. A fan of the series and Blake's work, after reading the script he wisely withdrew. Kline would later play Dreyfus in the 2006 Steve Martin remake. Rowan Atkinson was also offered the part, but declined. Atkinson was a huge admirer of Sellers and the *Panther* films; in an episode of *Mr Bean* he pays homage by having a Pink Panther toy as a mascot on his desk during an exam.

Blake was certainly casting his net far and wide. Mathew Dunne, the son of stunt man Joe Dunne, was by then working in the film business and mentioned Hugh Laurie as a possibility but at the time he wasn't known internationally. Mathew was currently second assistant director on the Jack Ryan drama *Patriot Games*. 'Producer Tony Adams called me to sound out Harrison Ford to see if he would be interested in playing Clouseau's son. Harrison is actually a very funny guy and I mentioned it to him, but don't think for one moment he seriously considered it.'[14]

At the time a lawyer by the name of John Dellaverson, a partner in the law firm Loeb and Loeb and working out of Rome, was doing some legal work for Blake Edwards. Dellaverson also happened to represent Roberto Benigni. It was Tony Adams who first mentioned to Dellaverson the trouble they were having finding the right candidate for Clouseau's son. Dellaverson asked:

> Why didn't they consider Roberto. In my mind he resembled more of the Peter Sellers character. He was also a physical comedian, much more than, say, someone like Depardieu. And they said, 'Well, we've never heard of him.' I told them I would send over a few tapes.[15]

Roberto Benigni was a big comedy star in his homeland of Italy but pretty much unknown everywhere else, despite making a couple of Jim Jarmusch directed US independent movies, including 1986's *Down by Law*. Benigni's most recent film, *Johnny Stecchino*, a comedy in which he played a bus driver mistaken for a despised Mafia boss, was then one of the highest-grossing films of all-time in Italy.

Dellaverson heard back from Blake and Adams, they had talked to MGM, and yeah, they were interested now they had viewed some of his movies. 'Let's take a look at him.' Dellaverson put Benigni onto a flight to Los Angeles. 'And he met with Blake and Adams for breakfast and lunch and they liked him a lot.'[16] Things looked positive but there was hesitation from Benigni's side. For one thing there was the language barrier. 'Roberto's English was, let's say, marginal,' stresses Dellaverson.[17] Something else, too; Benigni liked to take personal creative control over what he did. Within the Italian film industry, he was insulated. He controlled the entire production. According to Dellaverson:

> People submitted things to him all the time, but he always took the same position which was, I'm not going to work for another director. I will direct myself and I'm going to write the stuff myself because I feel more comfortable. And that's what

> he did. I don't think he had ever acted in a picture, except for those Jim Jarmusch ones, that he didn't write and direct. So, his initial reaction was, I don't think I want to do this. But he had such a high regard for Blake that he said, OK.[18]

As a result of Benigni's involvement, Aurelio De Laurentiis, Dino's nephew and one of the most important distributors in Italy, paid $14m for the Italian-language distribution rights of *Son of the Pink Panther*. This accounted for more than half the budget. MGM provided the rest.

Along with the new names in the cast such as Robert Davi, who had recently played a Bond villain opposite Timothy Dalton in *Licence to Kill* (1989), the old crew were back for one last hurrah. We have Herbert Lom as Dreyfus, Burt Kwouk as Cato and Graham Stark as Auguste Balls. Blake hoped Elke Sommer would reprise her role as Maria Gambrelli, the character from *A Shot in The Dark* who turns out to be the mother of Jacques. 'I turned it down because you cannot replace Peter with another actor. I would not have been happy doing it. My heart didn't want to do it.'[19] Next, Blake and Benigni made a pilgrimage to the home of Sophia Loren to personally ask her to play Maria. While flattered, the legendary actress declined the offer. Blake ended up casting Claudia Cardinale, who had played the role of the princess in the original 1963 *Pink Panther*.

Principal photography began in June 1992 and once again Blake took his company to Nice, then on to Marseilles and Monte Carlo. In Nice, due to unforeseen circumstances, Blake was unable to stay at his favourite hotel. Instead, he was put up in the same hotel as the crew, still a very good hotel, but not up to his usual grand standards. The management gave Blake a suite on the top floor and the whole place was redecorated in time for a visit to the location by Julie Andrews. 'It was all stripped down,' recalls John Allenby, the prop master on the film. 'Fire proof carpets brought from London, new curtains and all the furniture, fittings, everything was brand spanking new. They spent a fortune on it.'[20] As prop master, it was Allenby and his team's job to get it all ready in time.

> We were waiting for Blake to turn up to give the ok on it. He came into this suite and looked around and he couldn't fault it. He only said one thing. On the big sofa there were these cushions that our set decorator had got, and Blake looked at these cushions and said, 'You'll have to change them, Julie won't like them.' That was all he could say.[21]

After five weeks in the South of France, the production relocated to Jordan to shoot a climactic battle sequence. The Royal Jordanian Army loaned fifty Special Forces paratroopers and two helicopters. The soldiers were not paid for their appearance. Six paratroopers who performed a rigorous helicopter jump were presented with video copies of *The Sound of Music*, signed by Julie. Production concluded at Pinewood studios.

The writing was on the wall very early regarding *Son of the Pink Panther* when MGM decided not to hold any press screenings. As with *Curse*, the hope had been to release more sequels with Benigni reprising his role as Gambrelli. During filming Benigni had endeared himself to the cast and crew. 'He was very easy going,' recalls production designer Peter Mullins. 'And Blake seemed to get on well with him.'[22] John Allenby liked Benigni, too. 'He was a smashing bloke, really nice. And I thought he played the part quite well.'[23] Benigni approached the part in a much more physical way than Sellers ever did. His is a much broader comedy performance, playing Gambrelli almost as a clown.

As usual it was up to the public to pass judgement on the new *Panther* and they stayed away in droves. The only country where the film performed well at the box office was Italy. And there was a very good reason for that, as John Dellaverson explains. 'In Italy pictures are dubbed, they're not subtitled, so Roberto basically rewrote the script and voiced himself in Italian. So, the movie went from being not funny at all in English to very funny in Italian.'[24]

Maybe in the end the language barrier proved to be an unsurmountable obstacle. As Dellaverson states:

> Roberto is revered as a comic genius with the Italian language. It's very hard to be funny in another language. Even if you're quite fluent, which he absolutely was not. And I don't think there was anyone there to make that bridge. Blake couldn't understand him well enough as an Italian comic and Roberto didn't know enough English to make it funny. You needed someone who understood his humour, what made him funny.[25]

The critics were equally ungenerous, such as this well-aimed punch to the solar plexus from the *LA Times*:

> Edwards actually sets the stage at the end for a sequel. Is there anybody out there who would want to see it? More to

> the point, would Edwards want to make it? His work here is so spiritless that the idea of his doing a sequel is positively harrowing. Either that or it's the best joke in the movie.

At least Benigni managed to escape the farrago relatively unscathed. In 1997 he wrote, directed, and starred in the comedy drama *Life Is Beautiful*, for which he won the Academy Award for Best Actor, the first for a foreign language performance since Sophia Loren's triumph with *Two Women* in 1960. Dellaverson:

> I don't know if there would have been a *Life Is Beautiful* for the world market if there had been no *Son of The Pink Panther*. In other words, Roberto started to think about making films with an international appeal. His Italian movies were completely Italian. They were very successful in Italy but not really elsewhere. But *Life Is Beautiful* was a massive hit all over the world.[26]

This was a sad end to the Blake Edwards/*Pink Panther* franchise. 'It was rubbish,' said Burt Kwouk, not holding back. 'Cato was only in it so they could say, 'Cato's in it!' It was part of the package. I did some stuff with Benigni, who's very inventive, but he got no direction.'[27] It appears that by this time even Blake had had enough, not just with the *Pink Panther*, but with making movies. 'Blake was a bit nonchalant about the whole film,' claims John Allenby. 'He wasn't really interested in it that much. He was leaving more stuff for his son Geoffrey to shoot.'[28] It is no surprise to learn that *Son of the Pink Panther* was the last film Blake Edwards directed. Poignantly, too, it was also the last film to be scored by Henry Mancini.

For the regulars on the crew, too, it was the end of a journey, the end of what had been a wild ride. Peter Mullins, production designer on six of the films:

> They were wonderful to work on. You didn't realise at the time how marvellous they were. At the time it was a job, and they were quite tough to do because Blake was charming and nice, but he could be difficult, and there were Peter's moods. So, there was tension. But they were great fun to do.[29]

Chapter 10

THE AMERICAN CLOUSEAU

After the dismal failure of *Son of the Pink Panther*, both artistically and commercially, eyebrows must have been raised when, in the late 1990s, rumours began to circulate that MGM/UA were preparing a reboot of the series. Some of the top comedy names in Hollywood were linked to the role of Clouseau, principally Robin Williams and Jim Carrey. Williams was a self-confessed fan of Sellers. 'For me, the most influential actor in film was Peter Sellers because of the *Pink Panther* but mainly because of *Dr Strangelove*.'[1] Jim Carrey, too, was a fan, watching and studying all of Sellers' movies as a young comedian.

It turned out that the *Pink Panther*'s comeback had much to do with the spectacular reboot of the Bond franchise with 1995's *GoldenEye*, after the series had been in production limbo for six years and commentators were saying Bond had been played out and didn't match the times. The man given the task of breathing new life into the *Pink Panther* was Ivan Reitman, who had a lot of comedy hits to his name like *Ghostbusters*, *Stripes*, and *Twins*.

In 1998, Michael Saltzman, a modestly successful young TV comedy writer/producer on sitcoms such as *Murphy Brown*, was approached by Jeff Kleeman, an executive at MGM/UA; both had been roommates at Yale and best man at each other's weddings. Kleeman had played a pivotal role in shepherding *GoldenEye* to success and the next Pierce Brosnan 007 films. The MGM/UA board looked around to see what was next, and the other most famous property they owned was the *Pink Panther*. And so it was a case of, let's do the *Pink Panther* for the new generation, as they did with Bond. With Reitman's team taking meetings with prospective writers, some of them top calibre, Kleeman got Michael included, knowing he was a big *Pink Panther* and Peter Sellers fan. 'I had no real film experience,' confesses Michael. 'So going in I thought it was a long shot.'[2]

To his surprise, Michael passed muster and was asked to go see Reitman.

> It was one of the most contentious meetings I've ever had. Ivan would say, how do you think the film should go, and every answer I gave seemed to be wrong. It was like he would ask, what colour do you think the sky should be in the movie and I said, blue, and he'd say, wrong. It should be green. And in my head, I was going, this meeting is not going well.[3]

The irony was that Michael was a fan of Reitman's work. Getting up to leave, Michael mentioned a *Time* magazine review of one of Reitman's early films, *Meatballs*, and expressed his thoughts on the unfairness of the critic's left-field comment that the relationship between the Bill Murray character and the teenage boy seemed homosexual in nature. 'You know. I always thought that, too,' said Reitman. 'I always said I'd tell you that if I met you,' went Michael and left.[4]

Driving home, Michael called his wife, admitting there was no way he was going to be working on the film. A second call came though, it was Kleeman. 'Heh, great news, Ivan really liked you and wants you to be the writer on this movie.'[5] Michael was stunned, unable to fathom anything from the meeting that transpired, other than that one comment, that was a positive take away.

Asked to come up with a rough outline, Michael took inspiration from his favourite *Panther* film, *Return of the Pink Panther*, which for him was always the most cohesive of the series, the most grounded. 'I like a world that feels real and Clouseau is the crazy aspect in it.'[6] Michael had the story take place in the fashion industry and the head villain was a clothes designer. It was to begin, like *Return*, with an exciting and elaborate jewel heist. Clouseau is brought in to investigate and falls in love with a supermodel. 'For me, the world of fashion was a fun thing to parody with Clouseau, putting this klutz into this very stylised, high-end world.'[7]

Michael's first draft ended up very beholden to the Sellers films. 'I wasn't mimicking it, but I was true to that character.'[8] The studio read it and was very excited. Reitman really liked it, too, but wanted to incorporate some of his own ideas and so he and Michael set about writing a second draft together.

> There were two big innovations or changes that Ivan wanted from my initial draft and that departed from the previous

> *Panther* mythology. He wanted the film to be an origin movie. He wanted a younger Clouseau, just starting out. I think that was because he saw this as a series of movies and he wanted to start at ground zero, he didn't want it to be beholden to the Clouseau that previously existed. And the second thing he was looking to do was finding a way to integrate the animated Pink Panther character into the movie.[9]

Michael and Reitman came up with an idea that was a cross between *Roger Rabbit* and the famous 1950 James Stewart comedy *Harvey*, so only Clouseau could see the Pink Panther, and there would be moments where the panther complicated things for Clouseau but also helped him out. 'Ivan was very excited about the draft,' Michael recalls, 'and his people were saying, I think he's going to want to direct it, not just produce it, which was big news.'[10]

While all this was going on thoughts turned to who should play Clouseau. Michael was pushing for an unknown like Sacha Baron Cohen, then grabbing a lot of attention in the UK as a rising comedy star. 'I thought you wanted someone who the audience wouldn't have a pre-conception of, someone who would simply identify as Clouseau.'[11] The studio was committed to a star and they approached Kevin Spacey, then a hot property after *American Beauty* (1999). He had also hosted TV's *Saturday Night Live*, revealing a little-known comedic side. Michael reveals:

> They approached Spacey who was very intrigued about doing it, but because MGM was so intent on helping their stock price they made the announcement that Spacey was attached to the movie prior to any negotiated agreement and Spacey was livid. He said, screw it, I'm not doing it. MGM were apoplectic about this and said, 'Look, we understand you are a big art collector and Sotheby's are having an art auction, here's the catalogue, pick any painting you want and it's yours. That's our way of apologising to you and making this right.' He said, 'Alright, people make mistakes. Ok, I think I'll take this one.' And they say, 'That one's a little too pricey. Can you choose another one.' So, he said, 'That's it, I'm out.'[12]

When it came time to hand in the script, the executives preferred Michael's first draft. 'And Ivan was very thrown by this because he thought we had the right version.'[13] A big meeting was called where Jeff Kleeman had the script notes from Frank Mancuso, the studio head. Michael recalls:

> Ivan is already not happy because he's got advance word about what the premise of the notes are. I'm sitting there with him and Jeff offers up the first of Mancuso's notes and Ivan's response is, 'If I can just stop you there. That is, without a doubt, the stupid fuckingest note I've ever heard in my life. Next.' And it went downhill from there. So, I'm watching, like a tennis match, as these notes are given and Ivan is dismissing them and hating them.[14]

After about a dozen or so of these notes Kleeman turned to Michael, 'Well, Michael, you've just been sitting there quietly, which script do you like better.' This put Michael in an impossible situation. He decided the diplomatic approach was best. He liked both versions, he said, which was true, and was happy with whatever the studio and Reitman decided. 'And Ivan gave me a look of complete contempt, that I didn't rush to his side and say I much preferred the second version.'[15]

The meeting broke up and what Michael later heard was that as soon as Reitman got into the elevator with his posse of assistants he started to bad mouth and eviscerate the top brass at MGM/UA. The problem was there were a couple of employees in the lift with him, and as soon as Reitman got out, they told their bosses, 'wait till you hear what Ivan was saying about you'. The next thing, Reitman was off the picture. As for Michael, he was asked to do another draft based on his first one. He got to work, finished it, and was told they were sending it out to top flight directors like Mike Nichols. Within days of this happening there was a big shake up at the studio and all the executives who loved Michael's script were moved on. Reitman was brought back onto the project and Michael was out in the cold; although he would eventually get a co-story credit.

One of the first things Reitman did on his return was bring in a new writer, Len Blum, who he had worked with before. Blum did a rewrite, changing the story from the world of fashion, due to the release in 2001 of another comedy film set in the fashion world, *Zoolander*, to that of football. Clouseau is assigned to solve the murder of a famous football coach and the theft of the Pink Panther diamond. Another reason for the football setting was to attract the interest of Mike Meyers, an avid Liverpool fan. Myers was big on Sellers, too, growing up watching his movies on TV, and was attached to the project for a while – that was until the release of his third Austin Powers film, *Goldmember* in 2002. MGM, who distributed the Bonds, took umbrage over the title, and threatened legal action. And Myers was like, 'wait a minute, so the company who I'm about to make a movie with is suing me. I'm not doing that.' So, Myers was out. Next to come into the reckoning was Chris Tucker, hot after the *Rush Hour* movies. That never went anywhere either. Then Reitman dropped out and things looked bleak.

That was until Steve Martin was asked to do the film. Martin was a huge admirer of sellers and had been a guest at the Hawaii junket and premiere for *Revenge of the Pink Panther*. At the time he was making the film *Cheaper by the Dozen* (2003) with a young director by the name of Shawn Levy. 'Steve came to me one day and said, "I'm thinking of playing Clouseau in a new *Pink Panther*, wanna do it with me?" I was so flattered and inspired, it didn't take long for me to say yes.'[16]

Not only was Martin stepping into the shoes of Sellers, Shawn had the awesome responsibility of taking over from Blake Edwards on what was a beloved franchise. But that didn't faze him at all.

> I was a much younger and dumber man then, and so I don't recall thinking any of this through very deeply. For me, the decision was Steve Martin-inspired, and Steve Martin-motivated. Here was a living legend, asking me to direct him in his unique incarnation of an iconic character, on a script that he was going to rewrite himself – I got to 'Yes' pretty quickly. I think it was later that I fully grasped the depth of cultural love for this franchise and the audacity it took for Steve and I to relaunch it. In retrospect, I'm grateful for the slight myopia, as the pressure of assuming that mantle might have been paralyzing.[17]

Just coming off *Cheaper by the Dozen*, Shawn and Martin were used to working together and quickly hunkered down on the script, devoted to making Martin's Clouseau – his own Clouseau – as funny and singular as possible. Both shared many lunches where they would talk about and pitch ideas back and forth, and the ones that made them laugh mostly went into the script.

> Certainly, the most memorable of these riffs was the accent-coaching scene. I remember Steve pitching me, 'Hey,

> what if Clouseau has to go on assignment to the US, and so he hires a dialect coach to downplay his accent?' Boom. I knew instantly that this was a great idea. A simple premise that Steve Martin could crush in. If I'd learned anything from Steve, it was that sometimes comedy relies on THE IDEA, the right pairing of comedic concept, with character, with performer. Thus, was born the 'I would like to buy a hamburger' scene – a scene that not only brought the house down with laughter, but which remains the single most quoted scene from that movie, something Steve and I still find as bizarre as it is satisfying.[18]

From the start, Shawn wanted a strong supporting cast. In the pivotal role of Dreyfus, Kevin Kline was his first choice. It was reported that Jackie Chan was considered for the part of Cato, though in the end the character was deemed to be politically incorrect and replaced by a new character called Ponton, Clouseau's assistant, much like Hercule was in *A Shot in the Dark*. Shawn cast Jean Reno. In the role of Xania, a pop star who gets mixed up in the caper, Shawn had years before produced and directed Beyonce in a Disney Channel show. She was the perfect choice. Shawn recalls spending a day in the recording studio with the singer:

> We had to lay down some original tracks for the movie, and seeing Beyonce run a recording session, where she is both the performer and de facto producer … well, that was like watching a superhero execute their superpowers. Pure genius, instant instincts, and decisive leadership: pure, singular, God-given talent.[19]

Looking back, Shawn's fondest memory from his *Panther* film is one of laughter:

> I remember laughing over lunches during the writing process, on set literally each and every day, and then throughout the editorial and post-production stage of the movie. The lessons I learned about comedy from Steve Martin inform my work to this very day, and I feel proud to have played a small part in the legacy of this iconic comedic franchise.[20]

The plan was to open the new *Panther* in the summer of 2005 and while Shawn was happy with the finished result, when he showed it to audiences there was something holding them back from fully embracing it.

> After talking to focus groups and reading their responses, we realised that the movie had a fair bit of double-entendre racy innuendo that made parents uncomfortable. And let's face it: one doesn't make a *Pink Panther* movie for a small niche adult audience. So, we used both editing and additional photography to tweak the tone of the movie and make it a more broadly appealing family comedy. When the movie went on to become a big hit, we knew we had made the right decision.[21]

The Pink Panther eventually opened in the US in February 2006 and while it received mostly negative reviews was a commercial success. Inevitably, talk turned to doing a sequel, again with Steve Martin. But this time without Shawn Levy as director. 'I had already committed to making *Night at The Museum* before *Pink Panther* came out. So, there was never the option of me directing the sequel, though it was certainly gratifying to see audiences embrace our movie, and Steve as Clouseau.'[22] Shawn ended up as executive producer on the sequel.

A search for a new director led to Dutch-Norwegian filmmaker Harald Zwart. By then the script and concept was pretty much finished. 'I met Steve and I did my pitch on it,' says Harald. 'He saw what I'd done and we hit it off really nicely.'[23] This time Clouseau teams up with a squad of international detectives to stop a thief who specialises in stealing historical artefacts. This dream team of detectives required actors who had that kind of class, like Andy Garcia and Alfred Molina, but not necessarily comedy actors. 'Comedy can also be approached by people just playing it really seriously,' says Harald. 'It's when people push it too far and they're trying to be funny it sometimes falls flat.'[24] With Clouseau as the fool, the others had to be more restrained in the face of his antics.

With Kevin Kline not returning as Dreyfus, his place at the French Sûreté was taken by John Cleese. 'I was such a massive fan of *Fawlty Towers* and *Monty Python*,' says Harald, 'and between every take, if we were changing the scene, and John and I would be sitting around, I would say, "Tell me again about *Fawlty Towers*."[25] He was an amazing and generous person.' For Harald, Cleese was the master of serious deadpan. 'I've always found that the best comedic reaction is exactly what John Cleese is so very very good at, that absolute deadpan, where you can still see the wheels turning even though there's nothing happening in the face.'[26] In one scene Cleese bangs his head on a wall in exasperation.

> He did the first take and I was there thinking, that must have hurt, even though it was a fake wall. We look at the playback and John looks at me and says, 'I can do better.' 'Ok,' I say. And on the second take he just really goes for it, and that's the one we used.[27]

Also making a cameo appearance was Lily Tomlin, who had co-starred back in 1984 with Martin on the comedy *All of Me*. 'I think that might have been Steve's idea,' says Harald. 'They wanted to do something together again. It was a lot of fun.'[28]

Most of the film was shot on location in Boston. 'We just had three days in Paris,' says Harald. 'We shot what we needed there and then we went to Boston and everything was shot in libraries, old mansions, things like that.'[29] Harald knew that Martin and Cleese were old friends, but what surprised him was that Martin was very good friends with Mick Jagger. 'And Mick happened to be in Boston and Steve and he decided to go to dinner and I was invited. So, I had dinner with Mick Jagger and Steve Martin which was absolutely surreal.'[30]

It was an enjoyable shoot, according to Harald, no histrionics from the cast, no prima donna behaviour.

> They were all so generous about their own time. And because they weren't all leads in every scene, so sometimes they were background in somebody else's scene, they were just hanging around having fun. And Steve was so professional and sweet. He really wanted to make it his own and not try to be a copy of Sellers.[31]

That was the challenge, too, for Harald, not to be too influenced by the previous films. 'I never really considered the legacy aspect or what they'd done before. I tried to make it something that I love and that I own, and I think I succeeded in that.'[32] Harald had seen all the *Panther* films in the past, but deliberately didn't go back and run them again.

> I just wanted to somehow go in and own the material as it was presented to me. I didn't want to do a homage because you can

> upset the fans if you're trying but not doing it the right way. I wanted to make a cinematic experience, not a sequence of references.[33]

The film does pay homage in certain ways, the animated opening titles are present in both Steve Martin films, as is the classic Henry Mancini theme. On both soundtracks the saxophone player Plas Johnson, who featured on that original recording back in 1963, was invited back to play. At the time, he was still doing concerts but not many sessions. 'I remember him showing up at my studio,' recalls composer Christophe Beck.

> We said hello and he asked, 'Where do I go?' I told him to sit on this chair. He pulls out his saxophone, he looks up at me expectantly, and it was like, all you had to do was point at him and he would start playing that theme and when he started playing it, it was like, wow, that is the sound. It was amazing. He hadn't missed a step, even though he was in his late 70s. To me it was magic. And when we did the sequel, it was an easy decision again to have him come back.[34]

Christophe had worked with Shawn Levy before and when he was asked to score the first *Panther* recalls that he, along with Shawn and Steve Martin, sat down and watched all the Sellers movies. 'And as a kid I used to watch the *Pink Panther* cartoon show all the time and that theme just kept burrowing into my DNA.'[35]

The intention was to use the theme as frequently as possible in the first *Panther*, and in a lot of different ways. 'But the rest of the score was an opportunity for me to play with those notes,' says Christophe.

> We knew we wanted to have fun with the theme and we knew we wanted to place it in the context of a more contemporary, mainstream Hollywood-comedy type score with a lot of nods to the nostalgia of the period where these characters originally come from. There would be moments when I would feel the weight of the legacy of this music and the greatness of its composer on my shoulders, but I just focused on what was in front of me. It's not my job to be as great as Henry Mancini. My job was to honour his legacy and to help tell the story in

> the best way that I can. If I got into a frame of mind where I let that pressure get to me it just makes my job so much harder.[36]

It was always contemplated, on both movies, that for the title sequence they would go with as faithful and loving a re-recording of the original theme as possible. Christoph recalls:

> That involved picking the right room to record it in, picking the right microphones and making sure our drummer brought in a vintage drum kit, all these things to recreate the magic of that theme as faithfully as possible. I remember literally getting shivers down my spine when we put up the microphones and rehearsed that first take. It was incredible.[37]

The Pink Panther 2 opened in the States and the UK in February 2009 and met with a lukewarm response. The box office this time did not match the returns of the first one. Harald Zwart recalls that discussions were being held about where next for the franchise. He wasn't going to be involved anyway, having flown to Utah after the New York premiere to start work on a remake of *The Karate Kid*. In the end MGM called it quits. Comedies were becoming harder-edged, grittier, things like *The Hangover* (2009). By comparison the *Panther* looked like it belonged in another time.

Chapter 11

'UNTIL WE MEET AGAIN AND THE CASE IS SOLV-ED'

In the words of Burt Kwouk. 'The whole *Pink Panther* series doesn't seem like individual films to me. It just feels like one huge twelve-hour movie that took twenty years to shoot.'[1]

That's a nice way to sum everything up. Those films were special and retain a special quality today. The comedic genius that was Peter Sellers and the supreme talent that was Blake Edwards were a match made in heaven, even though it quite often felt like hell on the studio floor. But when it was working, together they created magic. And it was a joy to watch them at work, notes Gregg Champion:

> They had the script, but it was loose. Peter would always find bits of business and Blake was always looking for business. But there was a little gamesmanship. Sometimes Blake would show up late on the set, or Peter would show up late. Looking at it now, it seems a little immature and spoiled. And there was a lot of one-upmanship. Blake would have an idea and Peter would top it and ultimately one of them wouldn't be happy about something. That was their dynamic.[2]

Blake later spoke about Sellers, the fact that personally they didn't get along all that well. Herbert Lom was to sum up their relationship as like that of a screwball marriage. 'Comedy and combat in equal measure, and it was based on mutual need.'[3] The fact they were both perfectionists didn't help. The difference was, Blake had less complexities. With Sellers there was always something wrong. 'That was just his nature,' says Susan Wood. 'You and I could look at something he did and say, that was so funny. That was hysterical. And he would look at it and see all the faults. Yeah, he would say, but did you see that, did you see this.'[4]

Blake said that the pain and anguish caused working with Sellers was ultimately worth it. That some of the best times of his professional life were spent with Sellers, and some of the worst, too. 'You couldn't like him. You might feel sorry for him. You might like something he's done. But to truly like the man. He was not a likable man. There were times when it almost bordered on evil.'[5]

What they did share was a common love of comedy, and a certain childlike quality that was domineering and powerful. The difference was Blake recognised that and Sellers didn't. It was a love/hate relationship. Although in many ways the two men were very alike. Producer David Chasman was to call their relationship, 'a horrible marriage that produced beautiful babies'.[6]

Sellers did resent the fact that Blake exerted so much control, not just as the director but in writing the scripts. What he did take great personal pride in was his creation and playing of Inspector Clouseau. That was undeniably his and his alone. 'I think he loved the fact that he had created this character,' says Susan Wood. 'He was quite proud of that and the work he had done.'[7] On the set he easily slid into that persona. He became Clouseau,' says Dyan Cannon. 'It was just another facet of Peter, so he didn't really have to shift a lot of gears. He just easily slid into it because he understood that character so much. And he felt safe there. It was so close to his heart.'[8] Elke Sommer agrees: 'He totally became Clouseau. And he enjoyed playing that part tremendously.'[9]

People wondered why Blake kept on making *Pink Panther* films. Well, money. And why not. You knew they were going to make some money. Maybe not the kind of money the early ones got. But a lot of people would go to see them out of interest or nostalgia. In any case, after *Son of the Pink Panther* Blake never made another film. Instead, he began to focus on theatre. He was behind a stage version of his film *Victor/Victoria*, which opened on Broadway in 1995 with Julie Andrews reprising her screen role. It ran for two years. Blake then collaborated with English composer and lyricist Leslie Bricusse on a *Pink Panther* musical. It never materialised.

Working with Blake on the *Victor/Victoria* stage show was Tony Adams. He had been with Blake now since the early '70s, as his problem solver and facilitator. 'With Blake there was always an issue with something,' says Jeffrey Auerbach. 'And Tony would fix it. But it always had a real cost and put a lot of pressure on him. He was great at it, but sometimes the bullshit would be a lot to deal with. After that experience on *Victor/Victoria* Tony reached a point where he said, "no, I think this is what I'm going to be doing".'[10] Adams left Blake's employ and struck out on his own as a theatre producer.

With several Broadway and off-Broadway productions behind him, in 2002 Adams made a deal with Marvel to make a musical based on Spider-Man. A huge fan of U2, he approached Bono and The Edge to be involved in the project. There were endless problems trying to put the show together and Adams regularly confided in Auerbach about the troubles he was having. 'I was worried about the stress Tony was under, but he had dealt with it all his professional life.'[11]

In October 2005 Adams and U2 arranged to meet in New York to sign contracts. 'Tony was there,' says Jeffrey Auerbach, 'Paul McGuinness, U2's manager and The Edge. They went over the final page of the contract and The Edge went, 'Great, let me get a pen.' He got up to go get a pen and when he turned around Tony was convulsing on the floor.'[12] He was rushed to hospital.

Auerbach was in a meeting when he got the call that Adams had suffered a stroke. He left, packed, and flew into New York that day. 'I got to the hospital and I went up to his room and just sat there alone with him all night.'[13] Adams' family had all arrived and soon his brothers and sisters flew in from Ireland. He never regained consciousness. The decision was taken to switch off the life support machine. 'And in a matter of a moment it was done,' says Jeffrey. 'He was gone.'[14] Adams was only 52.

Blake and Julie were devastated by the loss of Tony Adams. Blake had by this time all but retired. He wasn't in too good a shape either. Physically he had deteriorated and had begun to walk with a cane. Soon he would need a wheelchair.

On 30 September 2010, the Academy of Motion Picture Arts and Sciences hosted 'An Evening with Blake Edwards' on the stage of the Samuel Goldwyn Theatre on Wilshire Boulevard in Beverly Hills; Blake's home patch. An enthusiastic audience of almost a thousand people turned up to watch and listen to Blake discuss his life and career. Sat with Blake on the stage was Walter Mirisch and the two old friends talked for nearly two hours. Blake was in fine form and enjoying the opportunity to reminisce, but Mirisch could see that he was obviously failing and physically straining. He recalled:

> When our conversation concluded, the entire assemblage of the theatre rose to give a standing ovation to Blake. He was sitting in a wheelchair, and I watched him make a herculean

> effort to rise and acknowledge the applause of his audience one last time. He said to me quietly, 'I must stand up for them.' Holding my arm for support, he waved his other arm in a fond farewell.[15]

Two months later Blake passed away.

PINK-OGRAPHY

THE PINK PANTHER **(1963)**
Director: Blake Edwards
Producer: Martin Jurow
Writers: Maurice Richlin and Blake Edwards
Director of Photography: Philip Lathrop
Music: Henry Mancini
Cast: David Niven, Peter Sellers, Robert Wagner, Capucine, Claudia Cardinale, Brenda de Banzie, Colin Gordon, John Le Mesurier, James Lanphier.

A SHOT IN THE DARK **(1964)**
Director: Blake Edwards
Producer: Blake Edwards
Writers: Blake Edwards and William Peter Blatty
Director of Photography: Christopher Challis
Music: Henry Mancini
Cast: Peter Sellers, Elke Sommer, George Sanders, Herbert Lom, Tracy Reed, Graham Stark, Burt Kwouk, David Lodge, Moira Redmond, Andre Maranne, Martin Benson, Reginald Beckwith, Douglas Wilmer and introducing Turk Thrust.

INSPECTOR CLOUSEAU **(1968)**
Director: Bud Yorkin
Producer: Lewis Rachmil
Writers: Tom Waldman and Frank Waldman
Director of Photography: Arthur Ibbetson
Music: Ken Thorne
Cast: Alan Arkin, Frank Finlay, Delia Boccardo, Barry Foster, Patrick Cargill, Beryl Reid, Clive Francis, Michael Ripper, Eric Pohlmann.

***RETURN OF THE PINK PANTHER* (1975)**
Director: Blake Edwards
Producer: Blake Edwards
Writers: Blake Edwards and Frank Waldman
Director of Photography: Geoffrey Unsworth
Music: Henry Mancini
Cast: Peter Sellers, Christopher Plummer, Catherine Schell, Herbert Lom, Peter Arne, Burt Kwouk, Peter Jeffrey, David Lodge, Graham Stark, Eric Pohlmann, Andre Maranne, Victor Spinetti, John Bluthal, Mike Grady.

***THE PINK PANTHER STRIKES AGAIN* (1976)**
Director: Blake Edwards
Producer: Blake Edwards
Writers: Blake Edwards and Frank Waldman
Director of Photography: Harry Waxman
Music: Henry Mancini
Cast: Peter Sellers, Herbert Lom, Lesley-Anne Down, Burt Kwouk, Colin Blakely, Leonard Rossiter, Andre Maranne, Richard Vernon, Dudley Sutton, Michael Robbins, Graham Stark, Geoffrey Bayldon, Omar Sharif.

***REVENGE OF THE PINK PANTHER* (1978)**
Director: Blake Edwards
Producer: Blake Edwards
Writers: Frank Waldman, Ron Clark and Blake Edwards
Director of Photography: Ernest Day
Music: Henry Mancini
Cast: Peter Sellers, Dyan Cannon, Herbert Lom, Burt Kwouk, Robert Webber, Tony Beckley, Robert Loggia, Paul Stewart, Andre Maranne, Graham Stark, Alfie Bass, Sue Lloyd, Douglas Wilmer.

***TRAIL OF THE PINK PANTHER* (1982)**
Director: Blake Edwards
Producers: Blake Edwards and Tony Adams
Writers: Frank Waldman, Tom Waldman, Blake Edwards, Geoffrey Edwards
Director of Photography: Dick Bush
Music: Henry Mancini
Cast: Peter Sellers, David Niven, Herbert Lom, Richard Mulligan, Joanna Lumley, Capucine, Robert Loggia, Harvey Korman, Burt Kwouk, Graham Stark, Peter Arne, Andre Maranne, Ronald Fraser.

***CURSE OF THE PINK PANTHER* (1983)**
Director: Blake Edwards
Producers: Blake Edwards and Tony Adams
Writers: Blake Edwards and Geoffrey Edwards
Director of Photography: Dick Bush
Music: Henry Mancini
Cast: David Niven, Robert Wagner, Herbert Lom, Joanna Lumley, Capucine, Robert Loggia, Harvey Korman, Burt Kwouk, Ted Wass, Roger Moore, Leslie Ash, Denise Crosby, Graham Stark, Andre Maranne, Patti Davis, Michael Elphick, Ed Parker.

***SON OF THE PINK PANTHER* (1993)**
Director: Blake Edwards
Producer: Tony Adams
Writers: Blake Edwards, Madeline Sunshine and Steven Sunshine
Director of Photography: Dick Bush
Music: Henry Mancini
Cast: Roberto Benigni, Herbert Lom, Claudia Cardinale, Shabana Azmi, Debrah Farentino, Jennifer Edwards, Robert Davi, Anton Rodgers, Burt Kwouk, Graham Stark.

***THE PINK PANTHER* (2006)**
Director: Shawn Levy
Producer: Robert Simonds
Writers: Len Blum and Steve Martin
Director of Photography: Jonathan Brown
Music: Christophe Beck
Cast: Steve Martin, Kevin Kline, Jean Reno, Emily Mortimer, Henry Czerny, Roger Rees, Beyonce Knowles.

***THE PINK PANTHER 2* (2009)**
Director: Harald Zwart
Producer: Robert Simonds
Writers: Scott Neustadter, Michael H. Weber and Steve Martin
Director of Photography: Denis Crossan
Music: Christophe Beck
Cast: Steve Martin, Jean Reno, Emily Mortimer, Andy Garcia, Alfred Molina, Yuki Matsuzaki, Aishwarya Rai Bachchan, John Cleese, Lily Tomlin, Jeremy Irons, Johnny Hallyday.

ENDNOTES

Chapter 1: The Pink Panther

1. Maurice Richlin memoirs
2. Ibid
3. Ibid
4. *Los Angeles Times*, May 1991
5. Ibid
6. Village Voice, May 1971
7. Maurice Richlin memoirs
8. Ibid
9. Ibid
10. Ibid
11. Ibid
12. MGM DVD documentary
13. Casetext.com
14. Maurice Richlin memoirs
15. Henry Mancini, *Did They Mention the Music* (Contemporary Books, 1989)
16. Maurice Richlin memoirs
17. Robert Wagner, author interview
18. Martin Jurow, *Seein' Stars: A Show Biz Odyssey* (Southern Methodist University Press, 2001)
19. John Miller, *Peter Ustinov: The Gift of Laughter* (Weidenfeld and Nicolson, 2002)
20. Robert Wagner, author interview
21. *Variety*, January 1963
22. MGM DVD documentary

23. Robert Wagner, author interview
24. *D magazine*, March 1985
25. Graham Stark, author interview
26. Henry Mancini, *Did They Mention the Music* (Contemporary Books, 1989)
27. Alexander Walker, *Peter Sellers: The Authorized biography* (Weidenfeld and Nicolson, 1981)
28. Ibid
29. MGM DVD documentary
30. *The Times*, September 1975
31. *The New York Times*, January 1964
32. Sam Wasson, *A Splurch in the Kisser: The Movies of Blake Edwards* (Wesleyan University Press, 2009)
33. Robert Wagner, author interview
34. Alexander Walker, *Peter Sellers: The Authorized biography* (Weidenfeld and Nicolson, 1981)
35. MGM DVD documentary
36. Maurice Richlin memoirs
37. Henry Mancini, *Did They Mention the Music* (Contemporary Books, 1989)
38. Robert Wagner, author interview
39. Ibid
40. Ibid
41. Ibid
42. Ibid
43. Ibid
44. Ibid
45. Italymagazine.com, April 2012
46. Graham Lord, *Niv: The authorised biography of David Niven* (Orion, 2003)
47. Susan Wood, author interview
48. Robert Wagner, author interview
49. bakertoons.blogspot.com, December 2010
50. Monica Mancini, author interview
51. Ibid
52. Henry Mancini, *Did They Mention the Music* (Contemporary Books, 1989)
53. Graham Stark, author interview
54. Robert Wagner, author interview

Chapter 2: A Shot in the Dark

1. Rob Edelman and Audrey Kupferberg, *Matthau: A Life* (Taylor Trade Publishing, 2002)
2. Chris Coppel, author interview
3. William Peter Blatty, *Finding Peter* (Regnery Publishing, 2015)
4. *Austin Chronicle*, March 2000
5. Michael Sellers, *P.S. I love You: Peter Sellers* (Collins, 1981)
6. David V. Picker, *Musts, Maybes, and Nevers: A Book About the Movies* (CreateSpace Independent Publishing Platform, 2013)
7. William Peter Blatty, *Finding Peter* (Regnery Publishing, 2015)
8. Elke Sommer, author interview
9. Ibid
10. Ibid
11. Terry Ackland-Snow, author interview
12. Elke Sommer, author interview
13. Ibid
14. Ibid
15. Ibid
16. Burt Kwouk, author interview
17. Michael Sellers, Gary Morecambe, *Sellers on Sellers*, (André Deutsch, 2000)
18. Ibid
19. Burt Kwouk, author interview
20. Cyd Child, author interview
21. Michael Birkett, author interview
22. Ibid
23. Michael Sellers, Gary Morecambe, *Sellers on Sellers* (André Deutsch, 2000)
24. *The Scotsman*, June 2002
25. *The Independent*, December 2004
26. MGM DVD documentary
27. *Sight and Sound*, Spring 1964
28. Brian W. Cook, author interview
29. Ibid
30. Ibid
31. Ibid
32. Ibid
33. Graham Stark, author interview

34. Elke Sommer, author interview
35. Ibid
36. Ibid
37. Ibid
38. Ibid
39. Ibid
40. Ibid
41. *Playboy*, December 1982
42. Henry Mancini, *Did They Mention the Music* (Contemporary Books, 1989)
43. Ibid
44. Alexander Walker, *Peter Sellers: The Authorized biography* (Weidenfeld and Nicolson, 1981)
45. Elke Sommer, author interview
46. Monica Mancini, author interview
47. Ibid
48. Walter Mirisch, *I Thought We Were Making Movies, Not History* (University of Wisconsin, 2008)
49. *Playboy*, December 1982
50. *Austin Chronicle*, March 2000
51. Maurice Richlin memoirs
52. Graham Stark, author interview

Chapter 3: Inspector Clouseau

1. *The Pink Panther: Behind the Feline* documentary
2. Walter Mirisch, *I Thought We Were Making Movies, Not History* (University of Wisconsin, 2008)
3. Graham Stark, *Remembering Peter Sellers* (Robson Books, 1990)
4. Bobbie Wygant archive
5. Ibid
6. Walter Mirisch, *I Thought We Were Making Movies, Not History* (University of Wisconsin, 2008)
7. Ibid
8. Alexander Walker, *Peter Sellers: The Authorized biography* (Weidenfeld and Nicolson, 1981)
9. Emory University, August 2010
10. Clive Francis, author interview

11. Ibid
12. Ibid
13. Ibid
14. Ibid
15. Walter Mirisch, *I Thought We Were Making Movies, Not History* (University of Wisconsin, 2008)
16. *The Independent*, May 2021
17. TVacademy.com
18. *The Scotsman*, June 2002

Chapter 4: The Return of the Pink Panther

1. *Playboy*, December 1982
2. Ibid
3. *The Times*, February 1974
4. Ibid
5. Susan Wood, author interview
6. Ibid
7. *Photoplay*, June 1971
8. *Playboy*, December 1982
9. Lew Grade, *Still Dancing: My Story* (Collins, 1987)
10. Psychotronic magazine, May 2017
11. Catherine Schell, author interview
12. Ibid
13. Ibid
14. Ibid
15. Ibid
16. Ibid
17. Graham Stark, author interview
18. Ibid
19. Ibid
20. Peter Samuelson, author interview
21. Ibid
22. Ibid
23. Ibid
24. Ibid
25. Ibid
26. Ibid

27. Ibid
28. Ibid
29. Ibid
30. Michael Sellers, Gary Morecambe, *Sellers on Sellers* (André Deutsch, 2000)
31. Christopher Plummer, *In Spite of Myself* (Doubleday, 2008)
32. Peter Samuelson, author interview
33. Ibid
34. Ibid
35. Mike Grady, author interview
36. Ibid
37. Ibid
38. Ibid
39. Ibid
40. Peter Samuelson, author interview
41. Carol Cleveland, author interview
42. Ibid
43. Ibid
44. Ibid
45. Ibid
46. Ibid
47. Ibid
48. Ibid
49. Peter Samuelson, author interview
50. Ibid
51. Catherine Schell, author interview
52. Ibid
53. Ibid
54. Ibid
55. Ibid
56. Ibid
57. Joe Dunne, author interview
58. Mathew Dunne, author interview
59. Ibid
60. Ibid
61. Ibid
62. Catherine Schell, author interview
63. Ibid
64. Ibid

65. Peter Samuelson, author interview
66. Ibid
67. Ibid
68. Christopher Plummer, *In Spite of Myself* (Doubleday, 2008)
69. Playboy, December 1982
70. Mike Grady, author interview
71. Ibid
72. John Allenby, author interview
73. Ibid
74. Peter Mullins, author interview
75. Ibid
76. Ibid
77. Mike Grady, author interview
78. Christopher Plummer, *In Spite of Myself* (Doubleday, 2008)
79. Mathew Dunne, author interview
80. Ibid
81. Cyd Child, author interview
82. Ibid
83. Ibid
84. Ibid
85. Tony White, author interview
86. Ibid
87. Ibid
88. Ibid
89. Ibid
90. *The Guardian*, December 1975
91. Tony White, author interview
92. Mike Grady, author interview
93. Ibid
94. Ibid
95. Ibid
96. Victor Spinetti, *Up Front* (Robson books, 2006)
97. Ibid
98. Mike Grady, author interview
99. Ibid
100. Monica Mancini, author interview
101. John Le Mesurier, *A Jobbing Actor* (Elm Tree Books, 1984)
102. Peter Samuelson, author interview
103. Christopher Plummer, *In Spite of Myself* (Doubleday, 2008)

104. Ibid
105. Catherine Schell, author interview
106. Susan Wood, author interview

Chapter 5: The Pink Panther Strikes Again

1. Susan Wood, author interview
2. Ibid
3. Lesley-Anne Down, author interview
4. Ibid
5. Julie Andrews, *Home Work: A Memoir of my Hollywood Years* (Weidenfeld & Nicolson, 2019)
6. Ibid
7. Susan Wood, author interview
8. Burt Kwouk, author interview
9. *Cinema Museum*, November 2010
10. Graham Stark, author interview
11. Ibid
12. Ibid
13. Ibid
14. *Curious Case of Inspector Clouseau*, Channel 4 2002
15. BBC Radio 4 *The Film Programme*, October 2008
16. Peter Mullins, author interview
17. Lesley-Anne Down, author interview
18. Ibid
19. Graham Stark, author interview
20. Alexander Walker, *Peter Sellers: The Authorized biography* (Weidenfeld and Nicolson, 1981)
21. Julie Andrews, *Home Work: A Memoir of my Hollywood Years* (Weidenfeld & Nicolson, 2019)
22. Peter Mullins, author interview
23. Jeffrey Auerbach, author interview
24. Ibid
25. Ibid
26. Ibid
27. Ibid
28. Gregg Champion, author interview
29. Mathew Dunne, author interview

30. Lesley-Anne Down, author interview
31. Ibid
32. Ibid
33. Ibid
34. Ibid
35. Ibid
36. Ibid
37. Ibid
38. Ibid
39. Ibid
40. Ibid
41. Ibid
42. Julie Andrews, *Home Work: A Memoir of my Hollywood Years* (Weidenfeld & Nicolson, 2019)
43. Lesley-Anne Down, author interview
44. Ibid
45. Ibid
46. Peter Mullins, author interview
47. Ibid
48. Ibid
49. Ibid
50. MGM DVD documentary
51. Susan Wood, author interview
52. *Curious Case of Inspector Clouseau*, Channel 4 2002
53. Joe Dunne, author interview
54. Ibid
55. Ibid
56. Ibid
57. Ibid
58. Ibid
59. Peter Mullins, author interview
60. Ibid
61. Ibid
62. Ibid
63. Cyd Child, author interview
64. Ibid
65. Ibid
66. Ibid
67. Ibid

68. Vic Armstrong, author interview
69. Ibid
70. Peter Mullins, author interview
71. Ibid
72. Ibid
73. Lesley-Anne Down, author interview
74. Ibid
75. Ibid
76. Peter Mullins, author interview
77. The Scotsman, June 2002
78. Roger Lewis, *The Life and Death of Peter Sellers* (Century, 1994)
79. Peter Mullins, author interview
80. Lesley-Anne Down, author interview
81. Ibid
82. Peter Mullins, author interview
83. Ibid
84. Tony White, author interview
85. Ibid
86. Ibid
87. Ibid
88. Ibid
89. Ibid
90. Ibid
91. Ibid
92. Ibid
93. American Film Institute
94. Lesley-Anne Down, author interview
95. Sam Wasson, *A Splurch in the Kisser: The Movies of Blake Edwards* (Wesleyan University Press, 2009)
96. TCM

Chapter 6: Revenge of the Pink Panther

1. *Playboy*, December 1982
2. Sam Wasson, *A Splurch in the Kisser: The Movies of Blake Edwards* (Wesleyan University Press, 2009)
3. Burt Kwouk, author interview
4. *Observer*, June 1975

5. *Curious Case of Inspector Clouseau*, Channel 4 2002
6. Julie Andrews, *Home Work: A Memoir of my Hollywood Years* (Weidenfeld & Nicolson, 2019)
7. Ibid
8. Ibid
9. Dyan Cannon, author interview
10. Ibid
11. Gregg Champion, author interview
12. Ibid
13. Ibid
14. Ibid
15. Ibid
16. Ibid
17. Julie Andrews, *Home Work: A Memoir of my Hollywood Years* (Weidenfeld & Nicolson, 2019)
18. Mathew Dunne, author interview
19. *Playboy*, December 1982
20. Ibid
21. Charlie Rose Show, November 1996
22. *Playboy*, December 1982
23. Julie Andrews, *Home Work: A Memoir of my Hollywood Years* (Weidenfeld & Nicolson, 2019)
24. Eric Pleskow, author interview
25. Ibid
26. Ibid
27. Ibid
28. Associated Press, December 1982
29. Ibid
30. Dyan Cannon, author interview
31. Ibid
32. Ibid
33. Ibid
34. Ibid
35. Gregg Champion, author interview
36. Ibid
37. Ibid
38. Ibid
39. Graham Stark, author interview
40. Ibid

41. Gregg Champion, author interview
42. Dyan Cannon, author interview
43. Ibid
44. Ibid
45. Graham Stark, *Remembering Peter Sellers* (Robson Books, 1990)
46. Peter Mullins, author interview
47. Ibid
48. Ibid
49. Ibid
50. Ibid
51. Ibid
52. Gregg Champion, author interview
53. Ibid
54. Television Academy.com
55. Ibid
56. Graham Stark, author interview
57. Ibid
58. Dyan Cannon, author interview
59. Ibid
60. *Playboy*, December 1982
61. Ibid
62. Terry Ackland-Snow, author interview
63. Valerie Leon, author interview
64. Ibid
65. Ibid
66. Gregg Champion, author interview
67. Roger Lewis, *The Life and Death of Peter Sellers* (Century, 1994)
68. Sam Wasson, *A Splurch in the Kisser: The Movies of Blake Edwards* (Wesleyan University Press, 2009)
69. Ibid
70. *Curious Case of Inspector Clouseau*, Channel 4 2002
71. Dyan Cannon, author interview
72. Gregg Champion, author interview
73. Ibid
74. Ibid
75. Julie Andrews, *Home Work: A Memoir of my Hollywood Years* (Weidenfeld & Nicolson, 2019)
76. Monica Mancini, author interview
77. Dyan Cannon, author interview

78. *Los Angeles Times*, January 1979
79. Eric Pleskow, author interview
80. The Scotsman, June 2002
81. Susan Wood, author interview

Chapter 7: The Panther That Never Was

1. Steven Bach, *Final Cut* (William Morrow & Co, 1985)
2. Adam Fields, author interview
3. Michael Sellers, *P.S. I love You: Peter Sellers* (Collins, 1981)
4. Susan Wood, author interview
5. Catherine Schell, author interview
6. Ibid
7. Elke Sommer, author interview
8. *Curious Case of Inspector Clouseau*, Channel 4 2002
9. Susan Wood, author interview
10. *Sunday Express*, August 1979
11. Susan Wood, author interview
12. Psychotronic magazine, May 2017
13. Adam Fields, author interview
14. Ibid
15. Ibid
16. Ibid
17. Ibid
18. Ibid
19. Ibid
20. Ibid
21. Ibid
22. Ibid
23. Ibid
24. Ibid
25. Ibid
26. Ibid
27. Steven Bach, *Final Cut* (William Morrow & Co, 1985)
28. Ibid
29. Ibid
30. Ibid
31. Ibid

32. Adam Fields, author interview
33. Susan Wood, author interview
34. Ibid
35. Ibid
36. Ed Sikov, *Mr Strangelove: A Biography of Peter Sellers* (Hachette, 2002)
37. Susan Wood, author interview
38. Ibid
39. Ibid
40. Ibid
41. Burt Kwouk, author interview
42. Julie Andrews, *Home Work: A Memoir of my Hollywood Years* (Weidenfeld & Nicolson, 2019)
43. Susan Wood, author interview
44. Denise Crosby, author interview
45. Peter Mullins, author interview
46. Burt Kwouk, author interview
47. Susan Wood, author interview
48. Ibid
49. Ibid
50. Ibid

Chapter 8: Flogging a Dead Panther

1. Graham Stark, author interview
2. Alan Tomkins, *Stars and Wars* (The History Press, 2015)
3. Peter Mullins, author interview
4. Ibid
5. Ibid
6. Joanna Lumley, *No Room for Secrets* (Michael Joseph, 2004)
7. Hjordisniven.com
8. Daniel Peacock, author interview
9. Ibid
10. Ibid
11. Ibid
12. Ibid
13. Denise Crosby, author interview
14. Peter Mullins, author interview

15. Denise Crosby, author interview
16. *The Times*, March 1985
17. Ted Wass, author interview
18. Ibid
19. Ibid
20. Ibid
21. Ibid
22. Ibid
23. Ibid
24. Ibid
25. Ibid
26. Ibid
27. Ibid
28. Ibid
29. Ibid
30. Ibid
31. Ibid
32. Ibid
33. Denise Crosby, author interview
34. Ibid
35. Ibid
36. Ibid
37. Ibid
38. Ibid
39. Ibid
40. Leslie Ash, author interview
41. Ibid
42. Ibid
43. Ibid
44. Ibid
45. Michael Elphick, *The Great Pretender* (The History Press, 2013)
46. Leslie Ash, author interview
47. Ibid
48. Ibid
49. Denise Crosby, author interview
50. Leslie Ash, author interview
51. Ted Wass, author interview
52. John Allenby, author interview
53. Ted Wass, author interview

54. Ibid
55. Leslie Ash, author interview
56. Ted Wass, author interview
57. Ibid
58. Ibid
59. Ibid
60. Leslie Ash, author interview
61. Ted Wass, author interview
62. Ibid
63. Ibid
64. Peter Mullins, author interview
65. Ibid
66. Julie Andrews, *Home Work: A Memoir of my Hollywood Years* (Weidenfeld & Nicolson, 2019)
67. Ted Wass, author interview
68. Ibid
69. Ibid

Chapter 9: The Italian Clouseau

1. Denise Crosby, author interview
2. Ibid
3. Don E. FauntLeRoy, author interview
4. Ibid
5. Ibid
6. Mathew Dunne, author interview
7. Jeffrey Auerbach, author interview
8. Ibid
9. Ibid
10. Ibid
11. Ibid
12. Ibid
13. *LA Times*, August 1993
14. Mathew Dunne, author interview
15. John Dellaverson, author interview
16. Ibid
17. Ibid
18. Ibid

19. Elke Sommer, author interview
20. John Allenby, author interview
21. Ibid
22. Peter Mullins, author interview
23. John Allenby, author interview
24. John Dellaverson, author interview
25. Ibid
26. Ibid
27. Psychotronic magazine, May 2017
28. John Allenby, author interview
29. Peter Mullins, author interview

Chapter 10: The American Clouseau

1. American Film Institute, January 2013
2. Michael Saltzman, author interview
3. Ibid
4. Ibid
5. Ibid
6. Ibid
7. Ibid
8. Ibid
9. Ibid
10. Ibid
11. Ibid
12. Ibid
13. Ibid
14. Ibid
15. Ibid
16. Shawn Levy, author interview
17. Ibid
18. Ibid
19. Ibid
20. Ibid
21. Ibid
22. Ibid
23. Harald Zwart, author interview
24. Ibid

25. Ibid
26. Ibid
27. Ibid
28. Ibid
29. Ibid
30. Ibid
31. Ibid
32. Ibid
33. Ibid
34. Christophe Beck, author interview
35. Ibid
36. Ibid
37. Ibid

Chapter 11: "Until We Meet Again and the Case is SOLV-ED"

1. Burt Kwouk, author interview
2. Gregg Champion, author interview
3. 78: Roger Lewis, *The Life and Death of Peter Sellers* (Century, 1994)
4. Susan Wood, author interview
5. CNN, July 2002
6. Sam Wasson, *A Splurch in the Kisser: The Movies of Blake Edwards* (Wesleyan University Press, 2009)
7. Susan Wood, author interview
8. Dyan Cannon, author interview
9. Elke Sommer, author interview
10. Jeffrey Auerbach, author interview
11. Ibid
12. Ibid
13. Ibid
14. Ibid
15. *Vanity Fair*, December 2010

BIBLIOGRAPHY

Evans, Peter, *Peter Sellers: The Mask Behind the Mask*, Leslie Frewin, 1969
Forbes, Bryan, *A Divided Life*, William Heinemann, 1992
Lewis, Roger, *The Life and Death of Peter Sellers*, Century, 1994
Sellers, Michael, *P. S. I Love You*, Collins, 1981
Stark, Graham, *Remembering Peter Sellers*, Robson books, 1990
Sikov, Ed, *Mr Strangelove*, Hyperion, 2002
Tomkins, Alan, *Stars and Wars: The Film Memoirs of Alan Tomkins*, The History Press, 2015
Vanderbeets, Richard, *George Sanders: An Exhausted Life*, Robson books, 1998
Wagner, Robert, *Pieces of My Heart*, Hutchinson, 2009
Walker, Alexander, *Peter Sellers: The Authorized Biography*, Weidenfeld and Nicolson, 1981